The Soviet Union in World Politics

KLAUS VON BEYME

St. Martins Press   New York

First published in the United States of America in 1987

Printed in Great Britain

ISBN 0-312-00436-2

Library of Congress Cataloging-in-Publication Data

Beyme, Klaus von.
  The Soviet Union in world politics.

  Bibliography: p.
  Includes index.
  1. Soviet Union——Foreign relations——1975–
I. Title.
DK282.B49 1987   327.47   87-1550
ISBN 0-312-00436-2

Contents

Tables

Abbreviations of periodicals

APSR — American Political Science Review

APuZG — Aus Politik und Zeitgeschichte. Supplement to the weekly newspaper Das Parlament

BioSt — Berichte des Bundesinstituts für ostwissenschaftliche und internationale Studien

BJPolS — British Journal of Political Science

EA — Europa Archiv

MEiMO — Mirovaya ekonomika i mezhdunarodnye otnosheniya

MO — Mezhdunarodnye otnosheniya

PoC — Problems of Communism

OE — Osteuropa

PVS — Politische Vierteljahresschrift

SI — Sotsiologicheskie issledovaniya

SGiP — Sovetskoe gosudarstvo i pravo

StiCC — Studies in Comparative Communism

Introduction

The present portrayal of Soviet foreign policy is based on a systematic approach rather than being arranged in an historical, chronological order. The points of departure for the individual chapters are the problems of the 1970s and 1980s. Historical flashbacks are included in each case, however, in order to enable a better understanding of the change that has come about in Soviet foreign policy.

The systematic approach has a number of advantages. Firstly fewer areas are faded out than in the historically arranged works, which generally give too little coverage to economic relations or transnational politics. Secondly, this approach makes it easier to work out the immanent conceptual framework of the Soviet actors. This calls for a more detailed examination of the Soviet literature in all fields. Many American works, in particular, frequently confine themselves to a couple of standard Soviet works and the current press. The sole West German synthesis on this subject even achieves the feat of getting by without any Soviet language publications at all.[1] An upright left-wing outlook obviously salves the conscience better when substituting for detailed reading than a 'bourgeois positivist' could ever hope for.

Examining the growing amount of Soviet literature is still a highly frustrating undertaking. The empirical content is on the increase and propagandist zeal is becoming more restrained. Yet despite this there are still tedious repetitions. The slightest of nuances in Soviet theory is important, however, since most publications are written by scientists who advise the foreign policy actors (see pp. 124–8). These books thus have a higher source value than their more interesting counterparts written by independent scholars in the West.

The approach taken towards the Soviet Union's self-conception does not imply the adoption of the theories of history that underly the Soviet theory of international politics.[2] Nevertheless, an explanation of the Soviet self conception ought to come before an assessment in order to prevent an over-hasty interpretation of Soviet actions on the basis of maxims that do not apply. Despite this warning, I am certain that there will again be critics who accuse the author of adopting the Soviet perspective. It is difficult to convey the fact that the analytical principles to which the author is committed can apply to other societies apart from Western societies. Some scientists engaged in research on socialism seem to think that these principles have to be handed in at Checkpoint Charlie and exchanged for a sound Western normativism the moment one approaches socialist society. The Western value standard creeps through the author's portrayal, which sets out to be objective, early enough as it is, even though the author knows himself to be free of all fear of contact with the testimony of Soviet self-conception.

Finally, this approach permits comparisons with the foreign policy of the chief opponent which would seem out of place in a chronological description. This does not simply mean a comparison of the Soviet Union and the USA along the lines of the classic 'tit for tat' argument—'and you treat your niggers badly',[3] but an analysis of the opponents of the Soviet Union, to whom the actors in Moscow attempt to respond either in anticipation or in retrospect. Many a Soviet reaction does not appear to be so out of line with this method as when Soviet foreign policy is merely derived from her general ideology. It is useful here that the author also dealt with subjects in Western systems as well. The ideological inflexibility and narrow methodical approach of many Eastern bloc-only researchers results from their withdrawal into a ghetto that has cut itself off from the continuing discussion framework of their particular subjects and which considers a combination of flat description and cold war mentality to be theory.

I owe my thanks to the Federal German Research Association (*Deutsche Forschungsgemeinschaft*) for their support of my two visits to Moscow in 1981 and 1982. Whilst research trips of this type cannot unmask Kremlin secrets they do perhaps make for a greater degree of empathy when approaching the subject than is to be found in many of those mockingly termed *'tak nazyvaemye Ostforshery'* (so-called Eastern bloc researchers) in the Soviet Union, whose knowledge of the country is restricted to childhood memories or fleeting congress trips.

1 The Soviet Union's Self-Conception in the Theory of International Politics

Fundamental concepts of self-conception: world system, world order, comparative strength of forces in the world, reshaping of international relations

The Soviet Union is a world power *sui generis* which does not lend itself to straightforward comparison with other countries. In the 1960s the theory of international relations in the Soviet Union was viewed as a theory that was strongly oriented towards the substantial, traditional power categories of the early period of discipline.[1] It was not until the 1970s that modern approaches began to figure in the Soviet theory of international relations, allowing a more analytical and less self-centred view of the international system and its interdependencies.[2]

The Soviet theory, on the one hand, casts the state and its instruments of power into the centre of the theory of international relations in completely traditional manner.[3] On the other hand, however, the state frequently performs functions which would come under transnational politics in Western countries and be covered by non-state actors. These include functions such as the centre of the Communist world movement and the supporter of national revolutionary liberation movements in the Third World. The social organisations, however, have relinquished their proper role to pursue truly transnational, and not simply masked international politics of the party. This has been particularly true since the ending of the Soviet Union's isolation and the establishment of general relations through USSR diplomatic and state channels has meant that the social organisations are no longer the sole communication link with other systems (as was frequently the case in the past).[4]

Although historians who have studied Soviet foreign policy have long warned against simply viewing foreign policy as a function of domestic Soviet development goals and have pleaded for more complex analytical models,[5] many of the conservative and neo-Marxist patterns of interpretation converge in their emphasis on the primacy of domestic policy. The first argues on the basis of the totalitarianism model and the second puts forward a 'bourgeoisation' of the new classes in the Soviet Union, who allegedly initiated coexistence and East–West co-operation in order to secure and increase the standard of living and privileges enjoyed by the 'new classes'.[6]

A number of observers see the aggressive component as becoming more intensified in the 1970s. Military strength underwent a *de facto* increase and was also upgraded in the priority catalogue of Soviet foreign policy. In addition, the Societ Union had only had traumatic experience of military weakness until then, yet lacked the experience of Japan, Germany or the USA (in Vietnam) to recognise that a policy of military strength can lead to defeat. It is thus suggested at times that Soviet foreign policy has recently been more concerned with expanding its influence than with achieving security.[7]

The interpretation of the role of the Soviet Union in world politics long oscillated between the two poles of primacy of domestic policy and primacy of foreign policy. Supporters of the totalitarianism theory, from Kennan through to Tucker,[8] place emphasis on the change in internal power structures.

As convergence theories increasingly came to overshadow the totalitarianism paradigm, a bigger role was taken up by explanations of Soviet foreign policy that were construed in terms of the situation in the international system. Marshall Shulman, for instance, made a conscious effort to break away from the 'Kremlin-astrological' aspects of a predominantly domestic policy perspective by largely basing his appraisal on 'the rational responsiveness to changes in the world environment and, above all, in power relations' instead of on some or other cryptic features of the Soviet leaders.[9]

The classification of driving forces behind Soviet foreign policy essentially counts as a primacy of domestic policy approach as well. Boris Meissner draws a distinction between three such forces: the world revolutionary impetus of Moscow as the centre of the Communist world movement, nationalism as a 'new incarnation of the Russian Empire'. The third driving force of totalitarianism proves almost to be a moderating element when it comes to foreign policy. True to the principle of the 'primacy of domestic policy', unconditional priority is accorded to the 'consolidation and securing of totalitarian single-party rule within the country, the actual bearer of which must be regarded as the party bureaucracy, over and above all goals of expansion and even over the maintenance of a specific stock of possessions'.[10]

There is no question but that the Soviet Union had to react in a much more intense and differentiated manner to the international system in the time after the Second World War and during her rise to second world power than beforehand. Studies on the history of Soviet foreign policy between the two world wars ran an even greater danger of absolutising the domestic policy aspect. Historians thus increasingly demanded more complex models and called for an investigation of the socio-economic change in the Soviet Union caused by 'changed international conditions' and for an investigation of the changes in the international system, in addition to the primacy of domestic policy.[11]

The question 'Is foreign policy really foreign policy?', which critical publicists have repeatedly raised about all systems, seems to suggest much more of an answer along primacy of domestic policy lines for socialist systems than for traditional great powers. After the Second World War a classification of the chief factors of the change pointed rather to a primacy of active forces from outside. Only two out of the six fundamental processes that were set against the simplicity of the totalitarianism model were of a domestic policy nature:

1 the switch in the international system from bipolarity to multipolarity;
2 the development of polycentrism in the Communist world movement;
3 the creation of military technology leading to stalemate in the potential total destruction of the relevant enemy in the world system;
4 the emergence of parity between the Soviet Union and the USA;
5 the move away from totalitarian system in Stalinism to an authoritarian, bureaucratic oligarchy;
6 the differences in leadership styles since Stalin.[12]

Even in the 1980s it has still been maintained that the domestic policy approach holds better heuristic and prognostic capacities than the system approach.[13] Instead of making such a global statement it would seem wiser to specify the limitation that, seen in the short term, the domestic policy approach has greater prognostic value. At the time of the change from Brezhnev to Andropov, this indeed predominated in almost all analyses. Long-term surveys, however, will also have to work with the world system perspective.

The influence of a world system perspective is becoming increasingly evident in Soviet publications as well. The strictured concept of foreign policy is being replaced by the analysis of international relations in the same way as in the West, though with a greater time lag. The domestic policy and revolutionary-centred equivocation about the foreign policy functions of the state from the era of the 'dictatorship of the proletariat' through to the 'state of the whole people', which predominated in the earlier literature,[14] has been superseded by a perspective which also places the Soviet Union in a context of action and reaction to outside influences.

This new perspective was also reflected in the uniquely detailed mention received by foreign policy in the Soviet Constitution. Article 29 of the new Soviet Union Constitution of 1977 has largely taken over the subheadings of the Final Act of the CSCE. In Article 28, however, the Soviet Union has set itself the goal of 'strengthening the position of world socialism' and 'supporting the struggle of peoples for national liberation and social progress'. This has frequently been interpreted as justification for an expansionist policy on the part of the USSR. The concept of 'Leninist peace policy', which is in need of interpretation, also by no means allows solely peaceful strategies, given the implicit committment to world revolution.[15] On the one hand, 'primacy of domestic policy' as a fundamental principle suggests the defensive, protective functions of the system, yet, on the other hand, the facets of centre of the world revolution and the traditional national and imperial goals of the Soviet Union are put forward as grounds for the aggressive component.[16]

In a system in which every book on so important a topic cannot be published without at least receiving approval for those in power, and where authors are frequently tied into the system of foreign policy consultation (see pp. 124–8), it is no longer possible to sum up the growing, increasingly differentiated literature exhaustively in a couple of lapidary set phrases of constitution, party statute and party congress resolutions. It is for this reason that the Soviet Union's self-conception, i.e. the way she expresses herself in her literature on the subject of international relations, is gaining increasing importance.

The constriction of the older discipline of foreign policy was given up even later than in Western countries. The acceptance of the concept 'international relations' already points to a system perspective that includes consideration of reciprocal processes. Of the six processes cited above which led to acceptance of the international world system perspective, the Soviet literature rejects bipolarity and multipolarity as being 'reactionary and utopian', particularly in the form of the superpowers theory.[17] The danger of a nuclear war, however, is also forcing the Soviet observer to adopt the bipolar system approach to international relations.[18] A system of 'universally planned peace' is offered as a model for a 'new system of international relations'.[19] Bipolarity is not only accepted *de facto* in strategic thinking (see pp.

151–4) but also any attempt to set up a multipolar system is branded, in the Soviet Union's own camp at least, as 'great power chauvinism', such as in the case of China. Only France has fared better here to date for propagandist reasons and on account of her irrelevance in terms of power politics (see pp. 43–4).

For a number of observers from the People's Democracies the mere existence of conflicting socio-economic systems is reason enough to view their relations from the perspective of a system of 'international relations'.[20] For the socialist camp, the system concept has even been constitutionally anchored in Article 30 of the Soviet Constitution, which makes reference to the 'socialist world system'. According to a commentary on the Constitution, it is not by chance that Article 30 contains two concepts: *'mirovaya sistema sotsializma'* (the socialist world system) takes in antagonistic relations as well (such as with China and Albania), whilst the expression *'sotsialisticheskoe sodruzhestvo'* (socialist co-operation, most frequently translated as socialist community) covers only those socialist countries whose relationship with the Soviet Union is marked by 'genuine friendship'.[21] Here again, the system concept reveals a degree of complexity that was lacking in the earlier Manichaean thinking of Soviet ideology. The 'concrete tasks of situation system analysis' based on the 'general laws of development of international relations', are set against the 'formal system analysis' of the bourgeois theory of international relations.[22]

Whilst the socio-economic structures of the states acting together admittedly determine the principles of international relations at each stage, the international system does possess a certain degree of autonomy. One can cite aphorisms of Marx, which are not further elaborated upon in the introduction to the 'Critique of Political Economy',[23] to the effect that 'international relations' are 'secondary and tertiary, altogether derived, transposed and not original production relations'.

The system of world economics, blocs and alliances is developing laws of its own, which cannot be straightforwardly derived from the production relations of a country. A sixfold typology is put forward for the current system of international relations to counter a bipolarity theory:

1   relations in 'real socialism';
2   relations amongst capitalist countries;
3   relations amongst countries of the Third World;
4   relations between socialism and capitalism—determined by the 'comparative strength of socialism and capitalism in the world arena';
5   relations between socialist countries and the Third World;

6   relations between countries of the capitalist world and those of the Third World.[24]

The chief contradiction between capitalism (which, although 'histori-cally condemned to demise' also has the capacity to adapt) and socialism (which constitutes the 'ascending line of historical development) is overshadowed by other contradictions — in particular by the relations of the developing countries in the international world system.

One of the most independent thinkers in the theory of international politics is Georgii Shakhnazarov. He attempted to place the dynamics of the system of international relations in a more rigid analytical framework by means of two concepts: the concept of comparative strength of forces and the term 'world order'. Comparisons of the strength of forces have been drawn up ever since the rise of the Soviet world power. But the comparative strength of forces (*sootnoshenie sil*) on a world scale was not covered as a theme in the context of the term 'peaceful coexistence' until the third edition of the Soviet Encyclopaedia.[25] Prior to this the concept and its synonyms had been largely comprehended in the sense of strategically coloured 'power balance theories'.[26] Yet even for a very non-military thinker such as Shakhnazarov, the concept has not fully lost all traces of its military strategic origin.[27]

Nevertheless, one should not allow oneself to be deceived: the exceedingly global manner in which reference is made to the comparative strength of forces shifting in favour of socialism also bears traits of face-saving following the withdrawal of earlier doctrines, such as the assertion that socialism was militarily superior.[28] The dynamic, competitive aspect has thus been shifted to politics and social evolution, yet at the same time the verbal military threat potential has been phased out in favour of a continued improvement in climate.

The growing interest in mathematical modelling of international relations is also new. The initial results of this, which include a diagram of the interaction of four states — as if there were currently four states that interacted without claims to power and on an equal footing — come close to the frequently criticised formalism of bourgeois system theory.[29]

The world modellers, who do not always come off well in Šach-nazarov's books for internal Soviet use,[30] increasingly fascinate him. He testifies that the 'Club of Rome', in particular, has overcome the 'narrow and egoistic horizon of bourgeois thinking'.[31]

The comparative strength of forces in the world and the concept of the 'reshaping of international relations' (*perestroika mezhdunarodnykh otnoshenii*) which is used in parallel, are presented as a global, irreversible historical process on all levels (economic, military, social and national). Socialism is no longer simply a veto power in this process but emerges as being in a position to determine the chief trends in international development. The comparative strength of class forces which comes out on the side of socialism is declared to be the foundation for the rebuilding of international relations. The reunification of Vietnam and the victory of socialism in Laos and Cambodia are employed as proof here of the far-reaching successes of world Communism.[32] The socialist countries' own influence is frequently exaggerated. The claim that nothing can happen in the world without the socialist camp's participation scarcely remains tenable as a global statement — one only has to think of the Camp David negotiations for a peace settlement in the Middle East and the Falklands war that the Soviets were only able to watch by satellite (see pp. 135–40).[33]

The system approach in the theory of international relations achieved its highest level of abstraction with Shakhnazarov in the concept of world order, which is defined as 'the totality of political principles, legal standards and conditions of the economic exchange' that emerge 'from the action of objective social development processes and social forces within an era'.[34] The politics of the states are seen as being supplemented by the transnational politics of the movements. The most influential movements (in order of importance) are the so-called 'key factors' of the current world order:[35]

1   the Communist world movement;
2   the national liberation movements of the Third World;
3   the movement of the states which do not belong to a pact;
4   social democracy.

Despite the sharp criticism of the 'politics of illusion' pursued by international social democracy,[36] the classification into three factors, which although effective are not necessarily allied to Communism, is pleasantly removed from earlier schematic, dichotomic classifications.

Despite all the rhetoric about the superiority of socialism which is still to be found in the standard textbooks, the internationally versed theoreticians in the Soviet Union do seem to be tending to accept a number of common premises for the solution of the problems of the world as a whole and to be correcting the one-sided optimism about socialism and the general pessimism about capitalism through differentiated judgements.[37]

The originally optimistic view of the international system proved to be mistaken in at least three areas:

1   The Soviet camp would gain increasing power. Although a number of states were indeed added to the socialist camp, the problems grew and inner cohesion tended rather to deteriorate, contrary to all forecasts.
2   The capitalist world, rocked by crises, would increasingly lose its significance *vis-à-vis* the socialist camp.

3   The Third World, once it had shaken off the shackles of imperialism, would unavoidably tend towards the Soviet camp.[38]

All three forecasts just did not happen. However, the counter assumptions about the socialist camp, ranging from pessimism about its imminent domination to optimism that such systems could not survive for long, also had to be modified in the West. Soviet successes are summed up in five points in the foreign policy theory of the Soviet Union:[39]

1   the achievement of recognition for the Western borders of the GDR, Czechoslovakia and Poland;
2   the warding off of American 'aggression' in Vietnam;
3   the fact that condemnation of Israel's aggression has become general throughout the world;
4   the reduction of America's intervention in the Third World;
5   the checking of Chinese aggression in South-East Asia.

The third point highlights the capacity of the Soviet Union's propaganda to turn even the defeats of Soviet foreign policy into alleged victories.

The role of ideology in international relations

Totalitarianism theoreticians in the West were inclined to stress the aspect of system maintenance and only ascribe secondary importance to the ideology of world revolution.[40] That, by comparison, was their most moderated contribution to the analysis of socialist systems. A number of analysts, however, considered world revolutionary expansionism to be just as much a driving force behind Soviet foreign policy as the defensive, system-upholding element of totalitarianism: 'the Soviet Union, through its ideological commitment, appears as a power which is striving for universal rule via a revolutionary structural change in the existing world of states'.[41]

A mere listing of driving forces, however, does not furnish a sufficiently complex picture of the motives behind foreign policy action. The adoption of the driving force concept from Marxism, which is closely connected with narrowly defined elements of the contradiction theory and the theory of the class struggle, in itself already seems rather strange.[42]

Not even the Soviet counter accusation of 'hegemony', which is understood as the endeavour to win leads in the military and economic sector which have already been lost, goes as far as this statement.[43]

A mere analysis of the rhetoric from 'peaceloving' to 'anti-imperialistic' and the epithets repeatedly used in the literature (with somewhat tiring monotony) for the Soviets' own foreign policy does not permit the conclusion that the revolutionary character is in the foreground, even if values such as 'pragmatism', 'flexibility' and 'willingness to compromise' still do not figure very prominently in the Soviet Union's assessment of herself.[44] Soviet pioneers in further development of the theory of international relations at times actually do face up to penetrating questions. When asked what he meant by the general expression 'improvement of the international situation as a whole', Georgii Arbatov replied: 'Not a worldwide socialist revolution, of course. I am referring to changes that are acceptable to both systems'.[45]

In terms of the Soviet Union's self-conception, ideology is coming to play an increasing role in the system confrontation. The stalemate that has resulted from the reciprocal nuclear threat has forced coexistence upon the camps. Soviet doctrine is thus attempting to save face. Since military confrontation would be increasingly suicidal and impossible, emphasis is being placed on the growing role of ideology in the system confrontation.[46]

It would be one-sided to ascribe too much importance to the general equivocation about adaptation in the daily output of ideology. This ideology output today no longer comes from a 'central office for eternal truths' in the Soviet Union either. B. N. Ponomarev, a candidate member of the Politburo since May 1972 and Head of the international department since 1955, certainly does not rank amongst the great innovators. It is not difficult to filter out aggressively sounding sentences from his many speeches and essays.[47] Yet more striking than the official and officious speeches of the politicians is the increasing differentiation in the formulation of ideology. In the 1970s, following the XXIV Party Congress in 1971, the Institute of World Economy and International Relations under Inozemtsev (up to 1982, until 1985 under Yakovlev) and the Institute of USA and Canadian Studies under Arbatov were increasingly frequently entrusted with the preliminary formulation of the Party's programmatic statements as well.[48]

Even Western interpreters who had long highlighted the expansionist features of Soviet foreign policy saw less emphasis on the world revolutionary element and a less pronounced world power consciousness in Brezhnev's policy speech at the XXVI Party Congress in 1981 than at the XXV Party Congress.[49] This analysis again assumes a pluralist negotiating process behind the ideology output. Whilst the Brezhnev speech of 1976 is presumed to have borne the signatures of ideologists such as Suslov and his colleague, Ponomarev, a more immediate group of staff in the Secretariat and the Central Committee apparatus (particularly from the Department of International Information) seems to have played a greater part in 1981. Foreign Minister Gromyko is said to have a mediating influence here.[50]

Analyses of press content have revealed that, by comparison with the Stalin and Khrushchev eras, even the Soviet press has gained increasing information value. Statements are worded carefully, yet still kept ambiguous in a large number of cases, partly to protect the author in a system which shies away from responsibility and partly to encourage the reader to draw fallacious, positive conclusions, which can then be denied if need be (if drawn into a tight corner at international level). Conscious lies have become rarer, however, even in Western estimations as well.[51]

The replacement of the totalitarianism paradigm in the analysis of socialist systems with convergence theories of differing shades has led to the influence of ideology being considered as slight in comparison to the practical politics of national interests. Many observers, however, still take a Soviet leadership belief in world revolution to be a constant factor.[52]

Alongside the lip service to world revolution, which can actually be found, even if in the less militant phrases of the theory of coexistence, an evolutionary interpretation of the processes in the world system predominates. 'Driving force' is the *Deus ex machina* here again, which has to help provide justification for the growing significance now accorded to intelligence in a system that which defines itself as a 'worker and peasant state' — the scientific, technical revolution (abbreviated in Russian to NTR). Whilst the scientific, technical revolution is used within the country by way of an evolutionary explanation for a large number of processes and for the alignment of classes, strata and groups in social structure analysis, when it comes to the system confrontation in foreign policy, it is the class conflict aspects on which value is placed. NTR counts as a 'qualitative leap forward in the field of mass communication media', which is not intended to have an unideological, evolutionary impact in the sense of convergence theories. It is rated as a means of re-ideologisation and mobilisation of the masses within capitalism as well, such that these masses will then allegedly respond in 'deep sympathy to the titanic effort being undertaken by the CPSU to create a better international climate'.[53] The fact that this truly observable increase in making the masses more sensitive through mass communications media is not simply proceeding at the cost of Western democracies but is also threatening 'real socialism' through erosion tendencies at the borders of the Soviet camp, is not yet acknowledged in this analysis.

The question as to 'does ideology matter?', which is repeatedly posed in the Western literature, still receives a positive answer from most analysts.[54] The approach that stresses the power interests of the Soviet empire creates far too artificial a contrast between power and ideology.

Nevertheless, it would be inappropriate to follow the example of earlier totalitarianism theories and always try to derive actual behaviour directly from the party's ideological statements.[55]

Ideology accounts for a large component of socialisation. Ideological phrases and interpretations are imperative in order to create continuity in foreign policy and are manifold in order to take in different interests. Hence it is indispensable to take a look at the domestic conditions that govern the foreign policy decision-making process in the Soviet Union.

2 The Foreign Policy Decision-Making Process in the Soviet Union

Two different approaches have been adopted in the attempt to provide an answer, on the basis of experience, to the question of the role played by the CPSU's ideological goals in foreign policy:

1   *Group and elite theory approaches* have diversified the image of the political decision-making élite.
2   *Politico-economic analyses* by scientists, who regard themselves as to the left of the 'real socialism' movement, tend instead to postulate the degeneration of the original ideology into power interests or even into internal economic interests.

The second approach subsists primarily by analogous reasoning. It works on the assumption that the Soviet élite in foreign policy is 'tactically counter-revolutionary'. An 'objective revolutionary element' still remains 'functional' however, beyond the intentions of this élite, 'in so far as under the conditions of system competition it is forced *de facto* to work with social groups and classes that are seeking to liberate themselves from the dominance of American capitalism or imperialism...'.[1] This approach touches on the sharp criticism that has been voiced by *émigrés* as to the motivation of the 'nomenclature class', in that it largely denies the Soviet Union's foreign policy leadership revolutionary, ideological motives and views the growing exchange of goods in East–West trade in terms of improved privileges for this group, particularly in consumer goods and food.[2] In line with the earlier totalitarianism theory, the left ascribes this leadership a uniform 'class interest'. Whilst *émigrés* at times venture comparisons with the nobility,[3] leftist critics of the Soviet Union instead tend to speak of a 'new bourgeoisie'. Both views have an undifferentiated approach in common.

Even the older totalitarianism theories never took a totally monolithic view of the system. The research interest that has frequently been mocked as 'Kremlinology' or even 'Kremlin astrology', however, still has to work with personalised conflict models to date, due to the lack of more detailed information. The situation is in part no different when it comes to the analysis of Western foreign policy. Here again, there is an area that has retained the greatest number of old reservation concepts from the *arcana imperii*. It is only at parliamentary level, if at all (and mainly for foreign trade problems), that foreign policy decision-making processes are tackled in detailed studies with a differentiated group approach. Élite theory and interest group assumptions have improved the insight into foreign policy decision-making process in the Soviet Union. But we should not delude ourselves — this remains the area of our study where we are most dependent on suppositions and indirect conclusions: 'a rogue who gives more than he has to offer'.

The decision-makers in Soviet foreign policy

There is no shortage of élite studies on the Soviet Union but the foreign policy sphere is not generally given separate treatment. Individual members of the foreign policy leadership rank amongst some of the top positions. When Andropov with his overseas and KGB experience took up the leading post in the Soviet Union in 1982, he was the first holder of the post to count amongst the foreign policy élite in many quarters and who, above all, had least experience in the area where the Soviet Union has the most problems, namely in economic affairs.

A sample of 93 leading positions included five further men predominantly involved in foreign policy:[4] Gromyko (Foreign Minister), Ponomarev (Head of the Department of International Information), Ruskakov (Head of the Department for Relations with the Communist and Workers' Parties of Socialist Countries), Kuznetsev (first Deputy Foreign Minister and Politburo Candidate) and Zamyatin (Head of the Department of International Information).

If the concept of top leadership is extended to take in the whole of the Central Committee, then this gives some 15 posts for 1980, which still represents a small minority for a body with 309 members (1981: 319). This inner circle displays different recruitment patterns from other countries in that nine of its members studied engineering, the vogue course of study during the Stalin era. The majority still came from the working class — an increasingly rare facet amongst the younger members as self-recruitment becomes increasingly established amongst executive staff and the intelligentsia.[5]

The whole of the foreign service has a representation of 25 persons in the Central Committee. Conclusions are drawn about the importance of diplomatic missions from rises and falls within the Central Committee. In 1981 the ambassadors to the Federal Republic of Germany and Italy were upgraded, whilst the ambassador to the People's Republic of China was 'demoted'.[6] It is striking that the majority of leadership positions are held by the same persons for long periods of time.

Apart from the social profiles of the top leaders we have little information on the foreign policy élite specifically. Whilst the cadre literature of the Soviet Union, for both party and state machinery, deals with transnational contacts between the party and other Communist parties it does not cover the staff engaged in international politics.[7]

The *Politburo*, which was known as the Presidium of the Central Committee of the CPSU from 1952 to 1966, is also the true holder of governmental and organisational power for foreign policy — not the government in the Council of Ministers and its presidium. Foreign statesmen, such as Brandt and Kissinger, who negotiated with Brezhnev were initially under the impression that the Secretary General regarded Prime Minister Kosygin as a partner jointly involved in decisions. Only later did Brezhnev emerge as the deciding actor, who at best made a semblance of being dependent upon others in order to win time.[8]

The full Politburo cannot deal with foreign policy all the time and hence it has a foreign policy committee. The make-up of this important leadership body is not known. Its membership is presumed to include the Minister of Defence, the Head of the KGB, the Chairman of the Council of Ministers, the Chairman of the Presidium of the Supreme Soviet — *de jure* the function of President in so far as this office was not yet amalgamated with the functions of Brezhnev under Podgornyi — and the Secretary of the Central Committee.[9] Execution of the decisions taken by the Politburo rests with the Secretary of the Central Committee and with the Council of Ministers.

Apart from the party's direct leadership in foreign policy the party also possesses channels through which it can exert indirect leadership in foreign policy — the foreign contacts of the CPSU and what remains of the party's foreign machinery since the dissolution of Comintern (1943) and Cominform (1956). Contacts with foreign Communist parties are differentiated according to ruling parties and non-ruling parties (see pp. 145–61).

The Foreign Ministry and the Diplomatic Corps

The descriptions of the foreign policy machinery given in Soviet works, such as in the standard work by Zorin, provide little elucidation. It is stressed that the make-up of the Foreign Ministry follows the standard pattern applied in most other countries. The Ministry has 17 territorial and 16 functional departments (e.g. consular department, protocol, legal and contract departments, press office, department for international organisations, department for foreign cultural relations, planning department, department for general foreign policy affairs). Apart from the Foreign Ministry, the Ministry of Foreign Trade and the foreign departments of a number of Ministries and other authorities (through to the foreign department of the Academy of Sciences) have foreign contacts, it being stressed that this is 'under the leadership of the Foreign Ministry of the Soviet Union'.[10] No references are made about potential problems of competence between the Foreign Ministry and the Ministry of Foreign Trade. A further body, 'the Collegium', which has been the subject of much speculation in the West,[11] also remains in semi-obscurity. This is an advisory body made up of the Minister, his deputies and 'a number of members'.[12]

It was only after the USSR had been constituted on 30 December 1922 that the Foreign Commissariat of the RSFSR was changed into an all-union People's Commissariat for Foreign Affairs. Chicherin had still signed the Treaty of Rapallo in April 1922 in the sole name of the RSFSR. The other Soviet Republics were simply allied in the form of a diplomatic union and the powers they delegated to Chicherin were confined to such resolutions as they had approved in November 1922.

It should not, however, be imagined that the independence of the other Soviet Republics was all that extensive at the time of the Treaty Federation. The Russian delegation at Brest-Litovsk was already attempting to speak on behalf of the other Republics. The Republics were ruled by Bolshevist minorities in many cases, who had neither fully established themselves vis-à-vis their civil war enemies nor were able to uphold their efforts for autonomy (which to some extent were perhaps intended seriously) vis-à-vis the hegemonic power of the RSFSR.[13]

A number of Republics attempted to save something of their outward sovereignty. The Ukranians, Rakovskii and Skrypnik, were still calling for a decentralised diplomatic service and decentralised foreign trade at the XII Party Congress. All that they achieved with this venture, however, was that Rakovskii, the Ukrainian Foreign Minister, was appointed second Deputy Foreign Commissar to Chicherin. In September 1923 the Ukrainian diplomatic service was merged with the Russian diplomatic service. A law passed in 1926 finally made it a punishable offence for civil servants of Union Republics to have contacts with foreign representatives other than through the prescribed official channels.[14]

The independence of the Union Republics became even more of a sham after the formation of the Union. The right to separation and the declaration of sovereignty for the individual Union Republics was scarcely taken seriously abroad, particularly since there were provisions in the criminal law that made canvassing for secession an offence. In Febuary 1944, at a time when victory was becoming a possibility and the starting postion for renegotiations had to be strengthened, Stalin made amendments to the 1936 Constitution improving the Union Republics' legal claims to subjection to international law. The 16 Union Republics (only 15 after the Karelian-Finnish Union Republic was degraded to an Autonomous Republic after exhausting its role as the irredenta collecting point for all Finns within the Soviet' sphere of control) were again granted the right to establish direct relations with other states. This step only took on significance for the Ukraine and Byelorussia with Roosevelt's concession in granting these two regions a seat in the UN. The old opinion that only sovereign states could be subjects of international law was being increasingly called into question in Western international law.[15] The Soviet theory took the path of least resistance, continuing to demand sovereignty for the Union Republics instead of calling for the subjection of non-sovereign states to international law. The continuity of the Republics' independence was exaggerated in the Soviet literature. The explanation given for the extension of competences in foreign policy was that the Republics had simply had a dormant sovereignty and hence 1944 did not mark an intrusion but merely the legal confirmation of competences that had never been withdrawn.[16]

Although the Soviet Union rapidly took on a conservative stance in the theory of constitutional and international law, she nonetheless at the outset attempted to revolutionise international law in the institutional sphere. It was not until 15 March 1946 that the People's Commissariats were given the name of Ministries again.[17] Diplomatic ranks had been abolished by decree in June 1918 and from then on the Soviet government had only been represented by authorised representatives (Polpred, from *polnomoshchenyi predstavitel*). This was much to the detriment of her own position, since foreign diplomats did not treat the authorised representatives as being of equal rank. The supplementary wording 'with the title of Ambassador' thus had to be conceded again as early as July 1924. When the Union was formed, the position of the representatives was removed from one of revolutionary arbitrariness and subjected to statutory regulation.[18] The final vestiges of revolutionary Soviet terminology were eliminated during the Second World War with the decree on the 'establishment of ranks for diplomatic representatives abroad' in May 1941. The designation of the ranks retained its party-orientation, however, in titles such as Authorised Representative and Secretary.

In parallel to the changes in the legal status of the Foreign Ministry and the diplomats far-reaching changes came about in the conception and organisation of the Office. The post-revolutionary People's Commissariat (*Narkomindel*) was primarily restricted to the management of diplomatic business. Whilst Trotsky constituted a powerful figure as the first Foreign Commissar, his opinion of the Office was very low:

> When I was given the Foreign Ministry, it looked as though it would be impossible to get a hold on the business — everyone from the Minister's aide to the typists was engaged in sabotage. The cupboards were locked and there were no keys. I turned to Markin, who knew the secret of direct action. A few diplomats were locked up for twenty-four hours and the next day Markin brought me the keys and invited me to the Ministry. But I was at Smolny engaged in the general tasks of the revolution. Markin thus became non-official Foreign Minister for a while. He soon saw through the workings of the Commissariat in his way and with a firm hand undertook a purge amongst the high-born and thievish diplomats, re-equipped the chancery, confiscated for the homeless wares smuggled in from abroad in diplomatic luggage, took the most informative secret documents out of the fireproof cabinets in the Ministry and published them as brochures with his own comments under his own responsibility. Markin was by no means an academic and he did not even write without making spelling mistakes. His annotations at times appeared strange due to the peculiarity of some of his thoughts. Overall though, he hit his diplomatic nail right on the head. Mr von Kühlmann and Czernin used to pounce greedily on Markin's little yellow book at Brest-Litovsk.[19]

After the episode with Trotsky in the Foreign Office, Lenin himself took over a considerable part of foreign policy business. He had a close confidential relationship with G.V. Chicherin, the Foreign Commissar (1918–30). But the highly cultured Foreign Minister did not hold the levers of power. After Lenin's death Chicherin himself reported that Lenin had dealt with all the details personally.[20]

Lenin praised the work of the Foreign Commissariat as an example to be followed by other Ministries: — With the exception of the People's Commissariat for Foreign Affairs, our state machinery is for the most part a relic of the old state machinery, to which only a few changes of any seriousness have been made.[21] The obstruction which Trotsky was recalling had provoked a much more intense counterblow in foreign policy and led to a radical purge. An initial version of Lenin's proposal for the XII Party Congress not only included a stringent new start but also highlighted the fact 'that the People's Commissariat for Foreign Affairs works under the direct leadership of our Central Committee'.[22]

Chicherin's successor in office, Litvinov (1930–39), gave the impression of having competence to act alone through the self-assured manner with which he appeared in Western capitals, and at times even triggered speculation about potential affiliation to a non-Stalinist (Bukharinist) faction.[23] He too had to go, though, when the Hitler-Stalin pact brought a change of course and it became evident who really held true power in foreign policy. Under Stalin the diplomatic service was even allocated the function of being a frequent transitory occupation for those in opposition before they fell victim to the purges.[24] This same pattern, although without the liquidation, was applied to Molotov after his removal from power when he was deployed to the insignificant post in Mongolia. All the same, most of the top men in the Foreign Office and in the chief embassies were spared the purges, perhaps out of consideration to the Western powers.[25]

Earlier group affiliations seem to have played no role. Mayskii (Ambassador in London) and Potemkin (Deputy Foreign Minister) were previously Mensheviks. Tryanovskii, the Ambassador to the USA, had had connections with the Bukharin group which was purged. Not even the author Ilya Ehrenburg, a close friend of Litvinov, was able to explain why the Foreign Minister had survived and reported that he always kept a revolver on his bedside table to escape arrest should he hear the customary ring on the bell in the night.[26]

After 1939 the survivors were generally moved off into insignificant posts. The second generation, the Gromyko cohort, was less cosmopolitan than the old generation of diplomats, where the revolutionary intelligentsia had predominated (70 per cent middle class, 17 per cent nobility, only 5 per cent workers).[27] From 1937 onwards there was an increase in the *apparatchik* type with their close links to the secret service (NKVD). Molotov was the embodiment of the new type of politician in foreign affairs — unconditionally devoted to Stalin and possessing little creativity. Even ambassadors from the socialist countries had the impression that 'Molotov did not hold the chief reins of Soviet foreign policy in his hands although he was Foreign Minister'.[28]

In the Khrushchev and Brezhnev era the influence of the Foreign Minister and the foreign policy decision-making élite broadened. Andropov's taking up office in 1982 can be interpreted as a further step in this direction, since Andropov had more experience in foreign and security policy than in economic policy. In the 1960s and 1970s individual diplomats of merit moved up the party hierarchy. These included Dobrynin, Ambassador in Washington as of 1961, and Kuznezev, first Deputy Foreign Minister. Gromyko also made his party career via diplomatic work. From 1943 to 1945 he was Ambassador in Washington. It was not until 1973 that he achieved admittance to the highest party body but this success was due more to a collective increase in governmental offices than to the isolated success of the Foreign

Minister, since Andropov, Head of the KGB, and Grechko, Minister of Defence, received the same promotion.[29]

After Gorbatchev's succession to power in July 1985 a substantial re-shuffling of personnel took place. Contrary to many expectations Gorbatchev did not follow the example of his last three predecessors who had assumed the function of head of the state (chairman of the presidium of the Supreme Soviet) in combination with the party leadership. Gromyko — the longest serving foreign minister since Metternich — was nominated head of the state. It was disputed among foreign observers whether this was a reward for Gromyko's assistance in Gorbatchev's rise to power, or whether Gorbatchev wanted to neutralize a potential rival through a formal elevation, as Khrushchev once had practiced with Voroshilov and Brezhnev with Podgornyi. Even Andropov is said to have offered this post to Chernenko, and took it over after the decline of the office by his rival.

Among the 13 members of the politbureau in July 1985 (12 in 1986), KGB chairman Chebrikov and the new foreign minister Shevardnadze were included. The foreign policy elite was also strongly represented among its deputy members. There were many speculations that Shevardnadze — not a trained career diplomat — would be substituted for the Ambassador to the United States, Dobrynin. During the nominations in the course of the 27th party meeting in 1986, however, he remained in office. Some interpreters believe that this decision was motivated by Gorbatchev's zeal to avoid having too powerful figures in the most important offices.

Memoirs of foreign diplomats as a source of insight into the Foreign Ministry are only slightly more revealing than the Soviet information itself. A British ambassador found the ornate skyscraper, which he likened to a 'vast yellow wedding cake' to be 'curiously empty, silent and lifeless' at least in the rooms accessible to Western visitors. Dealings with the ministry were likened to an old-fashioned slot machine: 'You put in the penny — your question — and in the end probably you will get something out, perhaps not what you wanted, an acid drop when you hoped for chocolate, but something, and you can sometimes expedite the process by shaking the machine. It is however useless to talk to it.'[30] Formal contacts were 'unproductive routine' one American ambassador recalls, and the topics of conversation were laid down firmly in advance.[31] On occasions, some of the more unconventional relationships in diplomacy developed, such as that between Hans Kroll, Ambassador of the Federal Republic of Germany, and Khrushchev. But this relationship too was accompanied by alternating waves of friendly gestures and outbursts of rage.[32]

The change in cadre training and the urbanisation of the new generation of diplomats also brought a change in the negotiating tactics applied in Soviet foreign policy. The declaratory, diplomatic style of Brest-Litovsk has given way to a harsh professionalism. Soviet negotiators still tend to use Litvinov's bargaining tactics, however, making over-high demands and only reducing these when a certain *rapprochement* has been achieved. Overall, the qualities of Soviet negotiation lie in repetition.[33] A large number of misunderstandings with Western negotiators result from differences in education and mentality. Soviet diplomats like to proceed from general proposals which they gradually substantiate, whilst Americans place the emphasis on technical detail.[34] The Americans thus become impatient right from the start with these playing-for-time tactics, which they regard as an obstruction, even though this is no more so than in Brest-Litovsk where Trotsky later prided himself on having dragged out the negotiations, albeit with the support of the opposite side who had applied the same tactics.[35]

The professional profile of the Soviet diplomat has undergone a pronounced change since the time of revolutionary 'People's diplomacy'. 'The shop' which Trotsky, according to some declarations, promised to shut up, has grown into the most powerful foreign policy apparatus in the world. Western diplomats who had to negotiate with their Soviet colleagues all give the same reports of a growing quality amongst the diplomatic staff. The Soviet diplomats are still regarded as being so indoctrinated, however, that they are scarcely able to report in a manner which we would term objective.[36] It is not always easy to determine whether gross misjudgements of fact are deliberate or the ideological 'line'. A West German ambassador in Moscow reported of Abrassimov, his Soviet colleague in office in East Berlin, that 'he didn't even know the Agreement had been concluded for the whole of Berlin and by no means just for West Berlin, and accused the Federal Government of offending against the spirit of the Agreement'.[37] Of Zarapkin, his Soviet colleague in Bonn, he reported, that when asked what would be the most lasting impression of his stay in Germany, Zarapkin had replied: 'Well, first of all, of course, the terrible situation of the German worker'.[38] Ignorance and a lack of discernment? Hardly.

A study of official statements and press releases provides us with more to weigh up in our judgement. The Soviet élite generally expresses itself with care, and declarations are generally kept ambiguous given the risk of responsibility in a bureaucratic, authoritarian regime. At times, official spokesmen have openly lied, such as during the Cuba crisis. Yet it was precisely the ensuing diplomatic humiliation that led to those engaged in foreign policy becoming more reticent. The standard procedure, however, is to sidestep into propaganda statements or into ambiguous formulations, which do not contain any lies but do make it easy for the reader or listener to draw false conclusions from the declaration.[39] The increasing scientific consultation does not necessarily imply liberalisation or democratisation,[40] but does mark a contribution towards more rational decision-making — a factor which does not always imply greater democracy in the West either, but tends to favour technocratic development instead. Added to this, it serves to intensify a certain pluralism within the decision-making process inside the party, since the groups also employ scientific factual knowledge to win through their opinion in the various bodies.

In the international organisations the Soviet Union is paying increasing attention to the quotas allocated to the Eastern bloc and is thus increasing the need for diplomats. Since there were not enough qualified cadres available to meet all her worldwide obligations, the Soviet Union initially sent staff to the politically-important organisations, such as the ILO and UNESCO, rather than to the numerous technical organisations that take up people with a high level of expert knowledge without producing any spectacular political successes.[41] Whereas Soviet foreign policy once set out with the call for the special status of diplomats to be phased out, she is now scrupulously intent on observing immunities and privileges.[42]

Co-operation in the scientific and cultural sphere has come to be regarded as increasingly important in the wake of the scientific and technical revolution. Cultural relationships have always played an important role since these allowed transnational politics to be conducted to the Soviet Union's advantage and gave an opportunity for countless, unsuspicious fellow-traveller organisations to be set up.

A study carried out for a committee of the American Senate estimated that the Soviet propaganda apparatus had half a million people working for it worldwide. The financial outlay was reckoned to be one hundred times greater than for the whole of the 'free world'.[43] Only a fraction of this generous estimate goes into propaganda, and not all persons employed on propaganda have this as their sole function.

The Soviet Union's self-conception stresses that the products of Soviet publicity abroad can no longer be ignored even by 'the ideological adversaries', but does no more than give a list of the institutions. Not even the number of copies of printed material for foreign countries is given (except in special cases).[44] The boundaries between information for abroad and cultural policy are also fluid. The successes of Soviet cultural policy are only undisputed in the Soviet Union's own version of affairs. Europe plays a major role in cultural policy. Although, in ideological terms, the Soviet Union has an ambivalent attitude to the bourgeois culture of the West, she still implicitly measures her own achievements against West European standards. Cultural exchanges are only authorised on a highly selective basis.[45] Complaints are voiced about the indiscriminating nature of the 'cultural market', which admits ideas of nationalism, chauvinism and Fascism.[46]

In a few areas, such as ballet, those in charge of Soviet cultural policy regard themselves as being in the lead. An American ambassador told of a dispute with Furtseva, the Minister in charge, who had accused American experts of wanting to come to Moscow for 'industrial espionage'.[47] Even when brilliant cultural performances are on offer, authorities on the matter do not consider them to have much of an influence on the attitudes of Western citizens towards the Soviet Union. The Bolshoi ballet 'cannot make a Leninist out of a Rotarian'.[48] First-class performances in Soviet culture are scarcely attributed to the regime. Cultural missions most easily gain renown in the West when they are shrouded in an aura of resistance and deviant behaviour, such as with Evtushenko.

A new dimension in foreign policy setbacks is linked to the increasing number of defections amongst artists and scientists. Khrushchev concludes his memoirs with thoughts of free emigration, making reference to the exodus of dissenters that had already taken place under Lenin. His comment on Ashkenasy's settling in London was: 'Well, so what then? Let them live where they want to live!'.[49] This type of generosity, which Khrushchev only felt to be right after his fall from power, is no longer so straightforwardly possible today, given the increased defection of members of ensembles and scientists at congresses. The Soviet Union even cancelled guest appearances of her own accord in 1980 after demanding virtual security from the USA that all Soviet artists would return home again afterwards — an undertaking that no Western country with the usual guarantee of asylum can be prepared to give. The boycott of the Olympic Games (Los Angeles, 1984) by a large number of Western powers also produced cancellations from the Soviet side, despite the fight that the Soviet Union otherwise puts up against embargo and boycott measures from the opposing side.[50]

Cadre training and political consultation

The foreign service was subjected to particularly intensive purges after the seizure of power, and hence cadre training experienced a bottleneck. The social profile of the older generation, which included large numbers of graduates in the engineering sciences, in itself showed that there was a lack of professionalised diplomats at the outset. In 1921, the year of famine, the supply of food was so catastrophic that many Foreign Ministry officials left their jobs. Chicherin turned to Lenin for help and he made sure that rations were provided.[51]

The present, fourth generation of diplomats counts as well-trained, competent and endowed with a high level of social prestige in Soviet society. The training department of the Foreign Ministry is responsible for training up-and-coming diplomats. This department is in charge of the diplomat school, the Moscow State Institute of International Relations (MGIMO), and the language institutes. Apart from these language institutes, graduates from the Pedagogical Institute of Foreign Languages and the Institute of World Economics and International Relations (IMEMO) also have access to the foreign service.[52]

The training scheme does not produce generalists. The Soviet diplomat is highly specialised and has a good knowledge of the region in which he is later to work. Soviet diplomats are regarded as competent and persevering. Even in disarmament negotiations they prefer their opposite numbers to have a strong position in their homelands and to adopt a firm and stringent negotiating position.[53] The increasing differentiation in the institutes that train future diplomats and make scientific political consultation possible is a development that began under Khrushchev and was sped up by Brezhnev. In the older generation under Chicherin the opinion that diplomacy was an art still predominated, true to the Lenin dictum that 'politics is a science and an art'.[54] The tendency for practicians to view their handiwork as more of an art than a science (which also prevailed amongst our political élite for a long time[55]) has still not fully disappeared from recent Soviet publications.[56] Overall, however, the foreign policy decision-making climate has become highly scientised. The Soviet literature puts forward the 'scientific and technical revolution' as the reason behind the change in international relations and in the ability of the cadres, and in particular the 'qualitative leap' of gaining influence over the masses through the media, which has brought an expansion in the potentials of foreign policy.[57] This allusion to 'People's diplomacy', however, is misleading. This was an instrument used to a much greater extent by Trotsky (who first delivered a speech to the railway workers at Brest-Litovsk before greeting the negotiators from the other side) and by Lenin and Chicherin. Present-day foreign policy propaganda is embedded in too much of a routine to be able to reproduce the revolutionary impetus of the combat period.

The Foreign Ministry and the Central Committee department are not able to carry out systematic investigations. An increasing division of labour is thus developing between politics and science. This, however, is marked by incomparably closer co-operation than in Western countries. The Academy of Sciences holds a key role in the preparatory phase of foreign policy decisions,[58] a role that it has already had in domestic policy cadre training and policy consultation since the 1930s.[59] Since then, a steady flow of new sciences has been introduced for the consultation process. Even political science has emerged of late — the science that was long viewed as a reactionary, bourgeois science, of which scientific Marxism-Leninism had no need.[60] Political science, which is now becoming established in the Soviet Union as a research subject, if not yet as a subject of instruction, is also changing the dialogue situation with

Western political science students. The latest products of the discussion, which display considerably more understanding and differentiation than earlier attempts, bear witness to this.[61]

It was only after Stalin's death that this upswing in science become possible in the foreign policy sphere. In 1949 the only institute that had dealt with world politics, Eugene Varga's Institute of World Economics and World Politics, was closed down following vehement attacks due to Varga's false prognoses.[62] The political élite of the post-Stalin era increasingly began to feel the gap. Mikoyan criticised the lack of scientific treatment of capitalism on behalf of the Khrushchev wing of the party at the XX Party Congress:

> We are lagging seriously behind in the study of the contemporary stage of capitalism. We are not conducting any far-reaching analysis of facts or figures but frequently confining ourselves to the extraction of individual facts on an impending crisis and the impoverishment of the working population for propaganda purposes. We are not making any coherent, in-depth assessment of the phenomena that are taking place in the lives of other countries.[63]

After the XX Party Congress in 1956 the former Varga Institute was set up again as part of the Academy of Sciences, under the title World Economics and International Relations (IMEMO). Varga came forward again in 1956 with initiatives for assessing the Suez crisis[64] but he was not entrusted with the leadership of the new institute for a second time although he had been rehabilitated. A.A. Arzumayan and Inozemtsev (1966–1982) had much more political influence as heads of the institute than scientific institutions in the West could ever have. From 1983–85 the former ambassador to Canada, Yakovlev, became the director of this institute. The rapid expansion of the institutes created serious problems in finding next-generation staff and resulted in an extraordinary career mobility for large numbers of young people.

A Soviet listing of the institutes that deal with international relations and disarmament questions gives five area studies institutes. The most influential is the Institute of American and Canadian Studies under the direction of Arbatov (founded in 1968). The other institutes cover the following regions: Africa (founded in 1954); Orient (Vostokovedeniya Institute, founded in 1930); Far East (founded in 1966); and Latin America (founded in 1961). The foundation dates of the institutes allow certain presumptions as to the expansion of attention thresholds in Soviet foreign policy. The Orient had held a key function in Soviet foreign policy ever since the Conference of Baku in 1920 and was not by chance the region that was subject to permanent scientific observation (see pp. 118–23). Alongside these, there are six institutes divided up on a functional basis: General History (founded in 1968); the Institute of State and Law (founded in 1925 under the title *Institut sovetskogo stroitel'stva* and given its present name in 1959 — it houses the headquarters of the Soviet Association of Political Sciences (the old-fashioned plural is still the preferred usage)); the Institute of USSR History (founded in 1968); the Institute of the International Workers' Movement (founded in 1966); the Institute of the Economics of the Socialist World System (founded in 1960); and the already mentioned Institute of World Economics and International Relations set up in 1956, which is ascribed the role of a leading scientific centre in this listing as well.

The growing co-ordination problems were tackled by the creation of a documentation centre, the Institute of Scientific Information for the Social Sciences (INION), founded in 1969. In addition, a Scientific Council of the Academy of Sciences for the history of USSR foreign policy and international relations was set up (in 1963). This assumes the co-ordination of the different efforts undertaken in the sphere of international politics.[65]

Finally, a joint venture was launched in 1979 by the Presidium of the Academy of Sciences and the State Committee of the USSR for Science and Technology under the title 'Scientific Council for Research into the Problems of Peace and Disarmament' under the leadership of Inozemtsev (up to 1982) with some 80 well-known scientists. This is occasionally regarded in the literature as being the equivalent of Western armament control institutions.[66]

Apart from their regular scientific work (which is already subject to political imperatives on many counts) all these institutes have to devote some 25 per cent of their time to special assignments, which American observers have described as 'classified work'.[67] This type of political consultation does not necessarily have to be associated with espionage work. It generally remains unpublished, however. There is all the same, only speculation as to the proportion of secret activity within Soviet foreign policy. One observer of the diplomatic scene maintained that 70 per cent of all diplomats were engaged *de facto* on work for the KGB.[68] The institutes have increasingly come to express more pragmatic opinions about the West and to apply realistic expertise to politics. They have not been afraid to admit, with reference to Lenin, that they 'have to learn from the West'.[69] On the other hand, however, the institute lauded its own closeness to the party, which was honoured with the admission of Inozemtsev as a Candidate Member to the Central Committee in 1971. Arbatov, the Director of the USA Institute, praised the IMEMO, to which all other institutes were in some way obliged and which had 'created a tradition'.[70] The institute's close ties with the chief ideologists Suslov and Ponomarev gave it a leading function in the production of ideology and science which was relevant to foreign policy. The 'scientific, technical' revolution was not simply a propaganda phrase here. True innovations emerged from the institute, such as the application of quantitative methods, and these are only gradually being adopted in other institutes, such as the Academy-Institute of State and Law and the Department of International Politics around Shakhnazarov.

Pluralism in the foreign policy decision-making process

Despite the dominance of the totalitarianism paradigm, even Western analysts have never viewed the Soviet decision-making structure in monolithic fashion. The earlier version of pluralism hypotheses comprised research into internal party factions, the later version involved the acceptance of pluralism approaches from research into Western decision-making processes.

The history of the CPSU is a history of group struggles. It has been stated, in somewhat schematic terms, that 'the conscience of the revolution', which still at times identifies the opposition groups within the party with the traditions of the Westerners against the Slavophiles, is always subordinate.[71] It is also true that even the left/right configuration taken from the 'trouser seat geography' of Western parliamentary seating arrangements proved unsuitable as a description in many respects, although even Lenin branded 'left-wing' deviationists in particular. Nevertheless, whole eras of foreign policy were classified as a turn to the right (1921, 1955/56) or a turn to the left (1946–58), whereby left was identified with purposeful Utopianism, optimism and 'red' enthusiasm, whilst right was classified as emphasis on pragmatism and pessimism in the assessment of one's own potentials and a technocratic expert mentality.[72] The problems of drawing up right and left classifications already became evident with the flexibility of a number of chief actors after Lenin. Stalin overcame the left-wing Trotskyist deviationists but as of 1928 went on to adopt a number of their theses in forced collectivisation, that had been upheld by Preobrazhenskii. Khrushchev took up Malenkov's plea for more consumer goods just as he had succeeded in asserting himself against Malenkov and thus underwent a diametrical change of fronts in a number of areas of politics. In foreign policy, moreover, the decisions taken in a large number of areas (such as policy in the Third World) were not greatly influenced by the differences in the party factions.[73]

As of the mid-1960s the totalitarianism paradigm increasingly came to be supplemented by considerations of impending pluralism. There was evidence of the expansion of the role of the social organisations in the post-Stalin era. But it was not these that were the equivalent but, at best, a type of 'apparatus pluralism'.[74] We have little detailed knowledge about the decision-making process in the party leadership bodies. Khrushchev once commented on this, saying that the Presidium of the Central Committee generally arrived at a common stand. If not, 'decisions are taken by a simple majority of votes'.[75] This emphasis on the collective nature of decisions, however, is one-sided precisely when it comes to the Khrushchev era. Khrushchev was guilty on many occasions in the eyes of the party of bypassing the competent party bodies and taking decisions by himself, of consulting with outsiders and 'old pals', such as with his son-in-law Adzhubei, and of pursuing an exuberant tourism diplomacy no longer sufficiently co-ordinated with the party. These accusations were levelled against him in Suslov's public prosecutor's speech in 1964.[76] Brezhnev once chatted about the practices within the Politburo to American journalists in 1973. From this it would appear that Politburo meetings are held every Thursday for three to four hours. Decisions are generally taken without a vote.[77] Increased group confrontation is illustrated by the confrontation with the anti-party group in 1957 which had criticised Khrushchev's independent style of leadership, by the confrontations following the Cuban fiasco in 1962, which led to his removal from office in 1964, by the endeavour to re-establish collective leadership and the undermining of this through a renewed accumulation of power by Brezhnev in the 1970s and finally by the preparations for the succession of Brezhnev at the start of the 1980s. Even supporters of the totalitarianism theory have decided upon a pluralist outlook: 'The dependancy upon certain group interests' has been attributed to the 'relaxation of the autocratic, totalitarian system of rule taken over from Stalin' and to the 'growing differentiation of the Soviet class society'.[78] There is agreement on the fact that it is not interest groups in the Western sense that are developing this influence but rather non-organised and to some extent latent interests within the central institutions of party and state. Whilst supporters of Western democracies tend to view this as progress, leftist critics of the Soviet Union are inclined to see further signs of a degeneration of real socialism, with the primacy of domestic policy being realised in a completely new, non-revolutionary sense, namely by way of an increasing dependence of foreign policy on internal social conditions.[79]

In domestic policy the group confrontations are frequently studied as retinues, in career policy terms,[80] or as policy coalitions (alongside interest and opinion groups) and factionalism in decision theory terms.[81] As in other systems, a greater degree of agreement prevails when it comes to foreign-policy decision situations. It is thus difficult to make out permanent opinion groups or even interest groups, quite apart from the fact that the veil of secrecy is much greater in foreign policy than in domestic policy decisions.

Opinion groups are frequently studied through the analysis of periodicals. The Federal Republic of Germany's *détente* policy after

1969, for instance, was taken up in the Soviet media with time lags and shifts in emphasis — first by *Novy Mir*, then by the economic periodical *Voprosy ekonomiki* and finally by the military periodical *Red Star*.[82] Opponents at times, however, assume there to be firmly-established opinion groups within the Soviet Union as well, such as when Khrushchev maintained that Malenkov and Beriya had wanted to liquidate the GDR and negotiate concessions for the reunification of Germany.[83] It is difficult to make out groups of 'hawks' and 'doves' that remain stable over the long term, in the way that people like to infer such groups from the media. No positive correlation has been found between domestic policy reformism and the promotion of international interdependence. At best a negative correlation exists: the avoidance of reform through the import of Western technology.[84] At all events, the stand in favour of economic co-operation may either stem from a conservative tendency to maximise military efforts or may imply the active promotion of *détente*, and hence it cannot be tied down to a single opinion group right from the start. The American literature makes frequent mention of pressure groups. The chief addressee is the Politburo. The most obvious way of ascertaining influences is from the degree of penetration that the groups have managed to achieve in the main bodies through direct representation. This indicator is only of limited information value, however. The group interests associated with the doves, who have the greatest interest in *détente* and coexistence, i.e. diplomacy, sector B of the economy (the consumer sector), agriculture and foreign trade bureaucracy, have only weak direct representation and yet still managed to assert themselves on occasions.[85] Even the military, who are frequently portrayed as the driving force behind the hawks, have on the whole tended to be under represented in the central bodies, apart from a short period in which Khrushchev allied himself to the military in order to fight the anti-party group around Malenkov and Molotov. With its contingent of 8.1 per cent the military group ranks only third in the Central Committee behind the party functionaries (40.9 per cent) and the state functionaries (30.4 per cent), and it is still not easy at that to distinguish between the professional soldier and the politofficer.[86] In the leading body of the Politburo, representation was only one full member in Defence Minister Ustinov. This admission to the highest party body also only came about at a late stage (1973). The eight ministers responsible for military production, who are likewise generally rated amongst the hawks, have all achieved full membership of the Central Committee almost as a matter of routine but have not managed the step up to the Politburo.[87]

Pressure group influences are not only able to act through direct representation in the leading party bodies but can also be effective by bringing indirect influence to bear. There has been much conjecture about this indirect lobbying but very little secured knowledge is available. The lobbying would be easier to detect in foreign policy actions within the socialist camp than in confrontation situations with the West when the lid of secrecy and solidarity is tightly closed. Attempts have been made to reconstruct the group activity at the time of intervention in Czechoslovakia and Afghanistan but too few case studies are available to venture generalisations about group cohesion within the party leadership. Even the little information that is available does not reveal any stable groups in the foreign policy decision-making process. Suslov and Ponomarev were rated as hawks in the East–West conflict. In the debate on the intervention in Czechoslovakia, on the other hand, they had more the effect of doves, being opposed to intervention with the force of arms in the interests of an ideologically unified socialist camp.[88] When it came to the Afghanistan crisis — already treated by many decision-makers as an internal block affair — Suslov acted more as an agitator.[89] A number of the group allocations that have been drawn up in the Western literature are based on an analysis of printed material put out by close associates of the exposed actors and by those engaged on their preliminary academic work. To draw conclusions from their statements as to the opinions of those for whom they are presumed to be working still remains hazardous. The case analyses generally proceed from a typology of the potential groups which may have brought influence to bear. The most important actors in foreign policy are the military and the security organs. The military are strictly subordinate to the political leadership. In the conflict with China, Moscow never tired of accusing the country of 'barracks Communism' with emergent Bonapartist tendencies. The army (including the politofficers, who no longer have anything like the independent status enjoyed by the *Politruks* of Stalin's time) is kept under close surveillance by the Secret Service. The military is tied by privileges and kept in its dependent position through the uncertainty that surrounds the individual's career prospects.[90]

Only once did it come to a trial of strength between the military and the party. Khrushchev had to make concessions in order to win the help of the military against Malenkov in Febuary 1955. Zhukov, a known opponent of Malenkov, was appointed Minister of Defence, Bulganin, a political general became Prime Minister and large numbers of the military received promotion. When Zhukov seemed to be gaining too much power,[91] chief exponents in the party, such as Suslov, lent Khrushchev their support in removing Zhukov from office. This was done under the accusation that the armed forces had been isolated from the party and that the Central Committee was intended to be kept out of decisions on important matters concerning the army and the navy.[92] For lack of information, Western research has tended largely to adopt the official version of anti-party behaviour. A re-examination of the conflict, however, shows this to have been more of a personal rivalry. After Khrushchev, reproaches of Bonapartism and the like were dropped and when Zhukov died in June 1974 he was awarded all the honours that had been denied him after his fall from power during his lifetime.[93]

One of the most eminent experts in the field of military research, Kolkowicz, has conceived of the relationship of the military to the party as being too conflict-oriented — probably under the impact of the Zhukov–Khrushchev conflicts. He drew a conceptual comparison between the elitism of the military and the egalitarianism of the party, seeing an ambition for professional autonomy set against subordination to the ideology. In his view, nationalism predominated amongst the soldiers, compared with the proletarian internationalism of the party.[94]

Occasional conflicts can repeatedly be detected from the 'language of conflict' of different periodicals. Yet, like all comparisons of technocrats and dogmatists, though to the 'strategic clique' versus the ideologists, it has not proved possible to verify the configuration of a simple dichotomy between the military and the party in general terms. Common features are more frequent among the two groups than the few occasions on which they hold different opinions. Participation has predominated in Soviet history and not a zero sum game between two parties to a conflict. The opinion that the party was keeping the military in check through an iron grip proved to be one-sided.[95]

There are presumably problems involved in assuming a uniform interest on the part of the army. Traditionally the land-based forces have predominated, yet with the advance of technology the navy and air force have come to gain ground, and this has doubtless not always served to promote common goals. There are only two issues on which the whole of the military is united: their personal pay and pensions and the financial allocations to the armed forces. Although socialist countries do not experience economic cycles, they do reveal political cycles, which can be best read off from the fluctuations in the national budget.[96] A change in office is frequently followed by a change in political preferences in the Soviet Union as well and this has at times led to increases in the defence budget.[97] Few secured findings are available as to a generalised system of horse-trading, whereby the priority of the party is recognised in return for concessions in armament wishes.[98] The party leadership itself is a most keen proponent of armament interests in the East–West conflict when little success seems to be in sight in other areas. The military–industrial complex model, initially developed for the USA, has also been applied to the Soviet Union. Whilst the USA has a military–industrial complex, it has been argued that in the case of the USSR, the whole system represents such a complex. In 1952 when the military was at the peak of its influence, 21.5 per cent of the seats on the Central Committee were held by the military and armaments experts from industry.[99] This does not say very much, however, in view of the lacking significance of the rest of the body, and similar figures could be brought into the comparison for other groups.

The extent to which Brezhnev was dependent on groups behind him is likewise disputed. When abroad he frequently presented himself as a 'nice man' who wished to give Western opponents the impression that his proposals ought to be accepted, since (as he let it be known) there were groups behind him who were pressing for tougher conditions.[100] Brezhnev repeatedly consulted his colleagues Kosygin and Podgorny at summit meetings, though it cannot be concluded from this that there was any restriction on his freedom to act. He may have used this as a negotiating trick in order to win time. Kissinger recalled: 'Of course, visibly depriving oneself of flexibility is also an effective bargaining device that I occasionally used myself'.[101] Consultations with the military, however, did not feature in these negotiating strategies, not even for the sake of appearances. The only factor which is certain is that the Soviet military does not behave any differently from other military leaderships. Khrushchev acknowledged in his memoirs that 'unfortunately, people at the top of the armed forces tend to greedily wish to extract as much as possible for their sector'.[102] Even a statement of this type, however, does not sufficiently distinguish the military from other interest groups.

The security forces are the second group which are claimed to exert an influence on foreign policy. The Committee for State Security (KGB) with its staff of 400 000 to 500 000 has the biggest security apparatus in the world. The CIA (its American counterpart), by contrast, is estimated to have a staff of no more than 20 000. When Andropov took over as head of the party he could not be compared with his predecessors from Dzerzhinskii through to Beriia in terms of fanaticism for repression, but he had, nonetheless been head of the KGB from 1967 to 1982. Although the foreign policy side of his career bears blemishes, as is illustrated by his role as ambassador to Hungary in crushing the uprising and in the two-faced treatment of Imre Nagy, head of the Hungarian government, who was later executed, Andropov ranks as more of a reformer. Andropov's promotion did not remain without its consequences. The first round of appointments brought his retinues from the KGB in his wake. The appointment which most surprised the experts was that of the head of the party from Azerbaidzhan to first Deputy Prime Minister at the first meeting of the Supreme Soviet held after Brezhnev's death in November 1982. The appointment was made despite the fact that he was a pure *apparatchik* for internal security and brought none of the qualifications in economics that most of the holders of top posts in the Soviet Union's machinery of government possessed.

The KGB has a pronounced influence on advisory schemes with the Third World and on the development of security forces in countries with a 'socialist orientation' that look to Moscow (see pp. 118–23). At times the KGB has even been accused of pursuing foreign policy on its own initiative with the aim of interfering in domestic policy. The repeated infringement of American and British diplomats' immunity in 1964 marks such a case. These violations were interpreted as acts of political sabotage against Khrushchev, in that they were irreconcilable with his efforts to achieve better diplomatic relations with the Western democracies and were designed to create difficulties for him in the foreign policy sphere. The KGB is known to have figured amongst the anti-Khrushchev coalition that brought about his fall.[103]

The groups within the internal bureaucracy that also engage in a certain measure of lobbying in the foreign policy sphere hardly represent permanently fixed policy coalitions in this field. Despite well-intentioned methodic advances, group research frequently fails to rise above the level of 'Kremlinology' and is forced to draw too many conclusions from single statements or actions by actors engaged in foreign policy field, which, in addition, frequently contradict each other. Virtually the whole spectrum of opinion has been voiced in publications as to the role of the KGB in Afghanistan. This has ranged from the version that the security organs were the driving force and had even created *faits accomplis* which the political leadership then had to reconstruct, to the view that the KGB had warned against intervention. The only reliable conclusion that can be drawn here is that the intensification of domestic repression which followed on from the intervention does not constitute sufficient evidence of the KGB's having wanted this intervention at foreign policy level as well.

3 The East–West Conflict

The development of the East–West conflict and the divergent images
of the decision-makers in the superpowers

Although the main shifts in the relative strength of forces within the
world are expected to occur in the developing countries (see pp. 118–23),
the East–West conflict remains the axis of orientation for the Soviet
Union. The Soviet Union has not, however, explicitly adopted the term
'bipolar world system'. This would have too many overtones of the
Chinese theory of the First World — the two 'superpowers'. The special
role of the two superpowers is only emphasised occasionally[1] but Soviet
observers work on the assumption that any improvement in the
relationship between the USSR and the USA will translate into
improvements for the world situation as a whole,[2] and hence a wish for
expansion in the role of the superpowers could be read into this.

In the Soviet theory's balance of forces model the East–West
relationship is still marked by pronounced asymmetries:

1   In the era of coexistence, 'imperialism' constitutes the sole *danger
     to world peace*,[3] whilst Western observers for the most part
     assume American foreign policy to be status quo oriented and the
     Soviet Union to be endangering the balance by increasingly
     stepping up her superiority in the field of conventional weapons
     and Eurostrategical weapons.[4]

2   The Soviet Union views her *leadership role* in the socialist camp
     as marking a *new quality* of relationship and diplomacy amongst

sovereign states. In the capitalist world, by contrast, she sees a quasi-Darwinistic, 'bitter struggle between states'.[5] American observers view the asymmetry in precisely the reverse manner, in the low level of control that the dominating American power has over her NATO allies.[6]

3   There are asymmetries in the *degree of security called for*. The Soviet Union works on the basis of four potential enemies (USA, Western Europe, China, Japan). The strategical parity on which the Soviets were insisting so firmly at the time they were lagging behind is no longer directly challenged today. It is, however, construed differently with a large number of regional and functional constraints. Paul Nitze, a vehement critic of the SALT Agreement once conjectured that the Soviet negotiators added up items in their own particular way and were therefore demanding a *de facto* lead on the West in terms of their security.[7]

The phases in which the contest between the Soviets and the Americans has sharply intensified are also due to a large extent to the failure of both sides to grasp the complexity and foundation of the other side's decisions.[8] False hopes and estimations led to disappointment on both sides, thereby worsening the image of the other world power.[9] In the Soviet Union, these disappointments chiefly included:

1   The feeling of having been *left in the lurch* as of 1944 with the *build-up of the front in France*. It was only the Soviet successes along the Western front that sped up the American and British plans, since the latter were concerned that they might only be able to advance into Central Europe too late. In the Soviet view, they wanted to 'land comfortably in France and reach Berlin without high losses'.[10]

2   The *tolerence of governments-in-exile in America*, particularly those of the Baltic states.

3   The *cancellation of the lend-lease agreement* with the Soviet Union, which withdrew the material aid that the Soviet Union needed.

4   The forcing of the withdrawal of Soviet troops from *Iran*. The transfer of the Soviet oil well concessions to American and British companies. Iran virtually became a Western satellite with Stalin receiving nothing in return.

5   The Soviet's *giving way in the Trieste conflict*, where Stalin provided no support for Titos annexation demands, similarly remained unrewarded in the Soviet view.

6   The UN fell increasingly *into the custody of the Americans*. Up until 1953 the USA frequently took shelter behind UN resolutions. The USA had a large number of satellites to support her in

the UN whilst no one took the two Soviet Republics that had been granted seats seriously.

7 The Soviet Union was not allowed to join in the *occupation of Japan*. The transfer of the Kurile Islands was soon regretted by the Americans.

8 Hints at *co-operation in the field of atomic energy came to nothing*, and the USA retained her lead here for four years. Although the Baruch Plan had proposed that atomic energy be placed under international control, the tests on the Bikini Islands created *faits accomplis* for the USA, suggesting that this had not been a serious offer of partnership.[11]

9 The *Marshall Plan* initiative, which contributed to the Soviet Union's increasingly cutting herself off.

The opposing list of occasions on which the USA has been snubbed by the Soviets is no shorter:

1 The non-fulfilment of the Roosevelt–Litvinov Agreement on the repayment of debts.

2 The Soviet Union's intervention in Spain.

3 The assault on Finland.

4 The co-operation with Hitler which meant that goods received by the Soviets were passed on to Germany.

5 Stalin's Poland policy, Katyn, the refusal to aid the Polish insurgents in 1944. The *faits accomplis* that led to the Oder–Neisse division.

6 The support given to Communist guerrillas in Greece. Stalin did, however, exert a moderating influence on Yugoslavia and Bulgaria on this point. Kardelj and Dimitrov were taken to task by Stalin at the start of 1948: 'No, you have no chance of success. Do you think that Great Britain and the United States — the United States, the most powerful country in the world — will allow you to break off their line of communication in the Mediterranean! Nonsense! And we haven't even got a navy. The uprising in Greece has got to stop, and as quickly as possible'.[12] Stalin obviously feared the independent power that would result from too many Balkan states under the Red Flag since this exchange took place at a time when Stalin was trying to talk Dimitrov and Kardelj out of the plans for a Balkan Confederation (see pp. 95–7).

7 The Sovietisation of the Soviet zone of occupation.

8 The unyielding attitude of the Soviet Union on the question of reparation, which meant that the American taxpayer paid the reparations indirectly via the allocations to the West German population.

9   The satellisation of Eastern Europe.

Overall, the Americans tried to display good naturedness for a fairly lengthy period of time. Up to 1946 this was true not only of the government but also of the American press, which was still reacting in mainly amicable tones as far as the Soviet Union was concerned at a time when Churchill was already talking of the 'Iron Curtain'.

Even during the Cold War the USA displayed a restraint *vis-à-vis* the Soviet Union which is unique in the history of great powers, given the military superiority of the USA. The USA did not succumb to the temptation to eliminate her Soviet rival, despite the occasional threats voiced by American presidents, such as in the Iran conflict in 1946, in the Korean war in 1953 and against China, to protect Taiwan, in 1958.[13] On the other hand, the Soviets once threatened the People's Republic of China with nuclear war in the 1969 conflict.[14]

Both the superpowers had an inadequate perception of the world situation during the post-war period:

1   The USA overlooked impending conflicts for too long. Roosevelt's blue-eyed naivity is still causing problems today, such as on the question as to whether the zones of influence were negotiated.
2   The USA did not predict the formation of the socialist camp and took no effective counter measures.
3   The USA did not accept the USSR's striving for equilibrium in time and use it to gain concessions whilst there was still something to be expected in return.

The Soviet Union held an ideological view of world development that was too carried away by the independent laws of world historical processes:

1   She assumed capitalism to be in deep crisis. The Soviet power in its youth had rapidly had to correct its chiliastic expectations of the collapse of the capitalist system,[15] and after the Second World War she relapsed into these expectations of collapse, although formulating them more carefully this time as a period of the 'decline of capitalism'.[16] Even these forecasts were regarded as so unconvincing by the leadership that the conflict with Eugen Varga blew up, resulting in the closure of his institute in 1949 (see Chapter 1).
2   The USSR further viewed the growth of the Soviet camp as inevitable. The growth that has been achieved to date (Cuba, Vietnam), however, has been forfeited again through centrifugal tendencies within the group of original members of the Council for Mutual Economic Aid (Comecon) (see Chapter 6).

3   Finally, the forecast of the official Soviet doctrine was based on the assumption that the socialist camp would inevitably gain allies in the Third World. It gained a few, lost others and many socialist developing countries were not prepared to accept friendship with the Soviet Union as being the chief criterion for socialist development (see pp. 118–23).

Alongside these false prognoses that the two chief victorious powers were drawing up in parallel to each other, there were also a number of instances in which they displayed similar behaviour in their more immediate environment, amounting to the respect of a limited sovereignty in their respective areas of influence. The American side at times applied an even more stringent yardstick here than in her own sphere of power.

Whilst the Brezhnev doctrine aroused great indignation in the West when it was applied in Czechoslovakia (1968), the Monroe Doctrine was scarcely noticed when it was applied in the Dominican Republic in 1965. If one compares intervention by *coups d'état* in the two powers' respective areas of influence, then the CIA emerges as being more active than the KGB, and the Truman Doctrine has been regarded as an extension of the Monroe Doctrine to cover the whole of the free world.[17] The two-camp hypothesis underlying Stalin's foreign policy came to be increasingly consolidated by the other side as well.

Despite the intensification of the Cold War and the increasing instances of mutual misinterpretation, both sides displayed surprising rationality in their management of the crises, which verged on armed confrontation. This holds particularly true for the four most serious crises: the Berlin blockade in 1948/49; the Korean war from 1950 to 1953; the Berlin crisis from 1958 to 1961; and the Cuban crisis in 1962.

Khrushchev's giving way in the Cuban crisis marked the beginning of his fall from power and led to a period of *détente*. Even the Soviet leadership was shocked by Khrushchev's high-handed action that had brought them to the verge of military conflict, and attempted to re-establish collective leadership and ensure a predictable foreign policy again. This rationality presumably cannot be comprehended in so formalised a manner as a number of deterrent theories, which read like the rules of a game, have assumed.[18] It was not so easy for the actors involved to analyse the situation as it was for the analysts later on. The Secret Services — on whom Soviet politicians tend to rely too heavily and who have a reputation of being good fact collectors but poor advisors — frequently made mistakes.

It was only afterwards that it became clear to the opponents of the Soviet Union that open conflict is most likely to occur either shortly before the currently weaker of the parties (in this case the Soviet Union) makes the equalising move, or shortly after it has made this move. The USA for a long time wavered between the two improbable variants (of a large power difference and a fully accepted equilibrium), deciding which course to follow, and this did nothing to reduce the danger of a crisis.[19] Despite a different degree of willingness to take on risks, the Soviet Union also kept to the old rules of diplomacy, keeping the instruments employed as minimal as possible, leaving a line of retreat open to her opponent and respecting the many interests of her opponent — particularly in the opponent's sphere of influence.[20]

From the actual behaviour of the actors in the Cold War it is possible to draw up a realistic image of the opposing side that contrasts the verbal opinions expressed by the leaderships and the publicists associated with them on many points. Despite the usual propaganda images that are cultivated of America, it cannot be denied that the basic Soviet attitude towards America, and not just that of the population, is positive. Lenin praised America as being exemplary on many points. A positive picture of America was even built up during the war, although the extent to which the Soviet victory had depended on supplies from America was concealed from the Soviet population. There may also be additional subconscious sympathies at play between the superpowers, based on a mix of a risen-power complex and the feeling of being lands of boundless possibilities compared with the 'morbid' European countries. The fact that the Americans can also have an ideology-ridden image of the Soviet adversary is all too often skimmed over in the literature, in line with the motto 'there's nobody here but us pragmatists'.[21]

Image research is just as asymmetrical as the images themselves. Although we have no results of opinion polls on the Soviet Union, there are certain indications that the West views the Soviet Union in a more negative light than vice versa. The percentage of those ill-disposed towards the Soviet Union fell only from 88 per cent in 1954 to 72 per cent in 1976.[22] Improvement has at best been registered in the shades of aggression attributed to the Soviet Union and to the Communist parties oriented towards her. The Eurobarometers show that the findings in Europe are only in part more favourable. In 1977 (prior to the spectacular deterioration in climate) 60 per cent of those in the Federal Republic of Germany did not believe that the Soviets were willing to come to an understanding with the West, and in 1976, 75 per cent of those in Great Britain viewed the Soviet Union as a military threat.[23] The EEC average for 1982 revealed that 45 per cent of those questioned felt the Soviets not to be at all trustworthy and 27 per cent felt them only to be partially trustworthy. The spread of this negative judgement ranged from 61 per cent in Luxemburg to 24 per cent in Greece.[24] In the Soviet Union there are only very few comments to go by, even from élites. A politician in the Soviet Union has to be even more on his guard against spontaneous comments than in the West. The comments made by Khrushchev during his retirement are atypical. In conversation with Eisenhower, Khrushchev admitted that there were 'good' and 'bad' people in both camps and even engaged in a comparison of the typical behaviour patterns of the military in the two systems.[25] Stirringly honest traits of individual Soviet leaders can also emerge posthumously from the memoirs of statesmen. After Brezhnev's death Willy Brandt reported that, on his visit to the Soviet Union, Brezhnev had even said 'I understand you, Willy Brandt, as far as the German question is concerned, but we two can do nothing about it at the moment'.[26] Individual examples of this type at best allow the conclusion that Soviet actors also do not always believe the negative things they at times say about other countries and that they have more differentiated image of their adversaries the better they know them.

Politicians and publicists in the Soviet Union have, however, also become more differentiated in their verbal expression. The theory of collapse is no longer openly advocated and crises are chiefly construed as cyclic and temporary, and no longer as the beginning of the end.[27] The wealth of detailed agreements reached with the United States is developing its own gravitation force and is no longer jeopardised with every outbreak of frost.[28] East–West relationships are leading to a 'business like co-operation' in *détente*. The danger of a nuclear war is no longer being treated lightly, as it was under Stalin and boasts about the United States being a 'paper tiger' have ceased.

The analysis of America is becoming more differentiated. The focus has shifted from the 'Wall Street' of anti-capitalist propaganda to the 'White House' and its policies.[29] Even the earlier lack of understanding for a system with separation of powers has improved. The growing role that has been accorded to the Senate in foreign policy since Carter is now receiving considerable attention.[30] On the other hand, though, the sole American opinion of the Soviet Union that is presented to Soviet citizens is the opinion of the narrowly defined circle of fellow travellers and sympathisers. These, the 'thinking Americans', are contrasted with the uninformed population, who cannot be expected to know the truth about the Soviet Union on account of the official propaganda.[31]

It is in the assessment of the American media that the Soviet literature has most difficulty. Facets of the Soviet system are repeatedly applied to the American system. The American media are frequently equated with the Soviet Union's own controlled press and their opinions ascribed to the American government.[32] Even if press opinions are not portrayed as aggressive acts, they are at least imputed with an America-centred world view, launched by 'monopolistic circles', which forms the basis for the American media and government propaganda.[33]

Soviet relations with Western Europe

Even though there have been many subconscious attempts in the West to define the Soviet Union out of the concept of 'Europe' (even on this side of the Urals), the Soviet Union herself certainly feels part of Europe. Highly topical enumerations are proudly prefaced by historical reminiscences in the manner: 'It was in Europe that the October Revolution took place... it was in Europe that the co-operation among socialist countries, unique to history, developed'.[34]

The concept of 'Western Europe' has less positive connotations. The Soviet leadership avoided the term 'Western Europe' as far as possible for a long time. The gradual acceptance of the term and its inclusion in Soviet linguistic usage is a function of the Soviet attitude towards the European community.[35]

Coexistence has comprised three principles since Khrushchev:

1 avoidance of war with the 'imperialist powers';
2 selective participation in the international division of labour and peaceful co-operation;
3 continuation of the struggle against the ideologies of 'antagonistic' systems.[36]

These three basic principles lead the Soviet Union to adopt a particular focus in her treatment of Western European countries:

1 The promotion of trends within Western European countries towards independence from the American protecting power, particularly in the military sector;
2 The endeavour to achieve more intensive, selective co-operation with the Europeans in exchange for good conduct on the Soviet side, particularly in the economic and cultural sector;
3 The exploitation of the greater contradictions that exist in many European systems to gain ground in the battle of the ideologies — either by promoting direct allies (Communist parties, see Chapter 8) or by reinforcing neutralistic, anti-imperialist groups, ranging from pacifist Christians to the ecological movements.

The basic principle at play here is thus to exploit the greater pluralism of Western nations to play the American and European partners off against each other, to profit from the differences that exist within Europe and to separate off the peripheral zones of American influence (Southern Europe, Scandinavian NATO countries) from the core zones (West Germany, Great Britain, Benelux countries) as far as possible.[37] During the de Gaulle era up to 1969, France seemed a suitable starting point for the *divide et impera* policy, on account of her moves to obtain a special status within NATO. The potential for co-operation, however, was limited here as well, not only in the economic sphere but also politically, since the French example was too individualistic and it proved impossible to find any equivalent follow-up. With France building up her own *force de frappe* the Western camp became even more unpredictable and the courting of the Chinese was interpreted by the Soviets as a call to behave 'as the French' in the socialist world camp as well.

During the 1960s the Soviet Union generally conducted her relations with the 'chief capitalist powers' in the order of USA, Great Britain and France.[38] As Gaullist foreign policy became increasingly independent, however, France progressed up the scale.[39] The chief difference compared with the 1960s is the inclusion of the Federal Republic of Germany amongst the chief capitalist states — in 1981 even above Great Britain.

As the treatment of relations with capitalist states has become more objective it has taken on a descriptive and less normative colouring. Only occasionally do harsh judgements betray the ranking accorded to a country, and in most cases conlusions have to be drawn from a range of factors. In the case of *France* and *Italy*, relations are predominantly characterised by the swearing of allegiance to traditional sympathies and sentimental values. Consideration of the strong Communist parties in these countries obviously colours the assessment of interstate relations here as well. Differences of opinion with France are formulated in the mildest of terms. The countries confine themselves to an acknowledge-ment of different views on issues such as: international disarmament talks, MBFR, and the ban on nuclear weapons tests.[40]

A Soviet introduction to military geography for soldiers in training nevertheless refers to the French position as 'constructive'.[41]

France also gets good marks as far as Soviet peace initiatives are concerned. When the Soviet Union invited the five nuclear powers to disarmament talks in 1971 only France reacted positively, whilst the USA and Great Britain gave evasive answers. China refused categorically.[42] The fact that the smallest atomic power had the most to gain (even if only by having its significance upgraded) was not taken into account here. France also receives constant praise for its co-operation in the German question — from its early 'recognition of the realities' in the two German states to its stand against 'West German pretensions' in West Berlin.[43]

The attributes used to introduce each of the European countries in a dry collection of facts on military geography are also revealing. The Federal Republic of Germany is 'a highly developed capitalist state' and Italy, nevertheless 'industrially developed', whilst *Great Britain* is simply termed the 'oldest capitalist country' with an immediate reference to its crises as being 'imperialism in decline'.[44]

Soviet portrayals show relations with Great Britain as being much more problematical than relations with France. Great Britain is criticised on account of her traditional privileged status within the Western alliance.[45] The decline of the system is frequently painted in the colours of the Varga era and associated with the 'outdated foreign policy' pursued by the country. Much is made of Great Britain's backsliding in the Cold War, particularly under Conservative governments.[46] One author even adopts poetical tones, 'cold mists at times prevail on the Thames' but these cannot hold up the 'warm winds of *détente*' for ever.[47] Although the Soviet Union otherwise tries not to establish any connection between good political conduct and trade relations, it has been hinted that outbursts of anti-Soviet propaganda have also damaged the countries' economic relations.[48]

Japan is treated in a very cool manner amongst the imperialist powers and the particular features of her 'imperialism' occupy much space prior to the dryly reported phase of 'normalisation of relations'.[49]

The Soviet Union's appraisal of relations with the *Federal Republic of Germany* shows the least degree of uniformity. The German question is regarded as having been settled in 1952. The Western powers were opposed to German unity. This assessment is still held to be correct today but is felt to be in need of differentiation.[50] The economic rise of the Federal Republic to become the 'strongest power in Western Europe' has a positive impact in terms of prestige yet, on the other hand, this increase in power also creates fears.[51] Up until 1969 the Federal Republic of Germany seemed to be an obstacle to *détente*. As of 1969, the new *Ostpolitik* made the Federal Republic into the outrider of *détente* in Europe, giving it a new rating in Soviet policy on Europe. Even during the Adenauer era, though, the relationship with the Federal Republic was not simply a stumbling block for Soviet policy through West Germany's decisive renunciation of an independent military role, however much the Federal Republic was repeatedly used as a scapegoat in propaganda to appeal to the sentiments and war memories of the Soviet Union's allies. Looking back, Khrushchev recalled of Adenauer that his own policy had always benefited from Adenauer's repeated public announcement of the fact that the Federal Republic would be the first country to be reduced to ashes and ruins in the event of a war. He summed up the benefit as follows: 'We were not only keeping our enemy number one at bay, Adenauer was also helping us to keep our other enemies at bay'.[52]

The Federal Republic is viewed as the USA's most important NATO partner in questions of decision-making as well, and hence particular attention is paid to West German *détente* efforts. On the other hand, however, the traditional underrating of the security interests of the smaller partner in both blocks means that repeated warnings issued to the Soviet Union by the Federal Republic to the effect that continued armament could become necessary are not taken seriously. *Ostpolitik* had aroused expectations which led to the disappointment at the Federal Republic's attitude towards the end of the 1970s being all the greater.[53]

The chief points on which the Federal Republic's policy is criticised are:

1 The shared blame in continued armament, which stemmed from a West German initiative.
2 Left-overs of *neo-fascism*.[54]
3 The attempt by the Federal Republic to exploit the possibilities open to it in *West Berlin* to the very limit of what even the Western powers could swallow[55] — a move that has even been reproached by Western observers at times.[56]
4 The dynamics of 'social democracy', which admittedly promoted *Ostpolitik* and *détente* but at the same time is striving to create a 'new centre of attraction'. The Soviets are essentially reproaching social democracy with what has become their own motto, namely the promotion of coexistence with increased ideological confrontation.[57] Social democracy was after all acknowledged to be the fourth efficient ideology in the general literature on world order[58] and was probably also somewhat overrated.

The foreign policy literature of the Soviet Union viewed social democracy (which was evidently the sole relevant and dangerous ideology sighted in Western Europe in the 1970s) as coupled to the endeavour for 'Europeanism', to mark a counterweight to the traditional 'Atlanticism'. A second direction of impact, namely towards 'trilateralism', stems from this and envisages the formation of three centres within the capitalist world camp, i.e. the USA, Western Europe and Japan.[59] Considerations based on prognoses that go even further than usual have at times been added on here — such as the potential development of an alliance between Japan and Western Europe on an 'anti-American platform' due to the growing trade protectionism of the Americans.[60]

The normalisation of German–Soviet relations had a two-fold advantage for the Soviets. On the one hand, the potential creation of new conflicts amongst the Western European allies relieved some of the burden on Soviet policy towards the West. The allies welcomed *Ostpolitik* verbally, and had after all, been pressing the Federal Republic to take this step for many years. As the policy began to work well, however, contrary to all expectations, it began to create new concern, particularly in France:

1 Fear that the French *status as a victorious power* would be weakened through a *rapprochement* of Bonn and Moscow.

2   Misgivings about the *special status of the GDR* in EEC trade through German-German privileges and success in trade with the East.

3   Concern that Bonn might seek reunification through a type of 'Finlandisation'. When no signs of a clearly definable Finlandisation of the Federal Republic were to be seen, the 'spirit of Rapallo' was claimed to be present in the special German–Soviet relations, which could increasingly force the Federal Republic into a neutralistic policy.[61] The then American ambassador in Moscow reported that *Ostpolitik* was also filling the security advisors of the American president with concern — misgivings that the ambassador in Moscow obviously did not share.[62]

4   The *neglection of obligations within the Western alliance* through security gained on the basis of bilateral agreements, such as the *Ostverträge* (Treaties with the East). France would have liked to keep the spirit of bilateralism that it was invoking against the USA well away from the Federal Republic of Germany.[63] On the other hand, the worries about the West Germans distancing themselves from the Alliance were so unfounded and the defence efforts of the Western European countries in the Alliance so lax that a discussion developed about redirecting American policy on Europe towards Bonn, as was unleashed by Fred Bergsten. Considerations of this nature could in turn only engender mistrust in Paris.[64]

Now that *Ostpolitik* has come up against its limits and with the Federal Republic's active role in the debate about the NATO two-track decision, it has been seen that the danger of a one-sided Soviet advantage through *Ostpolitik* was exaggerated.

Finlandisation trends in Western Europe?

All the Scandinavian countries are the object of Soviet courting, especially Finland and Iceland, and the growing role of the small countries in the changes of the international relations and the *perestroika* (see Chapter 1) is emphasised.[65] The country that generally receives best marks from the Soviets in an international comparison of Western Europe is *Finland*. Relations between the two countries developed so amicably in the Soviet view that Moscow was able to give up her naval base in Porkkala in 1955 even though the lease ran until 1997. It was stressed that when Port Arthur and Porkkala were given up the last military base on foreign territory had been cleared.[66]. In East–West relations, Finland has come to embody all Western fears of threat with the word 'Finlandisation', which some Finns consider to be the defamation of a neutral country.[67] Finland endeavours to pursue a policy of neutrality although the Friendship and Mutual Assistance Pact concluded with the Soviet Union in 1948 excludes the Soviet Union from this neutrality, since the Soviet Union is conceded powers of definition and joint decision in questions of threat analysis and the defence measures required for Finland.[68] The attempt by Max Jakobsons, the Finnish observer to the UN, to gain acceptance for the interpretation whereby Finland itself would take the initiative for such negotiations was opposed by the Soviet Union following the intervention in Czechoslovakia in 1968.[69] This Soviet claim has not as yet led to any large-scale involvement in foreign policy. Opportunities do however exist for intervention in domestic policy — although this is excluded in the Treaty — and these are already regarded as a curtailment of Finnish sovereignty today. They include a renunciation of the right of asylum *vis-à-vis* Soviet dissidents and the fact that Finland accepts frequent grading from the Soviet Union and a classification of Finnish politicians into responsible and irresponsible categories — with the attendant consequences on coalition building.

On the other hand, a large section of the Communist party has ventured to develop in the direction of Eurocommunism and the government openly criticised the Soviet Union in 1968 and 1980. Finlandisation at best emerges in the way in which criticism is worded, since the Soviet Union is not mentioned directly by name.[70] The literature highlights several distinctive features that go to make up Finlandisation, which constitutes an alternative Soviet strategy to direct revolutionisation of Western Europe by Communist parties, which has not proved very successful (see Chapter 8):[71]

1 responsiveness to Soviet political preferences;
2 avoidance of alliances with countries with which the Soviet Union is in conflict;
3 conservation of a neutral stand in war and peace;
4 keeping away from regional organisations rated as 'unfriendly' by Moscow;
5 co-operation in trade and cultural relations, tolerating advantages for the Soviet Union;
6 open to the penetration of Soviet ideas and media.

Finland, Austria and Afghanistan are named as examples of countries which would seem to be susceptible to a policy of this type. Other countries at risk primarily include Norway, Denmark and the Federal Republic of Germany. Even in the case of Austria most of the points do not apply. Afghanistan has passed through the phase of Finlandisation into a phase of open penetration. When it comes to the Federal Republic of Germany all one could cite would be a vague mistrust of *Ostpolitik*, coupled with the highly disputed assumption that only the Federal Republic made concessions in the Treaties with the East and the claim that the Schmidt government did not criticise human rights violations in the Soviet Union strongly enough during the Carter era.[72] It has not been possible to furnish evidence of a coherent strategy of Finlandisation towards Western Europe. A number of points of criticism levelled at the Western European allies by American authors have become groundless in the meantime with the recent 'power changes' in Denmark, Norway and the Federal Republic of Germany since 1981/82.

In the face of the growing independence in Europe, two different interpretations have come to be placed on one and the same phenomenon in Soviet literature, as needs require: in one instance the growing pluralism in America and in the relationship of the dominating American power towards her European allies it is praised for its pacification functions.[73] Whilst Soviet foreign policy makes every effort to divide up the Western world, Soviet publications make every effort to avoid emphasising the advantages of co-operation with one country as compared with others (with the exception of Finland which is always praised to the skies). When it comes to practical politics as well the Soviet Union now seems to be less openly intent on separating the Western allies from the Americans than before. Brezhnev once made a comment to this effect to Willy Brandt.[74] At a time when the Soviet Union is suffering internal bloc difficulties of her own she has begun to pay increasing tribute to the function of the blocs in maintaining the international order.

For the Soviet Union, Europe holds the advantage that it has not launched a human rights campaign in such an ideologically one-sided way as the USA under Carter. Schmidt and Giscard d'Estaing did not always support Carter in this. On the other hand, however, the Western European media have a much greater influence in Eastern Europe and thus constitute more of a danger to the Soviet claim to power.[75] A number of American authors have already seen a spiritual Finlandisation in this reticence on the part of the Europeans, whilst the Europeans rather believe themselves to be observing a few of the basic rules of non-intervention. Whilst the Soviet Union does in fact stress the collective responsibility for permanent violations of human rights[76] and for sensitisation in this question, which stemmed from the Final Act of Helsinki, she is inclined to reject any reference to internal Soviet practice as 'intervention'. In contrast to the Carter era, the Western European governments have made their opinions known but have not permanently posted them on billboards or mistaken governments for 'Radio Liberty' or Radio Free Europe'.

The new Europeanism is viewed more positively in the Soviet Union today, a fact which is not unconnected with the change in the Soviet attitude to the European Community. The Soviet Union had attempted to approach the European Community in the manner in which it treats its own camp, namely leaving everything to bilateral agreements so as to prevent the accumulation of a collective decision-making power.

At the start of the 1970s Soviet foreign policy began to venture into multilateral politics. CSCE and MBFR constituted two such steps. The French inclination towards bilateralism now proved to be more of a hindrance to *détente* in Europe. Publistic preparations for the change in attitude towards the EEC commenced at the start of the 1970s in the Institute of World Economics and International Relations. The view that first gained ground here was that the EEC was viable and that Soviet foreign policy had to take it seriously, particularly since the enlargement in 1973.[77] The consolidation of the Soviet Union's own camp now also seemed to ascribe a useful function in foreign policy to her opposing camp: the Soviets could demonstrate to their own allies in the Warsaw Pact and Comecon the need for solidarity and closed ranks in the face of attempts by the 'imperialists' to rally together.[78]

This *de facto* recognition was supplemented by a *de jure* recognition with the sending of an observer to Brussels.

The process of recognition has not, however, stopped publications from lending strong verbal support to the 'struggle of communist parties' in Western Europe against the 'Common Market' (still always placed in inverted commas) of the 'monopolies'. Large-scale differences in appraisal are blurred and the impression is given that the Federal German Communist Party and Italian Communist Party follow the same policy on this matter.[79]

In August 1973 the Secretary of Comecon made an unofficial proposal that contact be taken up. Delegations were sent to both sides and contact made. Soviet actors had had the satisfaction of seeing the contractual capacity of Comecon recognised by the Western powers in the meantime.[80] Given the emphasis placed on sovereignty within Comecon, the Western Europeans had doubted the capacity of Comecon to enter into commitments on behalf of its members until then.[81] Both sides are silent for various reasons on the fact that the hesitant attitude of the West Europeans hardly stems from legal concerns. The highly integrated EEC has a penchant for bilateralism in its dealings with the Eastern bloc, similar to that which the Soviet Union long cultivated *vis-à-vis* Western Europe. This stems from a wish not to strengthen the dependence of the individual economies of the people's democracies on Moscow through too much co-operation with Comecon.

During the era of coexistence, developments in the East–West conflict did not proceed in the direction of a convergence of the systems, as a number of theorists had hoped in the 1960's. Convergence assumptions have always been rejected by Soviet theory and rated as an attempt at ideological subversion. An unstable equilibrium has tended to develop between antagonism and convergence, for which the fitting designation 'antagonistic co-operation' has been found.[82]

4 Military and Security Policy

The Soviet concept of security

In the Soviet Union's self-conception socialism is identified with a policy of peace — 'socialism and peace are indivisible'.[1] This view holds that the only way for imperialism to be won over to concessions for greater security in the world is through the successes of socialist peace policy.

The Soviet Union is even less prepared to adopt terminology and concepts from the West in her thinking on security than in other areas. The predominance of the Americans for many years, however, has meant that some Western thought patterns have made their way into the Soviet discussion. The preference is still for Soviet words, however, rather than for adapted foreign words, so as to avoid any secondary connotations. The term 'defence' (*oborona*) marks the central concept. This is set against the basic Western concept of 'deterrence' (*ustrashenie*). In the Western discussion on deterrence the Soviet Union is frequently assumed to be a potential attacker, who can only be restrained in her will to expand by deterrence. The Soviet doctrine, on the other hand, does not assume any direct intention to attack on the part of the West — despite the constant accusations it levels against 'imperialism'.[2]

The West is, however, charged with a series of aggressive acts, which include:

1 intimidation (*ustrashenie*) through atomic blackmail.
2 Containment (*sderzhivanie*), pressure (*davlenie*) and duress (*prinuzhdenie*) are allegedly applied in order to limit the Soviet scope for action.[3]

3   The West's strategic thinking with its discussion on escalation
     steps and deterrence thresholds is taken as evidence of the fact that
     the USA still regards war as an instrument of politics. Soviet
     politicians get into difficulties on this last point since they do not
     like to let quotations from their military authors be put on a par
     with politics in the Kremlin. Arbatov once, quite rightly, said: 'It
     is the military's task to consider what they must do in the event of
     war breaking out. It does not follow from this that they regard a
     nuclear war as a serviceable element of foreign policy'.[4]

Soviet publications do not use the concept 'deterrence' but speak of the
'warding off of potential aggressors' instead. Whilst the Americans held
the lead in nuclear weapons the greatest danger in the eyes of the West
was that Soviet strategy might attempt to take Western Europe hostage.
Since the Soviet Union's deterrence potential has been able to stand up to
the Americans, Soviet publicists have turned the argument round: the
USA is charged with virtually wishing to take Western Europe hostage
by preparing for a possible attack from Western European soil with no
fear of a great counter attack on American territory. The Soviet answer is
now designed more to soothe the Western Europeans, stressing that there
cannot be a limited nuclear war.[5]

Soviet publications see the concrete threat to the Soviet Union as
deriving from a number of factors:

1   The Western world is using a policy of *intervention in the
     Third World* to secure supplies of raw materials. The Soviet
     support for national liberation movements, by contrast, is not
     rated as 'intervention' but as 'support' (which is permitted)
     whilst Western support for the counter-movements opposing the
     socialist-oriented liberation movements is regarded as inter-
     vention (*vmeshatel'stvo*).[6]
2   A policy of encirclement is still being pursued from the *USA's
     foreign bases.*[7]
3   The *non-signing of SALT II* is regarded as an attempt by the
     Americans to win back superiority. The NATO two-track
     decision is seen as a breach of the 1962 Agreement in which
     Khrushchev and Kennedy renounced the installation of new
     launcher missiles on territory immediately adjacent to the other
     Great Power.[8]
4   The Americans are accused of continued *development of reta-
     liation-proof weapon systems* — either because the other side does
     not yet possess them (neutron bomb) or because the reduction in
     warning time with the new Eurostrategical weapons (making
     them suitable for attacking purposes) means that, in the American
     doctrine, they will not necessarily trigger a counter-attack on

American territory when launched.[9] A number of Western publicists have conceded that the Soviet Union does accept the principle of mutually guaranteed second strike capability[10] and this can also be inferred from the above reproach against the USA. The agreement with Moscow on the non-building of anti-ballistic missiles (ABM) would seem to confirm this conclusion.

In the meantime the counter-accusation has not taken long to surface. Western observers suspect that even recently the Soviet leadership has been attempting to curtail the potential for a successful second strike by the opposing side. This stems from her endeavours to achieve *higher payloads* which could make the USA's strategic launcher missiles more vulnerable[11] (benevolent observers simply see this as compensation for a lack of precision) and from her forced-pace development of *civil defence*, which a number of critics of the regime feel makes it more probable that the party leadership is reckoning on surviving, despite heavy casualties amongst the population. This argument, however, has been just as vehemently disputed by pronounced critics amongst the *émigrés*. In their opinion, whilst the leadership knows that it can survive, it also knows that it can no longer expect any obedience from the survivors.[12] The Soviet side plays down its 117 000-man strong civil defence organisation (*grazhdanskaya oborona*, macabrely abbreviated to *grob*, which means 'coffin' in Russian)[13] and sees its function as the protection of reinforcements and the reconstruction of destroyed installations.

The Soviet Union tends to apply two different standards in her accusation that the USA is striving for retaliation-proof atomic weapons. Her SS20 and Backfire weapon systems count as modernised, medium-range weapons, which are allegedly already covered by the balance formulations worked out to date. The American Pershing II and the cruise missiles on the other hand, are rated as essentially new weapons.[14] Given the technological superiority of American systems the fear of a new quality of weapon may be understandable in psychological terms and not simply be upheld by way of propaganda. It then remains incomprehensible, however, why the Soviet Union should belittle her own innovations to such an extent when she lavishes such immense praise upon the scientific, technical revolution in all areas.

The layman will scarcely wish to venture a conclusive judgement on the military aspect of the controversy. An analysis of the political factors is, however, important. Even if the two great powers had the same medium-range potential, their weapon systems would not possess the same political quality. The SS20 holds a political value for the Soviet Union so long as it still remains feasible for Western Europe to be taken hostage. Pershing II, however, provides the USA with an additional option in the nature of warfare, which the Soviet Union can never attain for purely geographic reasons due to her lack of a wide approach (even Cuba would not have provided this in 1962) — unless she can win over the whole of Central America to the socialist camp. Since this Soviet hope is not likely to be fulfilled in the near future, the Soviet Union in 1983 threatened a build-up of submarine-based missiles off American waters in the event of the Pershing being deployed.

5   Finally, the West is accused of using the arms race to *show off its economic superiority* and thus gaining influence over the socialist countries' internal affairs.[15]

All these accusations take no account of the fact that Soviet policy has to bear part of the blame for America's twists to the arms spiral since the Reagan administration. The Soviet Union did not sufficiently honour the relative reduction in armament efforts during the initial period of *détente*. The West, on the other hand, made no allowance for the Soviets' inferiority complexes and was not prepared to tolerate a slight lead, since it did not take the theory of the Soviet Union's four potential enemies seriously. This theory has admittedly been subject to repeated, pronounced modification by the Soviet side as well. When asked the catch question as to whether four potential enemies could produce a claim for superiority from the Soviet Union, Arbatov replied:

Only a very poor policy could lead to a joint military coup by all four. This can be prevented by a good policy. For the rest, we are sufficiently well armed to repel any attack, but with 25 per cent of the national product and 15 per cent of the population of these four we can never be militarily stronger than all four together. Those who like to speak of the 'Soviet danger' remain silent on this.[16]

The Soviet military power and the comparative strength of military forces worldwide

The balance of suspicions in the foreign policy doctrines matches an endeavour to achieve a balance of forces. Once again, however, the Soviet concept of 'balance' ranks differently in the West. Balance is not rated as a desirable final state but as the lesser evil until such time as fullscale disarmament is achieved throughout the world. The USA is also accused of wanting to upset the existing balance.

Just as Soviet diplomats generally argue holistically, whilst Americans prefer to start with the details (see pp. 21–2), so Soviet strategists tend to stress the overall balance and reject the simple addition of regional imbalances. The Soviets' predominance in Europe is viewed as compensation for the predominance of American power in most areas of the world. The fact of the Soviet Union admitting to a regional imbalance in her favour at all is in itself relatively new. Brezhnev spoke more openly about the balance at the XXVI Party Congress than had been customary up until then. He gave the Soviet Union a slight lead in the field of Eurostrategical medium-range weapons and tanks, whilst attributing the Americans the advantage in strategical weapons and anti-tank weapons.[17]

An important factor in the Soviet doctrine is the Party which repeatedly upsets the balance. Soviet exponents of foreign policy upheld the theory that all the decisive military innovations which disturbed the balance and made nuclear war seem feasible and winnable came from the USA.[18] A comparison of the innovation steps in arms technology shows this view to be predominantly, although not globally, correct (see Table 4.1). In 1957 the Soviet Union went into the lead for the first time with intercontinental ballistic missiles (ICBM). The anti-ballistic missile (ABM), developed by the Soviet Union as of 1968, appears to be a defensive weapon at first sight. It is, however, quite rightly rated as a dangerous weapon, promoting aggression, since it makes nuclear wars seem easier to win. The Soviet Union endorsed this view at the start of the 1970s when she renounced further development of the ABM.

There is scarcely a field of East–West relations subject to so much dispute as the figures put forward for the comparative strength of military forces. Two methods are applied in the West to estimate military

Table 4.1
Major innovations in arms technology in the USA and USSR since 1945

Weapon systems	USA	USSR
Atom bomb (first fired)	1945	1949
Hydrogen bomb (first reaction)	1951	1953
Long-range bomber	1948/53/55	1956
Intercontinental ballistic missiles (ICBM) (test flight)	1958	1957
Nuclear submarines	1955/56	1962
Submarine-launched ballistic missiles (SLBM)	1959/60	1964/68
Anti-ballistic missiles (first fired)	1960	1961
Solid propellant ICBM	1962	1969
Multiple independently targetable re-entry vehicle (MIRV)	1970	1968/72
Neutron weapons (ER/RB)	1981	1973/75
Cruise missiles	1983	—
Manoeuvrable anti-radar vehicle (MARV)	1985	—

Source: D. S. Lutz: 'Zur Methodologie militärischer Kräftevergleiche', *PVS*, 1982, No. 1 (6–26), p. 9.

potential: a direct comparison of budgets; and an indirect cost comparison, also including estimates of the capacity of the arms industry. The first method raises problems since the dry set of figures that forms the published version of the Soviet budget conceals a part of the wages and maintenance costs for the army under various items of 'consumption'.

Part of the expenditure on infrastructure is concealed under budget items for civil institutions. Even weapons are frequently entered under 'inventory' or 'reserves'.[19] The government budget in the USA is considerably more transparent, although this does not prevent Soviet publicists from returning the accusations made against their own budget methods. 'Secret military expenditure' is alleged to be entered under 'space travel' and 'advance credits'.[20] A comparison of the percentage of gross natioanl product spent by the two superpowers on armaments provides little elucidation. The Soviet Union is reputed to spend 12 to 13 per cent of her national income[21] (maximum estimates run to 18 per cent)[22] on defence. Soviet publications assume approximately 6 per cent for the USA, a figure which tallies with that given by a large number of American authors.[23]

The scientific institutes which draw up quantitative comparisons of forces offer widely differing figures (see Table 4.2). In general, however, they do not present Soviet superiority in so blatant a light as do the popular publications, which use force comparisons for political mobilisation.[24] The unfairest portrayal of Soviet military strength was that given in the American government's brochure on *Soviet Military Power* in 1981. No mention was made of America's strength at all and the potential of the allies was not weighted.[25]

The superiority of the Warsaw Pact is easily demonstrated by indicators such as the percentage of gross national product (or national income) accounted for by military expenditure, or the number of soldiers under arms. If per capita military expenditure and the absolute level of expenditure on arms is included as well, then the fear of Soviet superiority is seen to be exaggerated. It is just as easy to prove one or the other theory with selected figures for individual types of weapons.

The Soviet Union has attained a lead in intercontinental ballistic missiles but this lead must not be viewed in isolation. The tendency for Soviet strategic doctrine to focus on a short war (this can be interpreted as a traumatic reaction to the long years of battles of annihilation in the Second World War and to the equally traumatic recognition that the West is superior in economic terms) led to the missile option being overemphasised *vis-à-vis* the air force under Khrushchev, though not without vehement internal disputes between leading military and political figures.[26] Whilst the Soviet Union was pinned down to a dual weapon system (ICBM-SLBM) in the strategic field, the USA developed

Table 4.2

Military expenditure, public expenditures per soldier and military manpower for selected member countries of the Warsaw Treaty Organization (WTO) and of the North Atlantic Treaty Organization (NATO) in current US dollars for 1965–84

	Warsaw Treaty Organization							North Atlantic Treaty Organization				
	Soviet Union	Bulgaria	Czechoslovakia	GDR	Poland	Romania	Hungary	USA	FRG	France	U.K.	Italy
Military expenditure in million $ US												
IISS 1967[a]	34.450	225	1.452	1.063	1.662	530	313	73.000	5.358	5.502	5.340	1.890
IISS 1969[b]	39.333	234	1.576	1.873	2.009	574	457	79.774	5.246	6.184	5.554	2.384
IISS 1975[c]	103.800	392	1.542	2.333	2.170	647	485	92.800	16.260	12.250	10.380	4.220
IISS 1980[d]	n.a.	1.140	3.520	4.790	4.670	1.470	1.080	142.700	25.120	20.220	24.448	6.580
IISS 1983[e]	n.a.?	1.681	4.618	8.685	5.766	1.576	1.631	239.400	22.375	21.654	24.469	9.698
SIPRI 1970[f]	42.619	279	(1.741)	1.990	2.224	748	513	77.827	6.188	6.014	5.850	2.506
SIPRI 1975[g]	61.100	472	2.271	2.821	2.965	1.029	649	90.948	15.198	13.034	11.348	4.744
SIPRI 1980[h]	116.900	(922)	(2.552)	(4.030)	(2.522)	(1.318)	753	111.236	22.003	19.498	16.187	6.324
SIPRI 1984[i]	[142.000]	[1.000]	(5.030)	(5.375)	(2.938)	(1.094)	(1.100)	200.329	26.992	27.896	30.497	11.435
Sivard 1975[j]	94.000	565	1.904	2.644	2.384	806	614	90.948	15.299	13.093	11.477	4.656
Sivard 1979[k]	114.000	940	2.250	3.930	3.900	1.420	1.020	122.279	24.796	22.663	19.156	7.762
Military expenditure per capita in $ US												
IISS 1967[a]	147	27	100	62	52	27	30	368	93	106	97	36
IISS 1969[b]	164	28	109	116	62	29	44	393	90	123	100	44
IISS 1975[c]	409	45	106	137	65	30	45	430	260	233	184	76
IISS 1980[d]	n.a.	128	229	285	131	66	101	644	410	374	437	n.a.
IISS 1983[e]	n.a.?	188	299	515	157	70	152	1.023	363	394	439	172
Sivard 1975[j]	370	65	129	157	70	38	58	426	247	249	205	83
Sivard 1979[k]	433	106	148	235	111	64	95	543	404	424	342	136

57

Table 4.2 (continued)

	Warsaw Treaty Organization							North Atlantic Treaty Organization				
	Soviet Union	Bulgaria	Czechoslovakia	GDR	Poland	Romania	Hungary	USA	FRG	France	U.K.	Italy
Military expenditure as % of GNP/GDP												
IISS 1965/1967[a]	9.0/9.6	2.9/3.0	5.7/5.7	3.0/3.7	5.1/5.4	3.2/3.1	2.7/2.6	8.0/9.8	4.4/4.3	5.6/5.3	6.3/5.7	2.9/2.9
IISS 1969[b]	8.5	2.8	5.6	5.9	5.0	2.9	3.4	8.6	3.5	4.4	5.1	2.9
IISS 1974[c]	10.6	2.7	3.8	5.4	3.6	1.6	2.3	6.0	3.6	3.4	5.2	2.8
IISS 1980[d]	11–13	2.1	2.8	6.3	2.4	1.4	2.1	5.2	3.3	3.9	4.9	2.4
IISS 1983[c]		3.2	3.8	5.7	2.7	1.5	2.2	7.4	3.4	4.2	5.5	2.8
SIPRI 1975[c]	5.0–11.6	3.7	4.7	(6.7)	3.6	?	(2.9)	6.1	3.6	3.7	5.1	2.9
SIPRI 1975[l]	9.1	(2.9)	(3.2)	(4.4)	(2.8)	2.0	2.2	5.6	3.3	4.1	5.1	2.4
SIPRI 1984[n]	n.a.	[3.1]	(3.2)	(4.7)	2.9	(1.5)	3.6	6.9	3.3	4.1	5.4	2.8
Military expenditure as % of government spending												
IISS 1975[c]	n.a.	6.0	7.3	7.9	7.0	4.0	3.5	26.6	24.7	19.1	10.8	8.6
IISS 1980[d]	n.a.	6.0	7.6	7.5	6.0	4.0	3.8	23.3	22.2	n.a.	10.7	n.a.
IISS 1983[c]	n.a.	5.9	8.2	8.3	7.1	4.4	4.1	29.6	23.2	18.7	13.7	5.1
Public expenditure per soldier in $ US												
Sivard 1972[o]	19 259	2 390	8 340	14 550	7 098	3 492	4 485	33 436	19 311	14 543	22 005	8 586
Sivard 1975[p]	26 294	3 717	9 520	18 490	8 137	4 713	5 848	42 699	30 907	26 082	33 267	11 059
Sivard 1979[q]	31 165	6 267	11 598	24 717	12 264	7 845	9 808	60 474	50 093	44 525	59 306	21 266
Numbers in armed forces												
IISS 1968[a]	3 220 000	?	225 000	126 000	274 000	173 000	?	3 500 000	456 000	505 000	427 000	365 000
IISS 1970[b]	3 305 000	?	168 000	129 000	242 000	181 000	?	3 161 000	466 000	506 000	390 000	413 000
IISS 1975[c]	3 575 000	152 000	200 000	143 000	293 000	171 000	105 000	2 130 000	495 000	502 500	345 100	421 000
IISS 1980[d]	3 568 000	149 000	195 000	162 000	317 500	184 500	93 000	2 050 000	495 000	494 700	329 200	366 000
IISS 1985[c]	n.a.	148 500	203 000	174 000	319 000	189 500	106 000	2 151 600	478 000	464 300	327 000	385 100

Estimated Reservists										
IISS 1968[a]	2 000 000	500 000	200 000	265 000	?	994 100	750 000	400 000	170 000	600 000
IISS 1970[b]	2 100 000	500 000	200 000	250 000	?	1 023 500	663 000	430 000	270 000	630 000
IISS 1975[c]	5 700 000	350 000	260 000	485 000	163 000	926 000	1 183 000	450 000	242 400	645 000
IISS 1980[d]	5 000 000	240 000	305 000	502 000	143 000	817 900	750 000	342 000	265 000	738 000
IISS 1985[e]	n.a.	795 000	650 000	565 000	143 000	1 212 300	770 000	393 000	294 500	799 000
Paramilitary forces										
IISS 1968[a]	250 000	40 000	340 000	50 000	?	—	30 000	75 000	—	105 000
IISS 1970[b]	230 000	35 000	73 500	50 000	?	—	18 500	75 000	—	76 000
IISS 1975[c]	430 000	20 000	80 000	45 000	20 000	—	20 000	73 000	—	80 000
IISS 1980[d]	460 000	189 000	571 500	737 000	75 000	n.a.	—	85 500	—	201 000
IISS 1985[e]	n.a	172 500	77 500	37 000	75 000	178 700	20 000	89 500	—	6 600

Compiled by Hans Günter Brauch, Institute of Political Science, Stuttgart University

Sources:

a   The International Institute for Strategic Studies (IISS): *The Military Balance 1968–1969 (MB 1968–1969)*, London 1968, pp. 55–57. (The data for the FRG do not include the financial assistance for West Berlin.)

b   IISS: *MB 1970–1971*, London 1970, pp. 110–112.

c   IISS: *MB 1975–1976*, London 1975, pp. 76–79.

d   IISS: *MB 1980–1981*, London 1980, p. 96.

e   IISS: *MB 1985–1986*, London 1985, p. 170.

f   *SIPRI Yearbook 1972, World Armaments and Disarmament*, Stockholm, New York, London 1972, pp. 82ff. The data for the WTO countries are given in current price figures in $ US at Benoit-Lubell exchange rates.

g   *SIPRI Yearbook 1977*, London 1977, pp. 222 ff.

h   *SIPRI Yearbook 1981*, London 1981, pp. 157 ff. The data are given in 1978 prices and exchange rates. All data for the WTO countries are based on *SIPRI Yearbook 1982*, London 1982, p. 141 at 1979 prices and exchange rates.

i   *SIPRI Yearbook 1985*, London 1985, pp. 272 ff. The data are given in 1980 prices and exchange rates. The data for Bulgaria are given for 1980, for Poland 1982 and for Czechoslovakia 1983.

j   Ruth Leger Sivard: *World Military and Social Expenditures 1978*, Washington 1978, pp. 21 and 24.

k   Sivard, op. cit., 1982, pp. 27–30

l   *SIPRI Yearbook 1977*, London 1977, pp. 224–226. The data refer to the net material product for the WTO countries and to the gross domestic product for the NATO countries.

m   *SIPRI Yearbook 1982*, London 1982, p. 150. The data for the Soviet Union and Romania are given for the year 1979.

n   *SIPRI Yearbook 1985*, London 1985, p. 280. The data for Bulgaria and Poland refer to the year 1981, for Czechoslovakia 1982, and for Hungary and Romania 1983.

o   Sivard, op. cit., 1974, p. 22.

p   Sivard, op. cit., 1978, p. 24.

q   Sivard, op. cit., 1982, p. 30.

a much more balanced triple weapon system (ICBM-SLBM-bombers), giving it greater potential for a flexible response to military challenges (see Table 4.3, lower section).

The scientific institutes are fully aware of the fact that a mere juxtaposition of numbers in East and West cannot produce a reliable comparison. The attempt to link launcher systems to specific targets was seen to require information on performance and target accuracy, which is only available with large gaps for the Soviet side in particular (see Table 4.3).

The American ICBM would seem to be highly vulnerable given the enormous Soviet payloads, but at no time has America's second strike capability been jeopardised. The ranking of the Soviet Backfire aircraft remains the subject of dispute, despite the Soviets' declaration in a letter to SALT II at the signing ceremony in Vienna in June 1979 that they would not use the Backfire for strategic, intercontinental missions, would limit the number of refuelable aircraft and would confine production to a maximum of 30 per annum. Soviet submarines count as inferior to American submarines and their SLMBs are considered less capable of survival than the American ones. The Soviets have won a temporary lead in anti-satellite satellites (killer satellites) but such gaps have never existed for long, given the general technical superiority of the USA. The Americans have the advantage when it comes to anti-ballistic missiles and unmanned cruise missiles — these may be slower than ballistic missiles but being smaller and flying closer to the earth they can penetrate the opponent's air space more easily than aircraft without being detected by radar systems.[27]

When comparing figures, consideration must also be given to the different defence mandates in East and West. In the air force an arms race is taking place between development of the American bomber and the Soviet air defences, which are regarded as superior.[28] The Soviet air force is designed more to support combat troops. Her bomber fleet is regarded as outdated and even with the high loss rates of American bombers — put at 15 to 50 per cent in the event of conflict — the Soviet Union still regards the American long-range bombers as an offensive threat, particularly since a number of American planners recommended NATO to focus its orientation on the destruction of Soviet surface-based defence systems in order to secure American 'sovereignty in the air'.[29]

The build-up of the Soviet navy likewise produced exaggerated counter-reactions in the West, given the lead held by the two chief seafaring nations, the USA and Great Britain, who are united in the Western alliance. Phrases are repeatedly quoted from Admiral Gorshkov's book, which sees a new centre of gravity emerging in the navy.[30] Not quoted is Gorshkov's commitment to a balance of fleet strengths, which reveals no endeavour for superiority at sea on the part of the Soviets. The

Western literature makes frequent reference to growth rates in ship building. The number of ships is not generally related to their tonnage, however.[31] A detailed comparison reveals that the Soviet Union is building more small boats to operate in her coastal waters whilst the USA is concentrating on ships suitable for operations on the high seas — once again regarded as weapons of attack by the Soviets. The Soviet Union has no aircraft carrier of American proportions suitable for offensive purposes. Her surface fighting ships cannot operate on the high seas without risk and without support from the air and hence the Soviet navy has a more limited radius of action than the American navy in the event of conflict. Additional limitations are placed on the operational capability of the Soviet navy by the fact that the NATO powers can readily control her departure routes in Northern Norway, the Baltic and the Dardanelles.

The defence mandate of the Soviet navy is considerably more limited than that of the USA.[32] In no other area is the weight of the USA's Western allies so great as in naval policy, whilst the naval strength of the Soviet allies appears insignificant. Even in the event of parity in Soviet and American naval strength, the West would presumably still retain a lead.

Soviet navalism, which has been a source of disquiet for Western politicians over recent years, has to be interpreted in predominantly political terms. The age of gunboat diplomacy would seem to be over but a number of equivalents still live on under the euphemism of 'naval diplomacy' in American policy too, particularly in the Caribbean. The offensive aspects of Soviet naval strength primarily serve the defensive function of protecting the Soviet Union's clientele — in particular Third World countries of 'socialist orientation'.[33] Soviet navalism is thus less of a threat in the East–West conflict than in the framework of military force applied in the Third World, at a level below the threshold of war (see pp. 135–9).

Standard numerical comparisons frequently overlook important factors in the East–West relationship:

1   *Qualitative military factors,* such as age, mobility, firepower and target accuracy, frequently receive too little coverage in numerical comparisons.[34] Doubts as to the equal standard of a number of Soviet weapon systems are only expressed in internal meetings or occasionally by the press, if at all.[35] The Soviet Union's inferiority in a large number of 'intelligent weapons' again formed the subject of malicious comments in the Lebanese proxy conflict of 1982. It is only of late that a technological gap to the West's disadvantage has been evoked.[36]

2   Relevant *factors of strategical policy,* such as the requirements that stem from dissimilar doctrines like NATO's front defence and the Warsaw Pact's forward defence, are frequently left out of

Table 4.3

Estimated US and Soviet strategic nuclear warheads

System	USA No. deployed	USA Warheads per launcher	USA Total warheads	System	Soviet Union No. deployed	Soviet Union Warheads per launcher	Soviet Union Total warheads
ICBM				ICBM			
Minuteman II	442[a]	1	442	SS-11 Mod 1	100	1[b] }	520[b]
				Mods 2/3	420	1[b] }	
Minuteman III	550	3	1650	SS-13	60	1	60
Titan	26	1	26	SS-17 Mods 1/2		(1 or 4)	—
				Mod 3	150	4	600
				SS-18 Mod 1	—	(1)	—[c]
				Mod 2	—	(8)	—[c]
				Mod 3	—	(1)	—[c]
				Mod 4	308	10	3080
				SS-19 Mod 2	—	(1)	—[c]
				Mod 3	360	6	2160
Sub-total (ICBM)	1018		2118	Sub-total (ICBM)	1398		6420
SLBM				SLBM			
Poseidon C-3	304	10[d]	3040	SS-N-5	39	1	39
Trident C-4	312	8[d]	2496	SS-N-6 Mod 1	—	(1)	—[c]
				Mod 2	—	(1)	—[c]
				Mod 3	336	(1)	336[c]

Type	US Launchers	US bombs/RV	US Warheads	USSR Launchers	USSR RV	USSR Warheads
SS-N-8 Mod 1				—	(1)	—[c]
Mod 2				292	(1)	292[c]
SS-N-17				12	1	12
SS-N-18 Mod 1				—	(3)	—[f]
Mod 2					(1)	
Mod 3				224	7	1568[f]
SS-N-20				60	9	540
SS-N-23				16	?	?
Sub-total (SLBM)	616		5536	979		2787+
Sub-total (ICBM and SLBM)			7654			9207+
Aircraft						
B-52G	90	20[h]	1800			
B-52H	90	8[h]	720			
Tu-95 Bear-B, -C, -G, -H				125	4[i]	500
Mya-4 Bison				45	4[i]	180
Sub-total (aircraft)	180		2520	170		680
Total			10174			9987+

a Eight other launchers are comms vehicles.
b There are three Mods: Mod 1 and Mod 2 have a single 1-MT RV; the three MRV on Mod 3 are counted as one RV.
c SS-17, Mods 1 and 2, SS-18 Mods 1, 2 and 3, and SS-19 Mod 2 may no longer be in service.
d May carry up to 14 RV.
e Very few Mod 1 believed in service; 2 MRV (counted as one RV).
f Assumes Mod 3 has replaced Mods 1 and 2.
g Due to approximation, these are not precise totals of the figures in the column.
h Assumes 12 ALCM, 4 SRAM, 4 gravity bombs for B-52G; 4 SRAM, 4 bombs for B-52H. These are operational, not maximum, loadings. SRAM counted as deliverable warhead.
i Tu-95: 1-2 AS-3/-4 ALCM, 2-3 bombs; Mya-4: 4 bombs.
Source: The International Institute for Strategic Studies (IISS), The Military Balance 1985-1986, London 1985.

account in numerical comparisons. The Warsaw Pact gauges its efforts for a short war and NATO more for a longer war.

Forward defence developed in the wake of the primacy of missiles during the Khrushchev era. This strategic doctrine is founded on the experience of two world wars, which brought immense losses for the USSR. Hence the Soviet Union is determined to shift any future attack to the opponent's territory as quickly as possible. These historical reminiscences conceal a highly topical reason. The Soviet forward defence is largely a response to NATO, which is equipping itself for a lengthier confrontation, in which its economic superiority (as in the Second World War) will have a favourable impact. A number of authors in the West even regard the West's condemnation of the Soviet doctrine as hypocritical. It is argued that NATO would also adopt this strategy (applied in the West by Israel, for instance) without second thoughts if it were in a position to do so in the conventional field.[37]

3   *Economic power* also has a role to play, even if confrontations cannot be expected to last for many years like the first two world wars. Western superiority in this sphere is generally played over by reference to the higher share of the Soviet economy working for defence. A number of estimates maintain that some 40 per cent (probably 14 per cent is meant) of the Soviet Union's total workforce is deployed in the military machine. It is concluded from this that whilst the USA 'has' a *military industrial complex* the whole of the Soviet Union 'is' such a complex.[38] Some of the figures mentioned contain contradictions. According to this source, 13 million workers are engaged on work for the Soviet military — taking the 1980 Soviet workforce statistics for 1980 of 112 million workers throughout the country, this would represent some 12 per cent.[39] Even more daring calculation feats in the sphere of productivity increases would have 21 million workers employed in the military industrial complex, accounting for some 15 per cent of the Soviet workforce.[40]

4   Despite the adoption of the bipolar approach in a large portion of the Soviet literature, reactions to international crises, especially in Asia, show that the Soviet Union still tends to think in *tripolar* terms when it comes to decisions on armaments and budget allocations for military purposes, taking the growth rates in allocations for military purposes in both the USA and China as a guide.[41] The USA has the advantage of not having had to seriously contend with a Chinese threat for a long time. The argument has only featured in Soviet–American talks in the case of anti-ballistic missiles. The 'Brzezinski strategy', which allegedly intends to

encircle the Soviet Union even more firmly with the aid of China, is a Soviet exaggeration. Nevertheless, it cannot be denied that prominent experts on the Soviet Union, such as Richard Pipes, who played a certain role in advising the President, deliberately propagated tripolar thinking against Nixon's recognition of the parity of two superpowers.[42]

How do Soviet publications view these numerical comparisons and the scientists' conflict that developed around them with increasing vigour in the West at the start of the 1980s? Soviet publications work on the basis that the 1970s was an era of virtual balance.[43] They concede that disarmament agreements to date (including SALT II) have not been able to stop the arms race or reduce military expenditure. They do, however, acknowledge that military expenditure would have risen even more drastically without SALT II.[44] Soviet publicists have even started to engage in numerical comparisons themselves of late, though without giving Soviet estimates and merely refuting allegedly incorrect CIA estimates of Soviet military potential.[45] As a rule, figures are taken from Western scientific institutes, in particular from the Stockholm SIPRI Institute, but also from official NATO and American government publications.[46]

American calculations of Soviet potential are accused of employing a trick, in that they allegedly apply American standards for the upkeep of the army.[47] The so-called Gerschenkron effect does indeed constitute a methodic problem here, as in other areas of the East–West comparison. It makes the performance of the opposing system appear higher when calculated in the opponent's currency.[48] Kennedy and Hatfield made a fitting remark as regards the concern about Soviet superiority: 'The administration claims we are behind the Soviets, but no one in authority, including President Reagan, would trade our deterrent for the Soviet forces'.[49]

Soviet policy on détente and disarmament

Détente embodies elements of both co-operation and conflict and hence, in the Soviet opinion, can only be regarded as a '*modus vivendi*' between two antagonistic systems.[50] *Détente* even involves an intensification of ideological competition whilst the increasingly pointless arms race is phased out and subjected to monitoring.

The key event that made the Soviet leadership prepared to accept disarmament was the Cuban crisis of 1962, which brought the world to the brink of a nuclear conflict. Although Soviet aid to North Vietnam from 1965 to 1972 caused a great deal of friction with the USA, Moscow was nonetheless prepared to conclude agreements with Washington — not least because of the growing competition with China. The first steps taken were the installation of the 'hot line' (1963) and the Test Ban Treaty. The Nuclear Non-Proliferation Treaty (1968) provided relatively few problems for the Soviet Union, since it established the hierarchy between nuclear and non-nuclear powers, which was much to the Soviet Union's liking in that it brought her additional recognition as a power of the world order.[51] In a message to the Congress, Nixon developed his doctrine which went further than the classic balance-of-power doctrine in that it allocated the superpowers joint functions of world order. Critics of the Nixon Doctrine set greater store by alliances of the old type, with a configuration of two or three against one (the Soviet Union).[52]

No other country of the world has launched so many peace offensives in propaganda campaigns as the Soviet Union. The UN, in particular, was kept busy by a continuous flood of new proposals. One of the most comprehensive initiatives was launched at the 31st UN General Assembly. A Soviet memorandum sums up the widely varied offers:[53]

1   end of the nuclear arms race, reduction and subsequent abolition of nuclear arms;
2   ban on all atomic weapon tests;
3   consolidation of the non-dissemination of atomic weapons;
4   ban on and destruction of (in so far as they exist) chemical weapons;
5   ban on developing new means of mass destruction;
6   reduction of conventional armed forces;
7   creation of peace zones in the Indian Ocean and other areas.

The first major agreements to which the Soviet Union gave her consent came in the early 1970s. The limitations of arms control policy, however, already became apparent with the SALT I Agreement of May 1972. Both sides agreed to curb undesirable and risky anti-ballistic missile systems, but ready-planned programmes were not impaired and the limitation amounted to quantitative modifications. The agreements did not hinder qualitative re-equipment with arms. SALT II was signed by President Carter in June 1979 but was not ratified by the American Senate. Reagan refused to set SALT II going again and instead entered a new round of START talks in Geneva.

At the beginning of the 1970s it proved possible to open the Conference on Security and Cooperation in Europe (CSCE), for which the Eastern bloc countries had long been campaigning. This produced the talks on mutual and balanced force reduction (MBFR). The several years of multilateral conference diplomacy, which culminated in the Final Act of Helsinki on 1 August 1975, not only constituted a success for Soviet foreign policy. They also provided a lift for dissidents and the human rights movement in the socialist countries, and for the first time brought the Soviet Union down from the high podestà of prosecutor into a European dock. The consequences became increasingly unpleasant for Soviet foreign policy as well, with instances such as the European Parliament in Strasbourg calling upon member states in January 1983 to speak out for the right of self-determination for the three Baltic states.[54] This new impetus also brought a number of drawbacks for the West, however, since it provided a point of departure for Carter's moralising human rights policy and brought a noticeable deterioration in the climate of East–West relations. The CSCE follow-up conference in Belgrade (1977/78) produced few resolutions of substance and even the MBFR results took their time in coming. In Madrid (1980/81) it proved impossible to reach agreement on the agenda for weeks on end. After the decision had been taken, with much difficulty, to suspend the talks, negotiations began again in 1982. Once again, however, the West launched further offensives, this time due primarily to the situation in Poland. Following this experience it seemed unlikely that the two sides would be interested in repeating the experiment; but the most visible symbol of *détente* policy in Europe recovered once more in Vienna in 1986.[55]

Differences also emerged in Madrid, however, in the interests of the USA and the Western European countries. Whilst the USA refused to negotiate on a business-as-usual basis and constantly reminded the Soviet Union of fulfilment of the obligations she had taken on with the Final Act of Helsinki, it was not in the interest of the European countries to put the trust-building potential of such conferences at stake by conducting 'psychological, punitive expeditions' against the Soviet Union.[56] In the face of the new bout of frost that settled on East–West relations, Soviet publicists came to place greater emphasis on the discontinuity and lacking trustworthiness of Western endeavours for *détente* than beforehand. In the Soviet view, peaceful coexistence constitutes a 'steadfast principle' in socialist countries but is the result of the conflict between hawks and doves in capitalist countries, the outcome of which cannot be reliably predicted.[57]

The Soviet Union has shown a lack of sensitivity for the pluralism of the Western camp in her disarmament proposals so far, although these have probably been well-intentioned in subjective terms.

A large number of the proposals are open to the suspicion that the Soviet Union wants to drive a wedge between the USA and her allies. This holds particularly true for the following Soviet initiatives:

1   The *special treatment of the nuclear powers*,[58] which can only lead to rivalries in the Western camp.
2   Proposals for *nuclear weapon-free zones* in Europe and Asia do not contain a sufficient offer in terms of areas of Soviet territory.[59]

3   *Threats* were repeatedly made against individual Western-European countries, such as in an Academy of Science publication, *Scientific Council for Research into the Problems of Peace and Disarmament*, entitled 'Europe faced with the choice: Confrontation or an Easing of Military Tension?'[60]

4   The *American allies' troops* are to be included in the disarmament agreements as well with no consideration to the far greater value that these troops hold as compared with the Soviet Union allies' troops, given the smaller conventional American presence in Western Europe.[61] In the eyes of some Western observers the troops of the Soviet Union's allies would only be allocated covering functions behind the front line, should the need arise. It was for this reason that Andropov's proposals to reduce the number of Soviet medium-range missiles in Europe to the number of British and French missiles were received with scepticism in the three Western capitals concerned.[62] France's special role within NATO is the subject of frequent praise (see pp. 42–5) but was not taken into account in proposals of this kind before Gorbatchev's new line in 1986.

5   The Soviet Union takes a *concept of strategic and tactical weapons* as the basis for disarmament negotiations, which relates specifically to the rivalry between the two superpowers and does not make sufficient allowance for Western-European concerns. Whereas the American missiles aimed at Soviet territory count as 'strategic', the Soviet weapon systems aimed at Western Europe are included under the tactical heading.[63] On the other hand, however, the USA has also been guilty of not paying enough attention to her allies' anxieties. The USA's awareness of her inferiority in the conventional field meant that she was repeatedly tempted to seek a way out via tactical nuclear weapons in Europe, with the result that her own allies began to feel they were being taken hostage by the dominating power.[64]

6   The Soviet Union complains that Western counter-proposals were expecting her to *withdraw* three times as many *troops* as the NATO countries. The Soviet Union quite openly expresses her fear that 'residual cadre units' could be maintained, whose equipment would remain in Europe and which could be quickly stocked up by an airlift in the event of conflict.[65] No mention is made of the fact that the West hedged similar concerns about well-intentioned Soviet gestures, such as the withdrawal of armoured divisions, 20 000 men strong, from the GDR,[66] which was strongly blown-up for propaganda purposes. Stocking-up residual units in the GDR by land ought to be even easier than arranging an American airlift.

7   The Soviet call for *liquidation of all foreign bases* is similarly not

quite fair on Western Europe's security requirements, given the geographical imbalance in the bloc leaders' respective distances from their allies.[67]

Other Soviet proposals stray so far into the realm of Utopia that they are frequently not taken seriously:

1   *Dissolution of the pact systems.* Even for Eurocommunist parties this remains at best a remote goal (see pp. 145–58). In view of her bilateral agreements the Soviet Union has no need even now of the Warsaw Pact in order to maintain her military penetration of Eastern Europe. The role of the Warsaw Pact is thus completely different from the significance of NATO for the integration of the West (see pp. 97–108).
2   The *abolition of all atomic weapons* is more of a declamatory proposal given the Western concept of deterrence.
3   The Soviet *dislike of controls* undermines the credibility of some of her proposals. Although emphasis is placed on the need for monitoring in the doctrine, when Soviet statements are put to the test only the Antarctic Treaty meets up to the ideal, since it covers an uninhabited area. For the rest, the discussion is largely halted by the principle of sovereignty, and the West is accused of perverting the principle of monitoring, in that it allegedly negotiates on the basis of 'first controls and then disarmament'.[68]

The question as to the credibility of Soviet moderation in the event of her having a certain military superiority or attaining this in the future is coupled to the question as to whether the Soviet leadership believes it can survive, or even win, a nuclear war. The answer which is frequently given in America as well is no.[69] One cannot conclude the contrary from the constant repetition of Lenin citations, in which Lenin quoted from Clausewitz, saying that 'war is the continuation of political intercourse with the intervention of other instruments'. He was quoting in a highly individual fashion, however, adding the words 'other — namely violent — instruments'.[70] Richard Pipes and other conservative advisors to the American government felt all the same that they had to assume the Soviet leadership to be working on the basis of a winnable nuclear war and hence to be resolutely striving for military superiority.[71] In contrast to this, there is something to be said for Arbatov's remark to the effect that the fundamental issues of highly-explosive politics cannot be subtly interpreted out of handbooks of military strategy.[72]

Part of the confidence gap that Soviet foreign policy has not so far been able to close in the West stems from the way in which she transposes her own bloc concept to the West. The other Warsaw Pact states played a subordinate role as independent actors with their own security interests.

The concerns of the NATO states are similarly not taken seriously, because the NATO two-track decision is viewed solely in terms of the two-fold option that it seems to open up for the Americans. Andropov's attempt to force parity between English and French Eurostrategic missiles on the one hand and Soviet Eurostrategic missiles on the other was also plagued by this dilemma.

Despite the verbal rejection of the bipolar approach, this point once again makes it clear that those engaged in Soviet foreign policy do indeed think in markedly bipolar terms. Where other states gain influence without the Soviets being sufficiently involved (such as in the Lebanon crisis in 1982), this is regarded as a serious crisis by the Soviet Union, even if she refrains from taking direct action.

The lack of consideration for the security interests of America's allies in Europe was also evident in Brezhnev's proposal of March 1979 that negotiations should be held on the renunciation of first use of nuclear and conventional weapons. The American guarantee of protection for countries such as the Federal Republic of Germany, which have renounced nuclear weapons, is tied to a first-strike capability. To renounce this capability would mean having to catch up in the field of conventional weapons.[73] This is hardly to be expected given the cost and the political resistance that would be encountered in America. The opinion that NATO is already almost as strong as the Warsaw Pact countries in the conventional field has remained a minority opinion to date, which excludes the West Russian military regions from the comparison of forces. Other calculations for soldiers in combat units work on the basis of a ratio of 1.2:1 in the Soviet Union's favour, which does not constitute a sufficiently large numerical advantage to tempt the Soviets into a lightning war.[74] Nevertheless, the West is predominantly of the opinion that America should not give up her nuclear first-strike option, in order to retain credibility for the concept of deterrence.[75] There are also voices emerging which see the deterrence doctrine as coming to an end when more accurately targetable and more reliable missile warheads make the possibility of taking the opponent's cities hostage in the counter-strike less feasible.[76]

The Soviet Union views this hardening of positions in a number of NATO partners as 'rash action',[77] whilst Western researchers increasingly regard the Soviet offer as not to be trusted so long as the Soviet Union continues to build up her first-strike capability.[78]

In view of the fact that it will not be possible to achieve a full consensus on parities in the foreseeable future, the West will presumably have to be content with the sufficiency principle.[79] At best it will prove possible to maintain a 'balance of imbalances', as currently exists in the intercontinental nuclear field.[80] Whilst it would be too difficult to secure strict parity at all times and in all regions, it ought to be feasible to secure global parity and second-strike capability. It is perhaps not by chance that the German politicans ready to make compromises today, such as Bahr and Gaus, have considered whether the West should not return to its old, pre-1967 concept of massive retaliation so as to avoid sinking the conflict thresholds in the East–West conflict and to offer the Soviets an alternative way out of their hypertrophic need for security. There are also competent voices in the West of the opinion that a potential nuclear superiority on the part of the Soviet Union would be irrelevant so long as there was still a 'balance of determination'. In this concept the defender has a greater determination to ward off a possible attack and is thus even able to offset a slight superiority in terms of potential.[81] The attacker on the other hand must be able to act relatively free of risk and thus requires considerable superiority in order to venture aggression. It is quite rightly thought to be unlikely that the Soviet politicians could derive a sufficient feeling of security to adopt a policy of attack from the small, hard-come-by advantages that they at times hammer out.

Furthermore, it is repeatedly assumed that the Soviet politicians work on the primacy of military thinking. The terminology, with its strong military slant (see pp. 3–13), would at times suggest this conclusion. There are, however, deterrent effects which stem from political considerations (over and above military risks) as to the advantage that the Soviet Union would gain from the integration of Western Europe into her domain and from the reunification of Germany in a socialist state, and these must not be forgotten alongside the large number of military scenarios.

The deployment of military instruments of power for political purposes

With the exception of the Cuban crisis — which initiated Krushchev's fall from power — the Soviet Union has so far avoided direct confrontation with the USA. The traditional type of power politics is rejected in theory, the power theory of the realist school is regarded in the Soviet doctrine *per se* as justification for a policy of military threat.[82]

In the era of coexistence the use of military power is rated as highly improbable on the basis of the three worlds. In the socialist camp the Brezhnev doctrine at times actually makes it seem imperative, and in the Third World the Soviet Union has even pledged herself constitutionally (Article 28) to support liberation movements, which could be stepped up as far as military engagement should the need arise. It is in her relationship with the first (capitalist) world that the Soviet Union has shown most restraint in the use of military power. There were four instances of confrontation during the Cold War which could have sparked off an armed conflict (see pp. 36–8) but both sides avoided an escalation.

Both superpowers have employed military power for political ends since the Second World War. In the case of the USA, over 200 instances have been recorded,[83] and for the Soviet Union there were 158 cases of military pressure being brought to bear in the period 1944 to 1979. Up until the Middle East war of 1967 the USA held a monopoly on intervention in the Third World[84] (see pp. 118–23). To begin with, the superpowers could only apply military pressure in their most immediate sphere of influence. In 1944/45 the Soviet Union attempted to retain the areas that she had already been granted in the agreements with Hitler. Outside her sphere of influence she proceeded with great care. She withdrew her troops from Iran, China (at the start of 1946) and Bornholm and dropped her territorial claims against Turkey. When the East European People's Democracies were set up a build-up of troops was ensured along the border in order to support the internal seizure of power by the Communists, such as along the Czechoslovakian border in February 1948. On the other hand, Stalin refrained from armed intervention against Yugoslavia after the break with Tito in 1948. Even in the Korean War no Soviet troops participated in the invasion of South Korea. The chief instances in which Soviet military potential has been employed as a threat or even for purposes of intervention since the Second World War are as follows:

November	1945	Penetration of Manchuria
February	1946	Establishment in Port Arthur and Dairen
March	1946	Border and Dardanelles dispute with Turkey
June	1948/49	Berlin blockade
	1950–53	Korean War
June	1953	GDR uprising
October	1956	Unrest in Poland
October	1956	Hungarian uprising
	1958–61	Berlin crisis
July	1962	Cuban crisis
	1965	Border dispute with China
	1965–72	Vietnam War
June	1967	Egyptian–Israeli War
August	1967–68	Intervention in Czechoslovakia
March	1969	Conflict with China
October	1973	Arab–Israeli War
July	1974	Cyprus conflict
	1975	Support of the MPLA in Angola

May	1977	Support of Ethiopia
February	1979	Sino–Vietnamese War
December	1979–?	Intervention in Afghanistan
	1980	Threat of intervention in Poland

In countless other instances the Soviet Union's foreign policy has been confined to verbal threats, such as in the Suez Crisis in 1956, to manoeuvres along the border (in Middle East conflicts) or to fleet movements (Lebanon crisis, 1958).[85] Naval units were at times employed for symbolic politics, such as to warn Yugoslavia in 1949 and Poland in 1956. In 1968 Soviet naval units put on a display in the Atlantic prior to the Soviet intervention in Czechoslovakia. In 1968 and 1971 the navy was used to intimidate Romania. All these incidents, however, concerned the Soviet Union's own sphere of influence. Outside this sphere, the navy was used more for purposes of co-operation, such as *vis-à-vis* France (1956) and *vis-à-vis* Egypt (on several occasions). At times naval diplomacy has been skilfully used for propaganda purposes during the withdrawal of Soviet troops, such as from China (Port Arthur and Dairen in 1955) and Romania (in 1969).

No Soviet ally in the Warsaw Pact has had to be protected against an attack from outside the socialist camp to date. There have, however, been several such incidents with Soviet allies in Asia: Korea in 1950 to 1953, North Vietnam in 1965 to 1972 and Vietnam in 1979 following the Chinese attack. The Soviets also rank Afghanistan as such a case. Even in the Third World, however, the alleged external threat here (from China and Pakistan) was for the most part simply regarded as a pretext. In the first three cases the Soviet use of military means was on a limited scale and confined essentially to military consultation, economic aid and the supply of arms.

The application of military power within the socialist camp has been most frequently directed against China. China ranks second to the Federal Republic of Germany (13 times) as the most frequent target of Soviet military threat (seven times). On one occasion the threats against China escalated to a threat to use nuclear weapons (1969).[86]

The Soviet Union only began to assert military power in the Third World as of 1957. Up to 1979 there were eight instances in which Moscow helped insurgents to fight an established regime. In ten further cases, Soviet foreign policy supported a national liberation movement against an established regime.[87] Part of the Soviet Union's military activity can be explained by her striving to achieve complete equality on a world scale. At times it is difficult to perceive the direct benefit of Soviet aid for the Soviet Union. A number of American authors also work on the basis that the Soviet Union has intervened less in the Third World than the Americans to date — this holds particularly true for the area covered by the Monroe doctrine. Even when it comes to indirect intervention via

Secret Services the KGB is at times said to proceed with no greater zeal than the CIA.[88]

Given the exceeding care taken by the Soviet Union in the handling of the Poland crisis in 1980 and her restraint in the Sino–Vietnamese conflict and on other occasions, a large portion of public world opinion would have been inclined to believe that the Soviet Union had come to adopt an increasing degree of moderation, had the Soviet leadership not committed the error of intervening in Afghanistan in December 1979. In many respects this application of military power was the first instance of its kind in history and was bound to create a particularly large measure of distrust in the West and the Third World:

1   The Soviet Union showed a *greater willingness to take on risks* than ever before, at least when viewed in retrospect. The Soviet leadership, however, must certainly have imagined that the risks of this armed conflict would be smaller.

2   No *proxy campaign* was employed to give the impression that the Soviet Union herself was not directly involved, as often happened elsewhere in the Third World (see pp. 118–44).

3   The intervention in Afghanistan had to be interpreted as an *expansion of the Brezhnev doctrine to Asia*. For the first time, the theory of the irreversibility of revolutionary processes had been transposed to the unsettled soil of a developing country outside the socialist camp. This was all the more surprising, since Afghanistan, although already deeply penetrated by Soviet influence, was still not universally classified as a country 'of socialist orientation' in 1980. One military textbook simply described Afghanistan as a 'democratic republic',[89] and Afghanistan was long rated as an outstanding example of the coexistence of a 'socialist great power' and a small 'independently evolving developing country'.[90]

4   Finally, this intervention marked a *relapse into Stalinist methods and prescriptivism*, which kindly-disposed observers had regarded as having been overcome. Direct Soviet involvement has been mooted in the murder of Amin.[91] The fact of Soviet publications declaring him to be a 'CIA agent' does not exactly weaken this suspicion.[92] The ordered request for help is presented as having been in line with the UN statutes and international law[93] but the credibility of this configuration is not improved by the flanking argument of 'imperialism as well', since a list of American interventions in Asia is supposed to prop up the legend of a forthcoming American intervention in Afghanistan.[94] In so far as the Soviet Union was citing international law, this shows she has a different understanding of the *right of intervention* from that

which prevails in the West. Those involved in Soviet foreign policy made increasing reference to a treaty and request for help from a friendly government. The treaties with the socialist countries even contain formal intervention clauses, particularly the treaty with the GDR.[95] As far as the Western camp is concerned, however, even the slightest non-monitored and non-official statement of opinion which penetrates the socialist camp is presented as intolerable interference which goes against the 'spirit of Helsinki'.

There has been much speculation about the motive behind this intervention but the Kremlin astrology method has not produced any conclusive judgement:

1   There was widespread presumption that the Soviet Union was attempting to advance towards the *energy sources of the Middle East*. This opinion was also fuelled by CIA presumptions that the Soviet Union could become an oil-importing country as of 1985, one of the most problematical false estimations of recent years. The majority of experts, by contrast, feel that despite the growing energy requirements within Comecon, the Soviet Union will not have to purchase large quantities of oil on the world market. Soviet foreign policy is not therefore under any duress to pursue an aggressive Middle East policy on grounds of an oil shortage. The further-reaching assumption that the Soviet Union wanted to create energy supply difficulties for her capitalist opponents and her advance towards the oil wells was based on the principle 'what hurts my neighbour is good for me' is likewise scarcely credible, since this would at best have a lasting impact on the West Europeans, thereby counteracting the Soviet courtship of the countries of Western Europe (see pp. 142–5).

2   The press has frequently seen a desire on the part of the Soviet Union to protect her own southern regions from the infectious germ of *Islamic fundamentalism* as being behind this intervention. This overlooks the fact that only some 8 per cent of Soviet Muslims are Shiites. Iran would have constituted a far greater danger here, yet the Soviets endeavoured to achieve correct relations with Iran (see pp. 124–8). The majority of Soviet Shiites are closer to the Iranian border than the Afghanistan border and are concentrated in Southern Azerbaidzhan. Soviet literature is still careful in discriminating Islam as a whole. In distant countries like Algeria, but also for the first phase of the Khomeini revolution, the modernising aspects of Islamic ideologies were emphasised.[96]

3   The intervention has been interpreted as a resultant in the *power struggle*. The ideologists such as Suslov and Ponomarev have (in this opinion) won through their policy of wide-area integration in the

face of the groups more intent on economic consolidation of the Soviet Union.[97]

Prudent analysts do not in the main regard this intervention as a further step in a demonological history of development from 'Berlin 1953 to Kabul 1979', in the way in which it was to some extent portrayed in the 1980 Federal German election campaign. Instead, it is rated more as a contradictory reaction from short-term considerations and miscalculations of the risk involved than as a deliberate break with Brezhnev's policy of *détente*.[98] The Soviet Union doubtlessly miscalculated the level of means that would be required to retain this satellite acquired in 1978 and she also misjudged the reaction of the Third World to her move. China and the USA were able to jointly toss their newly-established relations into a moral campaign against the Soviet Union. The fairly unanimous protest of the Islamic Foreign Ministers at the 1980 Islamic Conference[99] brought an unforeseen loss of confidence capital. Economic relations and Soviet good conduct in a number of political issues — such as exit permits for Jews in the Soviet Union — similarly suggest that Afghanistan was not intended as a conscious break with *détente* policy.[100]

An important lesson that the West ought to learn from the Afghanistan incident is that Western omissions may have contributed towards this Soviet adventure. It is not merely that Moscow judged the time to be right in view of the loss of American positions of influence in Iran. The USA had not put up sufficiently energetic resistance to the creeping satellisation that began long before 1978/79 and hence, despite verbal protests at isolated Soviet actions, had thereby suggested that Soviet dominance in this country would be potentially tolerated.

Theories which assume that the Soviet Union was simply showing her true face with the march into Afghanistan, revealing that *détente* had never been intended seriously, and theories that assumed a deliberate change of course on the part of Moscow[101] do not seem very probable given the overall picture of Soviet foreign policy at this time. The Soviet Union's judgement of America under Carter continued to be marked by moderation, despite the clear deterioration in relations. Reagan's election was also registered in a restrained manner. Soviet foreign policy attempted to maintain continuity and the status quo on all counts. When unexpected events occurred, such as the fall of the Shah in Iran (1979), the war between Iran and Iraq (1980ff.), the *rapprochement* between Egypt and Israel and the Chinese march into Vietnam (February 1979), the Soviet Union reacted carefully and did not let herself be drawn to intervention even though Soviet fears of encirclement were running high. A 'Brzezinski strategy' was even invented for propaganda purposes, which was allegedly aimed at a deliberate policy of encirclement on the part of the USA. Where factual evidence of a concerted Sino-American policy of encirclement was lacking, this was replaced by a couple of isolated quotations from Brzezinski's books where necessary.[102]

5 Soviet Economic Power and Foreign Trade with the Western World

Soviet economic potential

Soviet military strategy works on the basis that the socialist camp should not embark on a long, drawn-out conflict with the capitalist countries, since this would give the West a lead on account of its economic superiority (see pp. 51–77). Although the Soviet literature repeatedly maintains that the socialist economic system is superior, the Soviet leadership is clever enough not to build up its survival strategy on this illusion.

The Soviet Union's development of military power has frequently been interpreted as compensation for a lack of economic success on the world scale. This perspective must not be allowed to obscure the fact that, for a developing country which was set back a long way in its development by two world wars, the Soviet Union reveals an impressive balance of goods and services in some areas, despite all the shortcomings of the system. From her growing national income she has managed to secure both an increasing standard of living for her population and finance the tremendous outlay involved in her breakthrough to become an equal-status world power. In the course of this development, differences of opinion have at times prevailed between different groups within the party as to the priorities of budgetary policy (see pp. 10–13) but on the whole the establishment of a worldwide reputation for the Soviet Union has been accorded a high ranking by all groups.

Ever since the Soviet Union entered the circles of pentarchy there has been a discrepancy between her military power and the level of her economic development. Prior to the October Revolution, however,

Tsarist Russia was already the fifth strongest economic power in the world by virtue of her size alone. Growth since the October Revolution has been built up on a socialist variant of a big-push strategy and has been accompanied by large-scale human and social sacrifice in many areas. The Soviet Union developed an unparalleled capacity for capital accumulation and growth. A CIA report of 1982 set the annual growth in the Soviet Union at 4.7 per cent for the years 1950 to 1980, whilst the USA only registered an average growth of 3.4 per cent per annum in this same period.[1] Growth in labour productivity, technological quality and the quality of a large number of products, however, has not kept pace with this development, as can be seen from the rough output indicators which were long the preferred criteria of success for Soviet statistics.[2] Despite the continued growth optimism in the literature, Soviet growth has dropped sharply over recent years (in 1981 growth was some 1.5 per cent). The pace of military development has not slown down, however, and many observers do not expect this to happen in the near future either.[3] Only a few observers speculate about a slowing down of military efforts, forced upon the leadership by Soviet consumer revolts. Most experts instead assume great stability in the system inside the country, despite a growing dissenter movement in a number of centres of the Soviet system.[4] The Soviet Union has also cut down her claim in the economic competition in the Soviet theory as well. Little remains in the Soviet literature of the exuberance of the Khrushchev era, in which 'catching up and overtaking the USA' was treated as an imminent event. Only the left wing in America still voices the opinion that the Soviet Union will overtake the USA in the standard of living of its population over the next few generations.[5] The gap between the gross national products (national income) of the USA and the Soviet Union has, nonetheless, narrowed considerably to date. In 1950, Soviet national income represented 32.7 per cent of the American gross national product and in 1975 the figure was already 57 per cent.[6] All the same, the illusion of soon overtaking the West in economic terms has been replaced by more careful calculations as to the necessary restructuring of resources and the allocation of means.

The Soviet Union's trade with the West

The most important indication that the Soviet leadership was adopting a new course in the economic competition with the West came with the switch to a technology transfer from capitalist countries and the intensification of Soviet trade with the West.

Following the October Revolution the system was scarcely prepared for foreign trade with non-socialist countries as far as theory was concerned. 'Socialism in one country' required processing in terms of foreign trade theory, since Lenin had only left a theory about the imperialist phase of the world economy and not a foreign trade theory with instructions as to how a power in isolation was to behave *vis-à-vis* a capitalist world system.[7]

The labour theory of value, on which the Marxist–Leninist theory of economics was based, came up against particular difficulties in foreign trade — even in the exchange of goods between socialist countries. Non-identical production conditions meant that even socialist countries which had taken up the cause of overcoming 'unequal exchange' were not always able to exchange truly equivalent quantities of goods as expressed in terms of the quantity of labour involved. Conflicts not only developed between the Soviet Union and those Eastern bloc economies dependent upon her; even socialist countries whose relations were less characterised by the balance of power, such as China and Cuba, still became engaged in hefty controversies about the evaluation of the quantities of rice to be exchanged for sugar beet in the 1960s.[8]

The Soviet Union got round this dilemma in the initial phase by keeping foreign trade down to a minimum, although Lenin never put forward the pronounced concept of self-sufficiency, which some subsequent socialist systems came to adopt. The sound formula for socialism of 'Soviet power plus electrification' seemed to justify any means of rapidly achieving the second term of the equation, including the forced-pace transfer of technology from capitalist countries if need be. Only when the exchange of goods with the world outside took on greater dimensions did the socialist countries' foreign trade theory have to turn to the 'bourgeois' theory of comparative costs again. This is generally still clumsily circumvented in the Soviet theory with references to 'integration in the international division of labour' on the basis of 'mutual advantage'.[9]

The 'metaphysical preoccupation with ownership' that Lenin has been charged with (Wiles) meant that Lenin's chief efforts as far as theory was concerned were concentrated on establishing the monopoly on foreign trade. It was decreed as early as 29 December 1917 that licences for import and export could only be granted by the foreign trade department of the Commissariat for Trade and Industry. In April 1918 foreign trade was fully nationalised. The 1936 Constitution raised the principle of a state monopoly on foreign trade to constitutional status in its Article 14. The foreign trade monopoly did not remain undisputed within the party in its initial stages, particularly when the New Economic Policy (NEP) was introduced. Lenin nonetheless implemented the monopoly in strict fashion. Where he suspected that people were getting round the regulations he ordered that 'the guilty be found, so that we can let these scoundrels rot in prison'. He commanded that the foreign trade planners in the scientific and technical department of the Supreme Economic Council, 'these learned layabouts', be woken up so that 'we are informed in a reasonable, timely, practical and non-bureaucratic manner about European and American technology'.[10]

According to Soviet accounts, in the time before the Second World War the foreign trade monopoly served chiefly as a defence against economic offensives and attempts at infiltration by the capitalist countries. Value was placed on the assertion that the foreign trade monopoly was not a sacred cow and 'the question of the monopoly' was to be viewed 'in the light of the requirements of the particular stage of the socialist revolution'.[11] It thus became increasingly difficult to justify why the Soviet Union continued to uphold this principle after the Second World War, when she was a world power, and even forced it upon the smaller People's Democracies, where it only created pointless investment costs in some cases. Where People's Democracies began to slacken the monopoly, as in Czechoslovakia during the Dubček era, this was unrelentingly branded as deviation. The reason put forward for maintaining the foreign trade monopoly today is that it serves to co-ordinate the socialist economies and to create stable, long-term relations with developing countries and capitalist states.[12]

The marked emphasis placed on the national plan hinders the potential of enterprises to produce for foreign trade. Neither the price system (see pp. 97–108) nor other sources of information provide Soviet managers with sufficient information about market needs. An enterprise manager cannot even enter into trade relationships with another enterprise in the country on the domestic market without being subject to regulation from above. The intercalation of the ministry and the trade organisations under the ministry means that the enterprises are far removed from foreign trade and from the necessary knowledge about foreign markets. Soviet managers have little overseas experience and often have to be motivated with material incentives first before they will work for foreign trade.[13] Even where managers have the motivation, they often lack the know-how to produce goods of world quality. The Soviet literature has thus recently recommended that an improvement be brought about in top-level cadres' knowledge of foreign markets.[14] On the import side, foreign trade serves not least to overcome bottlenecks in domestic production. Weighing-up goods between the necessary use of scarce 'hard' currencies on the one hand and other plan targets on the other hand often restricts any expansion in foreign trade.[15] The Soviet currency is a purely internal currency. Even within the socialist camp, where world market price orientation could theoretically have been replaced by the creation of a 'socialist price system' for intra-bloc trade,[16] the unit of account of the transfer-rouble (*perevodnyi rubel*) was introduced by way of a collective currency for Comecon, with the functions of a price measure, payment medium and unit of account for joint investments.[17] Withdrawing the rouble from the world market has both its advantages and drawbacks. The advantage is that not all the inflationary trends and declines in the world market are able to undermine the internal bloc price system. The drawback would seem to be greater, though, in that by having two price systems inside and outside the socialist camp, the Comecon countries are not able to calculate benefit and detriment in the international division of labour with a sufficient degree of accuracy.[18] This drawback may be viewed lightly when it comes to the Soviet Union's trade with the West — particularly in the import of high-level technology, since it is a politically motivated price that is really being paid here after all. When it comes to expanding Soviet exports, however, the shortcoming is extremely serious. The non-convertibility of her currency means that the Soviet Union's trade relations (even within Comecon) are construed primarily in bilateral terms, and this has led to the co-operation between Comecon and the EEC, in particular, becoming a 'dialogue between the deaf and dumb' (see pp. 107–8).

The Western partners to Soviet foreign trade have experienced pronounced changes in their ranking over the course of history. In the initial phase of the Soviet system Great Britain still ranked top in Soviet foreign trade, then in the second half of the 1920s Great Britain was overtaken by Germany. Germany then dropped back during the National Socialist era and the USA pushed forward into the rank of chief trading partner during the war (see Table 5.1). This period of intensified trading relations with the USA is still beset with traumas in the Soviet literature today. Roosevelt is accused of trying to bleed the Soviet Union to death through inadequate supplies so as to be able to gain an advantage over the allies after the war.[19]

It was only after the Second World War that the Soviet Union became a world power. Even under socialist conditions the development of foreign

Table 5.1

Share of chief trading partners in Soviet foreign trade turnover (in %)

	1925/26	1929	1933	1938
Great Britain	24.0	14.2	14.0	19.6
Germany	19.7	22.7	27.7	5.5
USA	10.5	12.2	3.6	18.0
Iran	5.4	7.2	2.4	4.3
China	3.3	3.2	4.7	4.6
Netherlands	2.2	2.2	4.0	5.0
Belgium	1.4	1.3	3.4	6.5
Mongolia	0.5	1.4	6.6	4.0

Source: E. Shershnev: *On the Principle of Mutual Advantage. Soviet-American Economic Relations*, Moscow, Progress, 1978, p. 30.

trade was seen to be a function of the development of the country's economic power (see pp. 78–9). The Soviet Union's foreign trade, however, did not even develop in parallel to her economic power. Even Soviet authors openly admit today that the socialist camp still only accounts for a relatively small share of the worldwide production of major goods (see pp. 78–9). In cases where absolute figures produce too modest an impact, the growth rates for the 1970s are frequently quoted — even for goods such as motor cars, which for a long time did not enjoy a very high rating in production planning.

Growth rates of this type are also taken as proof of the fact that the 'restructuring of the world system' is in full swing (see pp. 97–108) and that the growing integration of the Comecon countries will guarantee this progress in the future as well (see pp. 97–108).[20]

Table 5.2

Comecon countries' share in selected products worldwide in %

	1970	1979
Steel	26.2	30.4
Natural gas	21.0	30.0
Cement	24.0	27.5
Electric energy	19.7	22.0
Oil	16.2	19.1
Automobiles	3.1	6.6

Source: O. T. Bogomolov (ed.): *Sotsializm i perestrojka mezhdunarodnykh ekonomicheskikh otnoshenii*, Moscow, MO, 1982, p. 25.

Foreign trade still only accounts for a very small share of Soviet national income. All the socialist countries together are said to hold a 12 per cent share in world trade. Here again, it is primarily the growth rates that are extolled. The USSR moved up from sixteenth place (1.5 per cent of world trade) to eighth place, with a share of some 4 per cent of world trade, after the war. No secret is made of the fact that this is still rather a modest result compared with the outriders of foreign trade in the West (USA 12.1 per cent, West Germany 9.6 per cent, Japan 6.6 per cent, France 5.9 per cent), but it is quite rightly pointed out that a big country rich in raw materials, like the Soviet Union, will become increasingly less dependent on foreign trade, measured in terms of the percentage of foreign trade making up national income. A type of unstable balance is assumed to exist on the world market — 'imperialism' is no longer strong enough to determine international economic relations on its own and socialism has not yet acquired the strength to fully reshape international economic relations on the basis of socialist principles.[21] This analysis of the Soviet Union's position in world trade provides the Soviet discussion with two directions of impulse. The first is a propagandist direction, aimed at collecting further points in the endeavour to restructure the world system. These efforts are generally classified under the heading 'economic diplomacy', which seeks to show up the class differences that exist on a world scale and use these to the advantage of the Soviet Union's own position.[22] On the other hand, however, capitalism still dominates on the world scale and hence the Soviet economy is forced to concern itself with the 'laws' of the capitalist world market. Even quantitative analyses and models are accepted here today, in order to improve the position of Soviet foreign trade policy.[23]

Growth in foreign trade has been conditioned not least by growth in trade with the West (see Table 5.3). For a time, foreign trade grew at a faster annual rate (10 to 12 per cent) than national income (4 to 6 per cent).[24] Both growth rates have slowed down in the meantime. The Soviet literature is still very optimistic about foreign trade with the West,[25] however, although intra-bloc trade has been pushed forward more again since 1975 (see pp. 106–8).

In her growing trade with the West the Soviet Union initially had the most intensive trade relations with the defeated countries she had been facing in the Second World War (Germany, Japan, Italy, Finland). This was all the more striking since the Soviet Union by no means had the most relaxed of political relations with these countries. In the 1970s trade with the West came to be largely disassociated from fluctuations in the political climate. Only Finland, which worked its way up from third to second place in trade with the Soviet Union at the end of the 1970s (see Table 5.4), has so far been suspected of being economically dependent on the Soviet Union. In the Soviet Union, on the other hand, Finland is upheld as a model case of good co-operation between East and West.[26]

The focus on Germany and Japan can be explained to some extent by Soviet concern about American sanctions. The USA was the country in the East–West conflict which was most inclined to declare all important categories of goods to be strategical goods and to subject trade to political considerations. Furthermore, Germany and Japan were latecomers to the world market and thus had spare capacity to offer during the boom period. Germany also had an old tradition of intensive trade and cultural relations with the Soviet Union. In 1977 Japan was the Soviet Union's second most important trading partner after the Federal Republic of Germany. In 1981 Japan fell back to fifth place (see Table 5.4). Even during the good times, trade with the Soviet Union accounted for only 4 per cent of Japanese foreign trade. Trade relations with Japan were not without political conflict and hence growth has stagnated over the past few years.[27] Soviet authors see American and Chinese pressure on Japan as being to blame for this.[28] Some of the difficulties which the Soviet Union came up against in Japan, however, have nothing to do with

Table 5.3
Growth in Soviet foreign trade in milliard roubles (converted at the exchange rate as of the 1961 currency reform)

	Turnover	Export	Import
1913	2.2	1.1	1.0
1917	2.2	0.3	1.9
1921/22	0.2	0.05	0.2
1922/23	0.2	0.1	0.1
1928	1.3	0.6	0.7
1932	1.0	0.4	0.5
1938	0.5	0.2	0.3
1946	1.3	0.6	0.7
1950	2.9	1.6	1.3
1955	5.8	3.1	2.7
1956	6.5	3.3	3.2
1957	7.5	3.9	3.6
1958	7.8	3.9	3.9
1959	9.5	4.9	4.6
1960	10.1	5.0	5.1
1961	10.6	5.4	5.2
1962	12.1	6.3	5.8
1963	12.9	6.5	6.4
1964	13.9	6.9	7.0
1965	14.6	7.4	7.2
1966	15.1	8.0	7.1
1967	16.4	8.7	7.7
1968	18.0	9.6	8.4
1969	19.8	10.5	9.3
1970	22.1	11.5	10.6
1971	23.6	12.4	11.2
1972	26.0	12.7	13.3
1973	31.3	15.8	15.5
1974	39.6	20.8	18.8
1975	50.7	24.0	26.7
1976	56.8	28.0	28.8
1977	63.3	33.2	30.1
1978	70.2	35.7	34.5
1979	80.3	42.4	37.9
1980	94.1	49.6	44.5
1981	109.7	57.1	52.6
1982	119.6	63.2	56.4
1983	127.5	67.9	59.6
1984	139.7	74.4	65.3

Sources: *Narodnoe khozyaystvo SSSR v 1922–1972 gg*, Moscow, Statistika, 1972, p. 491; *Vneshnyaya torgovlya SSSR v 1984 g*, Moscow, Finansy i statistika, 1985, p. 6.

external influences. They are the same difficulties that the Western OECD countries meet with on Japanese markets. They stem more from the cultural characteristics of the country than from a deliberately fashioned protectionist policy with its negative consequences of an imbalanced ratio of imports to exports.[29]

Table 5.4

The exchange of Soviet goods with capitalist countries (in % of total Soviet foreign trade)

	1977	1978	1979	1980	1981	1984
FRG	4.7	4.7	5.3	6.1	5.5	5.4
Finland	3.4	3.1	3.2	4.1	4.6	3.4
France	2.7	2.6	3.3	4.0	3.8	3.0
Italy	3.2	2.7	3.2	3.2	3.2	3.2
Japan	3.6	3.3	3.2	2.9	2.8	2.1
USA	2.4	2.6	3.5	1.6	1.7	2.2
Netherlands			1.4	1.5	1.4	1.4
Canada			0.6	1.1	1.3	1.0
Austria	1.0	0.9	1.0	1.0	1.2	1.2
Belgium		1.0		1.3	1.1	1.2
Switzerland				0.9	0.8	0.7
Sweden	0.8	0.7	1.0	0.7	0.6	0.6

Sources: *Vneshnyaya torgovlya SSSR v 1984 g*, Moscow, Finansy i statistika, 1985, p. 15, and earlier editions.

Over the past few years France and Italy have gained ground in Soviet trade with the West. Foreign trade with the USA, by contrast, was halved in 1980. The neutral countries such as Switzerland and Sweden play a subordinate role. Only Austria has intensified its foreign trade with the Soviet Union. This growth has been too insignificant, however, for it to be applied in support of the occasional Finlandisation theories (see pp. 46–50) put forward as far as the economy is concerned.

East–West trade has developed in such a way as to prevent any upset in the balance. The Comecon countries bulkhead off their domestic markets from the world market by means of import controls and price adjustments, in roughly the same way as the European Community operates on the agricultural market. The EEC countries, by contrast, protect themselves with import quotas, price review procedures and, if need be, anti-dumping duties. The latter are rarely necessary, since the socialist countries generally adjust their export prices to Western price levels themselves.[30]

Only occasionally has the Soviet Union coupled her trade relations with the West to political demands. Long-term considerations would also not allow this. The Soviet Union's opening up to trade with the West has been explained in part by the failure of domestic reforms and in part by the need to achieve relief on the consumer goods front, given the growing expectations on the part of the Soviet population, thereby allowing the country's own resources to be channelled into armaments.[31] Additional motives can be found in specific drawbacks of the Soviet economic system:

1   A *low innovation rate* compels the Soviet Union to close technology gaps through trade with the West. The benefit to the Soviet national economy of these imports of Western machines and equipment, however, is being rated increasingly sceptically.[32]

2   The *manpower shortage* which still prevails in the Soviet Union, in contrast to economies which are run on market economy lines, calls for increased use of high-level technology, which then has to be imported from abroad.

3   The need for the Soviet Union to *improve her export structure* so as not to remain predominantly a supplier of raw materials for all time, makes it essential for her to import high-level technology to begin with.[33]

The product structure of Soviet foreign trade is changing but Soviet exports are still made up predominantly of raw materials and semi-finished manufactures. The Soviet Union is following a pattern (even within her own bloc) which is otherwise found primarily in dependent economies. She has been able to register progress in machinery exports — in 1913 machinery accounted for only 0.3 per cent of total exports and in 1980 the figure was already 15.8 per cent. This must still be set against high figures on the import side, however. Imports of machinery and equipment have more than doubled as compared with pre-revolutionary times — from 16.6 per cent in 1913 to 46.7 per cent in 1984 (see Table 5.5). The proportion of high-grade finished products in foreign trade is still low (textile fibres 1.9 per cent, food stuffs 1.6 per cent), and these go first and foremost to Comecon and Third World countries. If imports and exports are compared with those of highly-developed countries then the disproportion of high-grade industrial goods becomes even more striking. In trade with the USA in 1981, 5.3 million roubles' worth of machinery and industrial equipment exports were set against 200 million roubles' worth of imports. In the case of the Federal Republic of Germany the ratio was less extreme with 16.1 to 920 million roubles.[34]

Percentages of this type are also affected by factors over which Soviet policy has no control. The energy crisis came as a windfall for the Soviet Union, increasing the share of energy carriers in foreign trade from 30 per cent (1973) to more than 40 per cent at the beginning of the 1980s. Oil and natural gas exports even accounted for almost 60 per cent of trade with the OECD countries. The Soviet Union was keen to push these supplies, since the sale of oil on Western markets proved more profitable than trade with Comecon partners, given the price explosion (see pp. 97–108).[35] Soviet publications maintain that the energy policy strategies adopted by the European countries (allegedly aimed at self-sufficiency through North Sea oil plus nuclear energy) are doomed to fail. The model of the

Table 5.5
Development of product structure in the Soviet exchange of trade (in %)

	Export						Import					
	1913	1938	1950	1960	1970	1984	1913	1938	1950	1960	1970	1984
Tools, machinery, means of transport	0.3	5.0	11.8	20.7	21.5	16.0	16.6	34.5	21.5	31.0	35.5	46.7
Fuels, electric energy	3.5	8.9	3.9	16.2	17.2	51.2	7.1	1.2	11.8	4.2	2.0	2.3
Ores, metals, metal products	2.8	3.9	11.3	20.4	19.6	10.4	6.9	29.8	15.0	15.6	9.6	5.3
Chemical products, rubber	1.2	4.0	4.3	2.9	3.5	3.7	7.9	5.2	6.9	6.0	5.7	3.2
Wood, cellulose, paper	10.9	20.3	3.1	5.5	6.5	2.8	3.3	0.8	3.8	1.9	2.1	0.4
Textile fibres, semi-finished products	8.9	4.3	11.2	6.4	3.4	1.9	18.3	10.0	7.7	6.5	4.8	0.3
Foodstuffs	54.7	29.5	20.6	13.1	8.4	1.6	21.2	12.7	17.5	13.1	15.8	17.4
Industrial consumer goods	4.7	7.9	4.9	2.9	2.7	2.2	10.3	1.0	7.4	16.9	18.3	15.6

Sources: *Narodnoe khozyaystvo SSSR v 1922–1972 gg*, Moscow, Statistika, 1972, p. 492; *Narodnoe khozyaystvo SSSR v 1980 g*, Moscow, Finansy i statistika, 1981, p. 540; *Narodnoe khozyaystvo SSSR 1922–1982 g*, Moscow, Finansy i statistika, 1982, p. 580; *Vneshnyaya torgovlya SSSR v 1984 g*, Moscow, Finansy i statistika, 1985, p. 18.

Comecon countries working in close co-operation with the Soviet Union is put forward as an alternative.[36] This sounds like an invitation to Finlandisation in energy policy and threatens to bring grist to the mill of the very opponents of more intense East–West trade. In non-scientific publications, which serve for foreign propaganda purposes, the West Europeans are urged to participate in this 'deal of the century' on labour market policy grounds too, and America's allies are presented with a gloomy picture of a permanent economic war between the EEC and America.[37]

The initial euphoria at the expansion of East–West trade gave way to greater realism on both sides.[38] On the Soviet side there were primarily four restrictions on trade with the West:

1   The forced-pace *integration of Comecon* as of 1975 (see pp. 97–8).
2   Credit restrictions and the constraints of a planned economy led early on to the preference for *trading in kind*, with goods being exchanged for other goods. This is meeting with growing restrictions in crisis-ridden market economies, however, where the state can only provide financial safeguards for foreign trade within certain limits.
3   Restrictions regarding the development of *joint ventures* in a large number of countries — these were only developed to a limited extent between the Comecon countries.[39] Despite constant verbal attacks, a certain admiration, and even an over-rating of multinational concerns can at times be detected in the Soviet Union. This perhaps heightens the care with which Soviet foreign trade functionaries deal with these concerns.
4   The socialist countries' *debts* are becoming an increasing barrier to East–West trade. The growing restrictions on credit in the West bring back traumatic memories of the post-revolutionary credit blockade during the civil war to Soviet publicists.[40] The Comecon countries' balance of trade deficit grew to DM 90.5 billion in the period 1970 to 1977, and in the case of the Soviet Union, to DM 34.4 billion. The figures extrapolated for Poland for the 1980s were much too low in many cases and the figures for the Soviet Union, by contrast, were exaggerated. The Soviet Union was able to finance almost half her imports from the West with energy carriers and raw materials. A number of the Soviet Union's allies, however, experienced payment difficulties.

In 1982 Poland, Romania and Vietnam occupied fourth, fifth and sixth places in the world ranking of countries that had to ask for a rescheduling of loans, behind Mexico, Argentina and Peru. The former had respective debts of 4.5, 4.0 and 3.5 billion dollars. In 1983 the socialist countries benefited from the decline of Deutsche Mark compared to the dollar which diminished the debts at least for the time being. Contrary to certain speculation and to the reservations of some banks (which are now only prepared to lend money to the Soviet Union under true market conditions[42]), the Soviet Union has not as yet had to suffer through loss of creditworthiness.[43] At the end of the 1970s she was even able to reduce her net debt through increased mineral oil exports and through the continuing rise in the price of crude oil, achieving considerable surpluses in her balance of trade with a number of West European countries.[44] The Soviet Union also held a further trump up her sleeve for covering short-term obligations. Some 5000 tons of gold were sold on the world market—roughly twice the amount that the Banque de France holds as reserves.[45] This trump was played in carefully measured doses, however, so as to avoid ruining the price of gold on the world market, in the Soviet Union's own interest.

The debts of the Eastern bloc countries have only represented an indirect burden on the Soviet Union to date. The Cuban outpost, however, does constitute a heavy burden on her budget (estimated at some 13 billion dollars in 1978).[46] The Soviet Union has frequently helped out in times of crisis, such as in Poland in 1981/82, but her help tends to be indirect (lost profits on foreign exchange, cushioning damage due to Poland's failure to deliver contractually-agreed supplies). The Soviet Union has not so far let herself be committed to an 'umbrella theory', whereby she would be liable for all her allies' debts.[47]

Western embargo policy *vis-à-vis* the Soviet Union

The restrictions on East–West trade on the Soviet side that are listed above have been set against limitations in the West's willingness to trade since 1947. It has been acknowledged that the Soviet Union has never interrupted strategically significant supplies of raw material to the West in times of political crisis. Even during the Vietnam war the USA always received the deliveries that had been agreed upon.[48] The USA, by contrast, frequently attempted to establish a link between good conduct in the political sphere and willingness to trade in the economic sphere. Since 1949 the export controls on technologies for delivery to socialist countries have been conducted on a multilateral basis, in an institution bearing the meaningless title of 'Consultative Group Coordination Committee' (abbreviated to Cocom). Cocom features in the Soviet literature as a NATO instrument deployed against the USSR in the Cold War, although its membership includes the non-NATO state of Japan and the West denies any formal relations with NATO.[49]

Cocom was still maintained during the era of *détente* although its agreements were repeatedly undermined by exemptions. In the 1970s there was a trend towards reducing the number of banned goods (in 1951 there were 270, in 1979 only 146).[50] Embargo policy developed into a bone of contention amongst the Western allies when the USA started imposing sanctions on individual Western European firms which were involved in the natural gas pipeline deal with the Soviet Union. Even Conservative governments in Great Britain and the Kohl government in the Federal Republic of Germany as of 1982 were not prepared to renounce this business. The USA found itself forced to withdraw the sanctions in November 1982 after agreement had been reached on a joint strategy for trade with the East.[51]

Much to the annoyance of those engaged in Soviet foreign policy, the USA has meted out different embargo policy treatment to the different socialist countries. Poland, Romania and China were confronted with the mildest trading restrictions,[52] and the Soviet Union with the harshest. The Soviet Union, however, developed ways of undermining the embargo policy. Countries such as Switzerland and Sweden with advanced technology on offer were not organised in Cocom. According to a Federal German government report, The Soviet Union was even able to obtain goods required for armament purposes by going via Canada and Switzerland.[53]

The Soviet literature rates Western embargo policy as a gigantic failure. The figures quoted in support of this theory are exceedingly global — during the first three years of the tenth five-year plan the USSR manufactured 130 billion roubles' worth of production equipment and only purchased 1.2 billion roubles' worth of similar equipment from the USA. Even the Soviet Union's dependence on the USA for grain is played down — the Soviet Union harvested 657 million tons of grain but only imported 32.5 million tons from the USA.[54] The courting for Soviet orders and the continued sales of grain after Reagan had succumbed to an effective agricultural lobby, did nothing to improve the credibility of American embargo policy in the industrial sphere in the West. When the Americans were endeavouring to conclude new agreements on grain sales in Autumn 1982, the Soviet Union was able to allow herself the triumph of letting the Americans wait.[55]

The Soviet Union does not provide any data of her own on the consequences of the embargo policy for individual sectors of industry but quotes Western sources instead. Khrushchev once poured ridicule on the West's embargo measures, relating that Soviet soldiers would presumably not be fit for operation now since they were having to hold up their trousers as the West had stopped the supply of buttons. Today, publications in the East tend to cite Western jokes, such as the statement by George W. Ball, an American diplomat, to the effect that the American refusal to supply goods which the Soviet Union could readily purchase elsewhere 'seemed not so much the carrying out of a rational foreign

Table 5.6
USSR wheat and feed grain imports by suppliers

	Grain crop Mil. M.T.	Wheat and feed grain imports Mil. Metric	Percentage distribution by supplier				
			USA	Canada	Argentina	Australia	Others
1972/73	168	22.5	60.8	22.7	0.5	4.0	12.0
1973/74	223	10.9	72.5	16.5	2.7	0.9	7.4
1974/75	196	5.5	41.8	5.4	32.7	16.4	3.7
1975/76	140	25.7	54.1	17.5	5.4	7.9	15.1
1976/77	224	10.1	73.3	13.9	2.9	5.0	4.9
1977/78	196	18.4	67.9	10.3	14.7	1.6	5.5
1978/79	237	15.1	74.2	13.9	9.3	0.7	1.9
1979/80	179	30.4	50.0	11.2	16.7	13.2	8.9
1980/81	189	34.0	23.5	20.0	32.6	8.5	15.4
1981/82	165	40.5	31.6	20.9	29.1	6.2	12.2

Source: M. Chapman and C. Marcy (eds): *Common Sense in US–Soviet Trade*, Washington, American Committee on East–West Accord, 1983, p. 120.

policy as self-flagellation on a national scale'.[56] In the case of Carter's grain embargo it was even a costly form of self-chastisement since the American share in Soviet grain imports went down from 74.2 per cent in 1978/79 to 31.6 per cent in 1981/82 (see Table 5.6). Findings, such as those of Adler-Karlsson, disclosing that embargoes can at best hold up the development of the Soviet national income by six months and development in the military and investment sector by a maximum of two months, are cited with satisfaction.[57] It is only the specialisation within Comecon that can be temporarily upset by boycott measures.[58]

There is also increased scepticism in the West as to whether the Soviet Union can be moved to concessions through positive and negative trade policy sanctions. The exaggerated concern of a number of Western observers that socialism could lose its specific characteristics and become increasingly aligned with capitalism,[59] is then also made groundless. Fears that East–West co-operation could lead to the creation of a Vodka-Cola complex, undermining the Soviet foreign trade monopoly and making the Soviet Union dependent on the West in the long term, and at the same time having a negative impact on the trade unions' wage policy in the West, belong very firmly in the realm of fiction.

Western corporations in the Soviet Union are totally subjected to Soviet planning and have no independent management. They are generally involved in offset transactions, limiting the return transfer of profits. Typical examples here are the agreements with Pepsi Cola (Pepsi in return for marketing Vodka in the West), the exchange of Soviet ammonia for American fertilisers and the European deal of natural gas in exchange for pipes. The USSR concluded some 45 offset agreements of this type in the 1970s. Soviet firms in the West build up just as little dependence on the capitalist world market and deal virtually exclusively in trading and marketing Soviet products, in transport and in the financing East–West trade.[60]

Not all the restrictions in East–West trade that Soviet publications castigate stem from boycotts. The restrictions on credit have not all been brought about by Western governments but are the result of the otherwise sharply criticised incapacity of the state to exercise control in capitalism. The fact that the crisis which Soviet publications repeatedly claim has gripped capitalism brings with it a fall in demand and reduced purchasing power is generally not mentioned.[61] Despite the Soviet crisis analysis for Western economies, there has been a sharp change in tone here as well. Less *schadenfreude* is in evidence than previously and fewer bold forecasts are made about the imminent collapse of capitalism than after the war. The Soviet advantage — 'the opponent's crisis' — has in turn been shifted to the Third World (as elsewhere in the East–West confrontation) (see Chapter 7). The Soviet Union reckons on better co-operation relations with the developing countries in the face of the 'decline of the imperialist powers'.[62]

It is, however, scarcely feasible to draw up a fair comparison when it comes to the policy of applying pressure. The Soviet Union has not allowed herself to be blackmailed into concessions by the West. Whether she herself would renounce the application of pressure if she held a stronger position in world trade has not been put to the test to date. Doubts can at best be fuelled by the experiences of weaker partners within the socialist camp. The Soviet Union initially tried out a policy of sanctions within her own camp, as with Yugoslavia from 1949 to 1953 (see Chapter 8). In later conflicts with Yugoslavia from 1958 to 1960, with China around 1960 and with Albania, the Soviet Union scarcely applied any embargo policy measures but simply a selective, non-discriminating reduction in trade.[63] The very generosity shown towards renegade Albania is particularly emphasised within the Soviet Union.[64] In her pro-Chinese phase, however, Albania immediately found a replacement for the blocked Soviet supplies and credit. An official Albanian party publication claims for the fourth five-year plan that 'the deficit was to be covered by the generous' internationalist aid of the People's Republic of China'.[65]

The Soviet Union has at times even been a boycott breaker in the international conflicts that developed between OPEC countries and the Western European countries, on account of the latters' policy on Israel, and has delivered oil to the Netherlands when supplies from the Arab countries had stopped. The need to improve her own foreign exchange situation was greater than the profuse verbal solidarity shown with the Arab countries.[66]

During the time of *détente*, economic relations have largely become disassociated from the ups and downs in the political situation. A type of *détente* within *détente* developed, and the two German states were also able to profit from this when the political climate in Europe worsened again towards the end of the 1970s.[67] The old liberal concept since Smith, Cobden and Constant that trade promotes peace — a theory that tended to be regarded with scepticism in the Western world, given the case history of the two world wars — has emigrated eastwards, as it were, into the socialist camp.[68] Sceptics in the West view the Soviet Union's large-scale trade with the West more as a consequence than as a cause of *détente*.[69]

The Soviet conflict with China embodies certain contradictions as regards the pacification effect of Western trade. Deeds that count as acts of peace in the Soviet Union are rated as warmongering by the Chinese and their growing trade with the West. The sole plausible explanation here is that the Chinese still abide by the 'inevitability of war' despite their foreign trade, up to three-quarters of which is conducted with capitalist countries.[70]

The Soviet Union also safeguards herself in terms of her own policy towards the West. She does not regard her Western trade as having an automatic pacification effect so long as the contradictions within capitalism make the latter unpredictable, and the multinational concerns, acting as a kind of secondary government, can counteract even peace-promoting government policies in the West.[71] All thinking based on motive powers, which would lead to a *rapprochement* of the system from meta-political levels, has been strictly rejected with the convergence theories to date. Western trade enjoys a high ranking in Soviet economic policy on pragmatic grounds. When it comes to reshaping the comparative strength of forces in the world, however, it would seem to be of secondary importance to other spheres.

6 Soviet Policy within the Socialist Camp

The formation of the Eastern bloc

One component of the processes which the foreign policy doctrine of the Soviet Union maintains will lead to the reshaping of the comparative strength of forces in the world is the growth of world socialism. It is noted with pride that the world socialist system covers one-third of the earth's surface and takes in one-third of the world's population. Although China has often been denied a socialist character (see pp. 109–17) it is always included in success ratings of this kind. The Soviet standard work, co-edited by Foreign Minister Gromyko, treats China in a separate chapter between the socialist and the capitalist countries. Apart from the Warsaw Pact and Comecon countries, the Soviets regard Yugoslavia, North Korea, Laos and Cambodia as belonging to the world socialist system. Albania receives special treatment at the end of the portrayals with the sentence 'the Soviet Union regards the situation between Albania and the USSR as abnormal and contrary to the cause of socialism as well as to the true interests of the populations of both countries'.[1] The Comecon countries rank as the centre of the socialist world. With slightly more than 10 per cent of the world population they generate one-third of world industrial production, one-fifth of world agricultural production and roughly one-quarter of world income.[2] In the Soviet view 'real socialism' — an expression that was used more frequently in the 1970s than today, as a counter concept to large numbers of Utopian ideas of neo-Marxism — has an influence extending well beyond the borders of the socialist countries due to its exemplary nature.[3]

The successes registered in the expansion of socialism after the Second World War cannot be overlooked. Following the October Revolution the Soviet Union was initially on her own. At the second Comintern Congress in 1920 the Soviet Union had promised that, in the cause of proletarian internationalism, the interests of the Soviet Union would also be subordinated to those of the international proletarian struggle. In fact, the reverse conclusion proved to be of greater political impact, namely that all socialist countries were obliged to give unconditional support to the Soviet Union in the name of internationalism (see pp. 3–9). Up until the Second World War no 'socialist camp' existed. Only Mongolia was made into a satellite in 1921 with the help of the Red Army, although Soviet Russia had recognised the sovereign rights of China to Outer Mongolia only a year before. This was a step which had serious consequences and which has marred Sino-Soviet relations to the present day.

Even after the second World War there is no evidence of a selective policy aimed at creating a socialist world system on the basis of a general plan. There would have been three potential routes for such a plan to follow:

1   The *annexation of the young People's Democracies* to the 'Fatherland of Socialism'. Ideas of this type were even discussed in Yugoslavia after the Second World War. Stalin opposed these plans. It has been suggested that the reason for his rejection lay in Soviet policy within the UN and in a concern for the Soviet Union's image abroad. This image had already suffered greatly through Stalin's insistence that the annexation of territories handed over to him by Hitler (Baltic States, Moldavia, Carpatho-Ukraine) be confirmed.[4]

2   The creation of *regional unions* of socialist states would have been less suspicious a route towards a large-scale socialist complex but this was again forbidden by Stalin — especially the plans for a federation for Bulgaria and Yugoslavia.[5] When the Bulgarian head of the party, Dimitrov, visited Stalin with a Yugoslavian delegation in January 1948, Stalin listened to the Federation plans and then barked back at him: 'Nonsense, you've rushed ahead there like a young member of the Comsomol. You wanted to amaze the world, as though you were still Secretary of Comintern.'[6]

3   The organisation of unity through a *network of bilateral relations* between the Soviet Union and the People's Democracies. This was the route that Stalin chose. It was not desirable for the People's Democracies to have close contacts with each other. It took time for the socialist camp to become legally secured. Between 1943

and 1949 there were only isolated bilateral treaties, of little political significance, pertaining to friendship, co-operation and mutual assistance. Foreign relations between the socialist countries remained at a rudimentary level. Foreign Minister conferences were convened only occasionally in order to work out a joint stand on the Germany question.[7]

The Soviet portrayal of this phase denies any 'export of revolution' and maintains that the exemplary role of the Soviet Union was extensively copied during this time.[8] The Western literature does not consider all the alignments to have been dictated by Moscow either. In many cases they were due to imitation effects within the national Communist parties — particularly in the GDR up to 1961.[9]

During this phase Soviet ambassadors quoted the party leaders in the People's Democracies at will and interfered in the parties' internal affairs. The army, secret police and to some extent the administration of the People's Democracies were interspersed with Soviet agents and at times with top executives from the Soviet Union. Some 17 000 Soviet officers — including Marshall Rokossovski — are reputed to have served in the Polish army. In many Communist parties an alignment in sensitive areas of security took on equal significance to ideologically conditioned self-alignment.

By the beginning of the 1980s the nature of the Soviet Union's relations to the other socialist states and parties had changed by comparison to the seizure of power phase. At the end of the 1940s Stalin used to summon the party leaders to the Crimea. Only Tito occasionally evaded these invitations and, much to Stalin's annoyance, sent deputies. At the start of the 1980s the Soviet Union had to send out invitations to win over the other socialist countries. According to the Soviet account, the meeting held in the Crimea in April 1980 clearly revealed the spontaneous solidarity of the brother parties with the 'revolution in Afghanistan'.[10] In reality, however, the Soviet Union had a hard job winning over her allies' comprehension for this policy.

The Council for Mutual Economic Aid and the Warsaw Pact

The first indication that relations in the socialist camp were to be placed on a multilateral footing came with the creation of the Council for Mutual Economic Aid in 1949. There were several reasons in Stalin's foreign policy for this new institution:[11]

1   The People's Democracies had been forbidden to accept *aid under the Marshall Plan*. This negative step by Moscow had to be offset by positive incentives.

2   A counterweight was to be created to the *OEEC* (later the OECD) of the Western European states.

3   A *co-ordination centre* was required for the blockade measures against Yugoslavia following the break between Tito and Stalin.

4   The *Sovietisation* of the People's Democracies was to be pursued in a more systematic fashion.

The earlier Comecon literature of the Soviet Union placed greater emphasis on the economic defence aspect of the initial years of Comecon than does the literature of today.[12] The over-hasty establishment of Comecon as a scarcely thought-out reaction to the West's economic and rebuilding initiatives is still having repercussions even now. The community has been beset by a number of problems right from the start:

1   *The hegemonial position of the Soviet Union*, which accounts for some 65 per cent of Comecon's national income, makes it difficult for co-operation to run on an equal footing — in contrast to the European Community where the predominant power of the camp is not a member.

2   Despite a common ideology, large-scale *differences exist in the steering system* and despite manifold declarations, plan co-ordination has remained largely confined to bilateral trade.[13] The Soviet literature does not deny the dominance of bilateral relations either. Comecon claims simply to be a major centre for integration.[14] During the period when experiments were being conducted with new planning methods, the Soviet Union had least inclination to allow far-reaching economic reforms and, indeed, has least cause to give priority treatment to reforms promoting foreign trade, since she is least dependent upon this trade.[15]

    Following the phase up to 1956 in which costly prestige objects such as steelworks were built, which later proved to be unprofitable, Comecon has of late been designated to promote a specialisation which will benefit all the Comecon countries.[16] Nothing is said in the Soviet literature about the many conflicts that have developed (particularly with Romania) concerning this specialisation. Western economists rate the benefit of this division of labour very differently. At the outset, in particular, the least developed countries (Bulgaria, Romania) and the most advanced countries (GDR, Czechoslovakia) seemed to derive a certain advantage from the co-operation. For countries at a midway stage of development, such as Poland, Comecon had neither a positive nor a negative impact.[17]

    One cannot, however, attribute all the successes and failures of socialist economies directly to Comecon or indirectly to Soviet foreign economic policy. Some countries were more strongly oriented towards the Soviet economy (e.g. Poland) and others deliberately oriented their economies towards the West (Romania). Poland even combined both features. Other countries, such as Bulgaria (with little ideological independence), did not fare badly with their specialisation (agriculture). The individual countries' literature generally attributes indisputably impressive growth rates achieved during the post-war period to the party of that particular country, whilst the Comecon literature ascribes it all in blanket fashion to Comecon. In contrast to the European Community, promotion measures in Comecon are not focused on the agricultural market but on industrial planning instead. When it comes to agriculture, the emphasis is, in turn, on the integration of industries that further process agricultural produce.[18]

3   The *differences in the development* of the socialist countries' economies are greater than those of other regional organisations, particularly since the accession of Mongolia (1962), Cuba (1972) and Vietnam (1978). For some sectors there is scarcely any data available on the developing countries within Comecon, and at times the data is left out again if it is not sufficiently flattering for the countries concerned.[19] The Comecon literature highlights the success that has been achieved in bringing the growth rates of the developed and the less developed socialist economies into line with one another.[20]

The integration of a number of developing countries outside Europe cannot hide the fact that co-operation is for the most part concentrated on Europe. The new countries have more of a function of a political signal within the community than any effective economic significance.[21] Mongolia marks an exception here — its intensive co-operation is so strongly focused on the Soviet Union that Comecon is marginalised by the very extent of Mongolia's dependence on the Soviet Union for supplies of machinery and industrial equipment.[22] Suspicions that the most recent accession, namely Vietnam (1978), had political, declamatory overtones are confirmed by the fact that the majority of Comecon countries only learned of Vietnam's application at the start of the XXXII Council Meeting — if Yugoslav information here is correct.[23]

The consequential economic burden of this policy of annexation on the Soviet Union is considerable, as was made clear by Cuba. The price was accepted for political reasons. It is suspected that the containment of Chinese influence in Southern Asia was behind the admission of Vietnam. Comecon will presumably put up resistance if the Soviet Union tries to take on further burdens. Afghanistan, South Yemen and Ethiopia are named as further

Table 6.1
Foreign trade interlinking in Comecon foreign trade as a percentage of GNP (1971)

Bulgaria	28.0
China	5.6
Czechoslovakia	32.0
GDR	24.0
Hungary	37.0
Poland	22.0
USSR	6.0

Sources: J. Bethkenhagen and H. Machowski: *Integration im Rat für gegenseitige Wirtschaftshilfe*, Berlin, Berlin Verlag, 1976, p. 82; W. Kraus: *Wirtschaftliche Entwicklung und sozialer Wandel in der VR China*, Berlin, Springer, 1979, p. 458.

candidates for Comecon membership in the West.[24] It should at all events be remembered that the cost-benefit calculation of a great power, which has committed itself to the growth of world socialism, cannot be assessed solely on criteria of economic rationality.

4   There is a much wider span in the *degree of interlinking in foreign trade* in the socialist countries than in the countries within the European Community.

When Comecon and the socialist camp were set up there was an unparalleled diversion of foreign trade flows. Countries such as Cuba, which had earlier only purchased marginal goods like Christmas tree decorations from Czechoslovakia, suddenly became entwined in much closer trade relations. A national domestic market even had to be torn apart in the GDR. Most of the Comecon countries had traditional relations with Western Europe which they then had to sever. Only Poland and Germany had had a considerable level of trade with the Soviet Union prior to 1945 (see Table 6.2).

It proved impossible to conjure up foreign trade from ideological exuberance. The consequence was systematic *'under-trading'*[25] which held great drawbacks for some of the socialist economies. It was not until the 1970s that this shortcoming was ironed out.

5   The socialist countries' currencies are all *internal currencies*. The Comecon economies lack fixture in an international price setting, which would align domestic prices to international price developments either with a fixed or a flexible rate of exchange. The 'anarchical price formation' on the world market is rejected but at the same time it is stressed that the prices on the socialist market cannot be fully uncoupled from world market prices. The Soviet

Table 6.2
Diversion of trade flows of subsequent Comecon countries towards the
Soviet Union

Soviet trade in million roubles at present-day exchange rate		1933	1946	1950
Bulgaria	Exports	0.2	75.5	90.0
	Imports	-	46.5	62.2
Germany/GDR	Exports	67.2	36.9	167.2
	Imports	116.1	45.3	144.1
Hungary	Exports	0.9	26.1	198.4
	Imports	3.8	29.0	181.4
Poland	Exports	4.0	95.8	217.3
	Imports	10.2	97.6	189.0
Romania	Exports	0.1	27.3	102.5
	Imports	-	20.2	125.3

Source: *RGW-DDR. 25 Jahre Zusammenarbeit*, Berlin, Akademieverlag, 1974, p. 45.

literature highlights the two-fold character of the system, with
national independence of each currency system on the one hand
and co-ordination within the socialist division of labour on the
other hand.[26]

Comecon's price policy protects the socialist camp from the
capitalist world market. Since the 1973 oil crisis the Soviet Union
has had to pass on part of the cost increase to the Comecon
countries. She based this price alignment on world market prices
over a period of five years. In 1975, however, the Soviet Union still
granted the Comecon countries considerable relief.

The socialist price system makes it difficult to pinpoint the price
discrimination and 'exploitation' repeatedly claimed by authors
criticising Comecon from the 'right' or from the 'left'.[27] Western
authors are also coming to view the problem in increasingly
differentiated terms. At most there is evidence of a certain price
discrimination for all concerned, although this stems from the lack
of a uniform socialist price system[28] and cannot be seen as an evil
intention on the part of individual actors or even Soviet foreign
policy.

6   Comecon has *no free market for the factors of capital and labour*
comparable to that of the European Community which would
stimulate the economy. The socialist market is largely construed
in terms of the exchange of trade. Criticism of this concept in the
earlier Comecon literature still delimited the socialist concept of
market from the 'bourgeois' concept in detailed terms.[29] In the

more recent literature, however, the dogmatism of the differences has become considerably weaker.[30]

Instead of having a capital market the Comecon countries practise a type of 'investment creation in kind'. This has been fittingly described as 'counter-trading extended over time'.[31] Joint ventures between socialist countries are focused largely on tapping sources of raw materials. The country providing the finance needs to have a direct demand before it can be prepared to invest in another socialist country, since there is no scope for monetary profit interests within Comecon. The foreign trade doctrine does not even admit rationalisation as an argument for countries to join together to produce cheaper goods. Instead, it is stressed that the chief concern is the 'satisfaction of needs in terms of utility value'.[32] There has not so far been any discussion in the literature as to whether the socialist countries that permit joint ventures with capitalist countries will be able to maintain this high goal, in view of the fact that their Western partners will scarcely be thinking in terms of utility value for their domestic populations.[33]

The socialist multinationals have not really acquired any new legal status so far and in the main adhere to the civil law model of an international economic order, thereby facilitating East–West co-operation (see pp. 79–89).[34]

The factor of *labour* is organised on a national basis to an even greater extent than the factor of capital. Only twenty thousand or so foreign workers have been established, these being chiefly in the GDR. In most cases, however, the workers represent a loan to the host country in the interests of the country supplying them. In the view of the publicists, the 'economic power of joint enterprises' is not only to be found in money and equipment but also in 'skilled manpower and management cadres'.[35] Comecon is aiming solely to achieve a greater balance in the demographic charts of its member countries so as to improve the manpower supply[36] and is not engaging in large-scale loan deals with the factor of labour, with all the social consequences that are unpleasantly familiar from Western economies.

7   Comecon is not aspiring to any *supranational institutions* like those within the European Community, which are developing a certain dynamism of their own to promote the process of integration. Even Western authors regard political pressure as a risky instrument of achieving further integration. The introduction of majority decisions are held to be unlikely since they would include that the Soviet Union renounces her veto power.[37] The supranationality of the EEC is sharply criticised from the East and denounced as an example of hegemonial dominance of the

monopolies (particularly the American monopolies) over the smaller national economies.[38]

This rejection of the EEC model, however, has made a virtue of necessity. The Soviet Union makes no reference today about the fact that from 1962 to 1964 she was all in favour of allowing the Comecon organs to make binding ex ante decisions rather than simply engaging in ex post co-ordination of the plan decisions taken by the individual countries. At that time, however, these Soviet Union initiatives failed, primarily due to resistance from Romania.[39]

The image of the European Community presented in the Comecon literature has changed. The EEC is now portrayed as an efficient partner organisation, and the expansion of trade between Comecon and the EEC is viewed with optimism.[40] Soviet publicists regret that the EEC does not consider Comecon as having contractual capacity, even though individual EEC countries do accept Comecon as a partner though the EEC have tried to co-ordinate the trade with Comecon countries since 1974.[41] The above-mentioned problems of price formation in state trading countries and the lack of convertible currencies have so far prevented trade between East and West from being placed on a multilateral footing.[42] Only in the case of Finland has Comecon figured to a greater extent as a negotiating partner. In the relationship between the EEC and Comecon there has been a partial switch of fronts — at one time it was the Soviet Union with her dislike of multilateral relations who was standing in the way. The EEC then came to promote bilateralism, seeing it as a means of allowing more individual treatment of the Eastern bloc countries and of reinforcing the trends towards autonomy within Comecon. In the West, Comecon has been widely thought to have competence solely in intra-bloc trade.[43] It had been hoped that the membership of a number of Eastern bloc countries in world economic organisations would promote multilateralism but the effects have likewise proved to be very limited.[44]

The dialogue between the EEC and Comecon remained a 'dialogue between the deaf and dumb'.[45]

Since there are no binding decisions from supranational institutions within Comecon, co-operative institutions have to take action in the event of conflict. Initially it was assumed that conflicts were settled by internal party law.[46] The growing number of internal conflicts within the socialist camp, however, meant that these general principles were no longer sufficient, and provisions for the arbitration of conflicts were expanded.[47]

There are few signs of any great measure of integration within Comecon. In contrast to the EEC, which is repeatedly postponing its stages of integration, Comecon does not indulge in any grand perspectives or schedules. Soviet periodisations are retrospective — the fourth and, for the time being, last stage in integration is deemed to have started with the acceptance of the complex programme in 1971.[48] Prospects for the future are left at best in the hands of the mysterious forces of the Scientific and Technical Revolution. Great value is placed on symbolic politics — the 'Community in Space' with ten flags flying in the universe, is hailed as a Comecon success[49] even though it marks a one-sided gesture of goodwill by Soviet foreign policy. The Soviet Union, moreover, has carefully guarded her monopoly in these areas of technology which also hold a military significance.

How far can Soviet foreign policy be shown to be a driving force behind Comecon? It would be wrong to take the hegemonial foundation of the institutions and conclude from it that Comecon was still a mere instrument of Soviet foreign policy today. In this age of polycentrism the regional Comecon organisations are coming to gain an increasing dynamism of their own. The policy of association has frequently been taken as evidence of a one-sided interest by Moscow here, as illustrated by the minimal consultation with which the Soviets prepared members for the accession of Vietnam in 1978. Even the policy of penetration of the African states, however, is no longer held up as a single-handed action on the part of the makers of Soviet foreign policy. Emphasis is instead placed on the growing interests that the smaller Comecon states have in co-operating with the Third World countries 'of socialist orientation'[50] (see Chapter 7).

The Soviet literature views the policy of association as evidence of Comecon's great successes. Yugoslavia was the first country to engage in co-operation and has been co-operating as a full member in 21 out of 32 Comecon institutions ever since. Co-operation relations were also established with non-socialist countries, however, such as with Finland in 1973 and with Iraq and Mexico in 1976. These countries do not participate in the Comecon institutions, though, since they have no foreign trade monopoly. The socialist countries of the Third World enjoy observer status and a number of them are negotiating association status along the lines of Yugoslavia. It is only with China that Comecon is no longer prepared to co-operate, a fact which is acknowledged by the Soviets as well.[51]

Internal trade within Comecon (which has frequently been taken as an indicator of the degree of integration of the socialist community) reached its peak from 1955 to 1962 and then fell steadily until 1975. Integration was made easier in the 1970s by the fact that the majority of Comecon countries ceased experimenting with spectacular economic reforms. At the same time it was made more difficult by a tacit consensus amongst most of those involved that national economic growth should be based more on imports of technology from the West. It was not until the mid-1970s that hard currency shortages in the socialist countries again proved to be a virtue in promoting a readiness to integrate. Poland and Romania now rank amongst the most deeply indebted countries of the world. This has again curtailed their scope for foreign policy *vis-à-vis* the Soviet Union.

Even before the end of the euphoric period of *détente* (as of about 1975) there was a trend towards consolidation of trade within Comecon on account of the rise in energy costs. The Soviet Union herself only set a good example in reintensifying her trade relations with Comecon partners up to 1978. In 1980, however, the level of Comecon trade fell below the 50 per cent mark again (see Table 6.3). The countries who had most foreign trade with Comecon after 1975, such as Cuba, were the most dependent countries. Even Romania, the country with the smallest share of Comecon trade increased its quotas up to 1979, only to fall back below the 1974 level again in 1980. When it came to trade with the West (see Table 6.4), Soviet comparisons show that the highest rates of increase were registered in Poland in 1965.[52] Romania's trade with the West was greater than her Comecon trade at the start of the 1970s. Only Hungary did not let itself be put off course and still had a rising percentage of Western trade after the 1973/74 crisis. The degree to which Comecon countries' foreign policy is independent of Soviet foreign policy thus correlates to a certain extent with the level of their Western trade.

Internal relations within Comecon are not simply a straightforward function of Soviet foreign policy either. The Soviet Union has frequently been unable to get her own way *vis-à-vis* her allies on matters of detail. In the eyes of Western economists there is no real dependence relationship anymore now.[53] Only Mongolia has been considered to be so dependent by economic scientists as to have been denoted a 'poor autonomous oblast in Siberia'.[54] The energy crisis as of 1973 brought a reintegration of many countries into trade within Comecon as of 1975. This even applies for Romania, which does not seem to have been supplying any more figures as to the share of capitalist countries in Romanian foreign trade for the Comecon statistics since 1976 (see Table 6.4). The People's Democracies had no alternative strategy for securing stable and reliable energy imports in the 1970s.[55]

The Soviet Union's hegemonial status is more pronounced in the military alliance than in economic integration. The Warsaw Pact has not, however, been an absolutely vital instrument of Soviet hegemony. A closely-knit mesh of bilateral treaties of alliance, which was much more in line with the concept on which the bloc was based, seems to suggest that the Warsaw Pact held political functions *vis-à-vis* the outside world.[56] Even the stationing of troops was settled on a bilateral basis, and the Pact's disciplining function was already covered by clauses in the friendship pacts, particularly by Article 18 of the friendship pact with the

Table 6.3
Comecon states' foreign trade amongst each other (turnover in %)

	1972	1973	1974	1975	1976	1977	1978	1979	1980	1981	1982	1983	1984
Bulgaria	78.1	77.2	70.2	73.8	76.6	78.0	78.4	75.7	72.8	70.6	73.0	76.8	78.5
Cuba	61.2	60.9	52.2	55.4	64.0	71.8	78.9	n.a.	n.a.	n.a.	81.5	83.1	80.4
Czechoslovakia	67.1	65.2	61.0	66.0	67.8	67.5	68.5	65.0	65.5	67.1	70.0	71.9	76.3
GDR	67.8	65.9	61.0	66.2	63.9	67.9	68.8	65.8	62.7	63.4	63.1	62.5	63.5
Hungary	65.0	63.1	59.0	66.1	54.3	53.4	52.1	52.0	49.6	51.3	51.7	49.6	48.8
Mongolia	95.4	95.1	95.9	96.2	97.2	96.2	96.8	96.9	97.7	97.1	96.9	97.2	97.4
Poland	59.4	53.4	47.0	49.7	50.2	53.2	54.7	54.7	53.3	59.7	54.3	68.4	72.9
Romania	46.6	43.2	34.7	38.0	39.2	41.9	39.7	35.4	34.0	38.7	43.7	47.7	52.6
USSR	59.6	54.0	48.9	51.8	50.8	52.2	55.7	51.9	48.6	47.6	49.1	51.2	52.9

Source: *Statisticheskii ezhegodnik stran-chlenov SEV*, Moscow, Finansy i statistika, 1985, p. 328 and earlier editions.

Table 6.4
Comecon states' foreign trade with developed capitalist countries (turnover in %)

	1972	1973	1974	1975	1976	1977	1978	1979	1980	1981	1982	1983	1984
Bulgaria	14.0	14.6	17.4	17.0	14.5	12.6	12.4	15.0	16.5	16.7	14.0	12.2	13.8
Cuba	25.1	26.9	36.8	31.5	25.4	20.0	13.8	n.a.	n.a.	n.a.	9.6	9.4	12.0
Czechoslovakia	21.4	23.6	25.9	22.4	21.7	21.1	20.7	22.1	23.0	20.9	18.4	16.6	15.2
GDR	25.8	27.9	30.9	25.9	28.3	23.7	22.7	26.0	27.4	28.5	28.1	29.4	29.0
Hungary	26.2	28.2	30.5	24.4	33.5	33.1	34.8	35.2	37.7	34.8	32.9	33.3	34.6
Mongolia	1.0	1.4	1.4	1.1	1.4	1.8	1.4	1.2	1.5	1.7	1.5	1.2	1.0
Poland	32.3	39.8	44.4	41.3	41.5	37.8	36.2	34.6	34.8	29.2	31.8	21.8	18.9
Romania	37.6	41.7	45.4	36.7	n.a.	n.a.	n.a.	n.a.	n.a.	n.a.	n.a.	n.a.	n.a.
USSR	22.6	26.6	31.3	31.3	32.9	29.6	28.0	32.1	33.6	32.2	31.6	30.1	30.0

Source: *Statisticheskii ezhegodnik stran-chlenov SEV*, Moscow, Finansy i statistika, 1985, p. 328 and earlier editions.

GDR, which concedes the right to intervention in the event of an apparent threat to security.[57] Countless other agreements with the GDR contain a sufficient number of ambiguous formulations that could provide a starting point for Soviet activity on its alliance partner's territory.[58]

When the Warsaw Pact was set up it evidently had a political bartering function *vis-à-vis* the outside world. The Soviet Union stressed the openness of her alliance in order to delay consolidation of the Western alliance.[59] The event which prompted the founding of the Warsaw Pact was the integration of the Federal Republic of Germany in NATO.[60] Alongside this factor, the need to place the stationing of troops on a new, multilateral basis also played a certain role. The necessity of securing the Soviet Union's *de facto* leadership role through a greater consensus in the military sphere probably represented a further reason for the establishment of the Warsaw Pact.[61]

The dominance of the leading power is even greater in the Warsaw Pact than in Comecon. The Soviet Union bears some 80 per cent of the Pact's defence burden and, in contrast to the USA in NATO, holds a monopoly on atomic weapons.[62] Despite this, even the Warsaw Pact is no longer viewed as a will-less instrument of Soviet foreign policy. Repeated conflicts have developed between the People's Democracies and the Soviet leading power about equipment with arms, in disputes concerning the occupation of the top posts in the Pact's institutions and about the degree of integration in the field of the armed forces.[63]

The event which led to the founding of the Warsaw Pact showed that the attraction for the smaller socialist countries in joining the Pact lay in the promise of protection against aggression from outside. As the Pact developed, however, it became increasingly evident that the Pact also constituted an instrument of discipline within the bloc. The gate of entry for this development was the mutual assistance clause of Article 4. The intervention in Hungary in 1956 and in Czechoslovakia in 1968 could scarcely be justified by this clause, particularly since there was not even a governmental request for mutual assistance in the case of the Czechoslovakian crisis. Reference was made instead to calls for help from leading Czechoslovakian personalities, to the alleged danger of a counter-revolution and to the interference of the imperialist camp. What came to be known as the Brezhnev Doctrine in the West was developed to counter the stealthy counter-revolution, which the Dubček regime was allegedly pursuing. A right of military intervention for the purpose of maintaining socialism was developed on the basis of a theory of the irreversibility of historical processes.[64] The Brezhnev Doctrine was made easier through the implementation of a Johnson Doctrine which was applied in the hegemonial sphere of power of the USA to control social change, promote intervention and consolidate the bloc. The doctrine of the ban on violence was given a new interpretation in Soviet international law, with the principle of non-aggression allegedly being rendered invalid by the socialist internationalism within the socialist camp.[65] The Soviet Union has retained the privilege of defining the principles of socialism for herself. New indicators were increasingly being developed within the Soviet theory of state to provide evidence that the principles of socialism were being abandoned — these included the undermining of the leading role of the party, the breaking-up of the foreign trade monopoly, a stealthy alignment to the theory of democratic socialism and tolerance of a growing independence within the trade unions. A number of these reproaches were well removed from the standard catalogue of nine points used to define socialism in the Soviet theory of state[66] and were developed specially to condemn Czechoslovakia.

The respect that the two superpowers have shown for their respective spheres of influence has favoured such doctrines of limited solidarity within the blocs. It has frequently been denied that there has been a kind of delimitation of spheres of interest since the Potsdam conference. American foreign policy, however, has only trespassed over the bloc boundaries for propaganda purposes, if at all, and made it clear right from the start that the USA cannot be expected to intervene in support of a People's Democracy in the Eastern Pact system. In 1975, one of the American Foreign Minister's staff, Sonnenfeldt, went as far as to declare that the USA's task included *inter alia* ensuring a development which would make the relationships between the Eastern Europeans and the Soviet Union into an 'organic' relationship. This statement, which was stylised into the Sonnenfeldt doctrine, was even regarded as constituting explicit recognition of the Brezhnev doctrine, a fact very much resented by Romania.[67] The acceptance of the Brezhnev doctrine was widely regarded as a contribution towards the maintenance of peace. This assumption has only become problematical since the Brezhnev Doctrine was applied for the first time to Third World countries of socialist orientation in Afghanistan (see pp. 75–7).

The Sino-Soviet conflict

Since 1960 the dynamism of the expansion of the Communist World movement (see pp. 145–61) has been slown down by the conflict between the two socialist great powers. Up until the end of the 1950s little of the fraternal strife within the socialist camp was evident to the world outside. In many cases the conflict was covered over by set-phrase compromises which Soviet advisors in China later interpreted as having been a sign of 'false friendship' right from the start.[68]

There were many reasons behind the Sino-Soviet conflict:

1 *Historical experience* of the alienation in the relationship between Stalin and Mao. The Chinese party came into power against Stalin's advice and without any notable Soviet aid. In internal talks with Communist leaders from other countries Stalin once even admitted that he had made a mistake with his advice to Mao to enter into an alliance with the Kuomintang: 'It has been shown that they were right and we were wrong'.[69]

2 *Political experience* of the Soviet Union acting like an imperialist power when negotiating advantages in China after the Second World War (border corrections to her advantage in Tannu Tuva in 1944, use of Port Arthur as a military basis, privileges in the commercial port of Dairen, defence of the independence of Outer Mongolia).[70]

3 *Ideological differences of opinion* after the heightening of the 'struggle between two lines' in 1956/57. In the Soviet view, Stalin's death and the criticism of him in the Soviet Union created the prerequisite 'for the glorification of Mao-Tse-Tung as the greatest and most brilliant man, as the leader of the world revolution'.[71] Personality cult apart, China started asserting for the first time in the de-Stalinisation debate that the Chinese party represented the 'better Marxist–Leninists'.[72]

4 Added to this came *economic differences of opinion* as to the wisest development strategy for China to follow. Soviet experts were given 'ugly American' treatment when they expressed their justifiable doubt about strategies which they felt, on good grounds, to be 'adventurous' (e.g. the Great Leap Forward of 1959/60).

5 *Divergences in foreign policy* on matters of world revolution in the Third World (which first emerged on an international scale at the 1955 Bandung Conference of Afro-Asian states) led to direct confrontation between the two socialist great powers. China began to develop a negative convergence theory in which Moscow was ranked with Washington under the heading of the 'first imperialist world' of the superpowers, whilst China sought to portray itself as the third force leading the developing countries.

6 The Soviet Union branded Chinese endeavours to achieve a *say in the Communist world movement* as attempted interference in Eastern Europe.[73]

China acted in an even more doctrinaire fashion than the Soviet Union in its demand for support of its own position from the smaller socialist countries. Only Romania, North Vietnam and Cuba, which resolved not to condemn Chinese policy, stood up to the Soviet pressure. For a time, only the small country of Albania was recognised by the Chinese as being 'socialist'. The cultural revolution and ideological sectarianism even led to the People's Republic of China isolating itself within the socialist camp to some extent.[74]

7   The *non-proliferation* of atomic weapons China had hoped for caused a good deal of feeling of discrimination in China.

8   *Territorial disputes* heightened the conflict. China had declared on several occasions that it had no territorial claims on the Soviet Union but did call for acknowledgement of the fact that the status quo of the border lines rested on the unequal treaties of the past.[75] In 1969 armed conflicts developed at the Ussuri river. For the very first time the theory that war had died out *ipso facto* in the resolution of conflicts in socialist systems was shown to be wrong.

Despite the deterioration in relations, the Soviet Union made a significant contribution to China's development with supplies of machinery and equipment. She did this under far more favourable conditions than she herself had received for aid from Western nations during the period of Soviet construction.[76] Up to 1959 one-sixth of Soviet machinery exports and three-quarters of all deliveries of complete factory plants went to the People's Republic of China. From 1958 onwards differences of opinion developed about the conditions under which credit was to be granted. As of 1956 China started taking precautions to become independent of Soviet supplies.[77] Even when the open conflict reached its climax in 1960, Moscow was still relatively generous in her policy on conditions of payment when China experienced a harvest failure.[78] The heightening of the conflict led to a drastic reduction in Soviet supplies of machinery and factory equipment. Only in the 1970s did more intense trading relations build up again, albeit at a considerably lower level. These were once more subject to surprisingly large fluctuations, however (see Table 6.5).

All in all, the Soviet Union has remained on top in the struggle with China for influence in the world and in the Communist world movement:

1   China courted the *countries of Western Europe*. Despite this, the search for a *modus vivendi* with the Soviet Union in the East–West conflict remained the priority (see Chapter 3).

2   China only succeeded in having one party (Romania) in the *Eastern bloc* not condemn the Chinese stand. China achieved modest successes in reconciliation with Yugoslavia, a country which had once sat in the Chinese ideological dock as being revisionist.

3   Despite all its efforts, China was less successful in the struggle for the *socialist countries of the Third World* than the Soviet Union. North Korea was much closer to the Chinese position in

Table 6.5
Soviet exports of machinery and industrial plant to China in thousand roubles

Year	Value	Year	Value	Year	Value
1949	17 373	1961	97 281	1973	74 918
1950	37 208	1962	24 594	1974	80 517
1951	98 833	1963	37 969	1975	69 617
1952	140 896	1964	51 944	1976	122 849
1953	145 217	1965	69 296	1977	64 194
1954	178 964	1966	77 596	1978	95 864
1955	206 615	1967	22 178	1979	100 627
1956	274 274	1968	13 409	1980	98 451
1957	244 401	1969	19 422	1981	17 477
1958	286 165	1970	13 581	1982	9 918
1959	537 768	1971	49 175	1983	45 635
1960	453 527	1972	75 830	1984	107 766

Source: *Vneshnyaya torgovlya SSSR v 1984 g*, Moscow, Finansy i statistika, 1985, p. 213 and earlier issues.

ideological terms than to the Soviet position. Economic and military co-operation with the Soviet Union, however, always kept Kim il Song at a critical distance from Peking.[79] In 1966, North Korea criticised both socialist great powers about their support for socialist movements in the Third World.[80] In North Vietnam, China only exerted the stronger influence for a limited period of time (1955 to 1957). From 1958 to 1973 North Vietnam set store by good relations with Moscow and received military aid from both countries. As of 1973 differences of opinion between China and Vietnam began to increase. In 1978 Vietnam was admitted to Comecon and built up into a bridgehead for Soviet influence in South-East Asia by means of increased economic aid. When it came to Cuba, China seemed to have a great deal in common with the country to begin with — particularly its independent route to the take-over of power by guerrilla warfare movements. Cuba's exposed position, however, made the country dependent upon Comecon aid and rapidly led to ill feeling between China and Cuba.

In 1966 the Chinese were accused of interference and trade relations deteriorated. Cuban and Chinese military advisors finally even found themselves acting directly against each other in the Angolan civil war.[81] In all three cases the Soviet Union profited from the friction between China and the smaller Third World socialist countries.

4   China at times exerted a great influence in *a number of national liberation movements* — particularly in East Africa. It was only the Soviet Union, however, which gained lasting allies in this area, such as in South Yemen and Ethiopia.[82] At times both sides

indulged in unreflected changes of alliance. When the Soviet Union achieved a dominating position in South Yemen, she lent her support to the PFLOAG guerrilla movement against the Sultan of Oman — the movement that had been supported by the Chinese up until then. China then switched overnight to the Sultan's side, which it had previously been helping to fight.[83]

5   The fact of China being a Third World country gave China a certain start when it came to the *non-aligned nations*. However, the Chinese tolerance of anti-Soviet military alliances (China even lent verbal support to NATO), the propagation of the inevitability of war and the Chinese contempt of efforts to create nuclear weapon-free zones and take small steps towards disarmament, weakened the Chinese position in the Third World.[84] When Cuba invited the tricontinental conference to Havana in January 1966, after relations with China had cooled down, the Soviets gave their support to this move, seeing it as a means of reducing Chinese influence in the Third World.[85]

6   China was only able to make a few temporary proselytes amongst the world's *Communist parties*, in South-East Asia and in the Pacific area (see pp. 153–5).

The Sino-Soviet conflict initially came as a relief to the Western world but in the long term the *schadenfreude* of the NATO countries at this split in the world socialist system proved to be short-sighted. The conflict had its repercussions on the East–West relationship. The Soviets began to step up their armament, and not just towards the West either. This triggered off heightened fears of threat in the West and did nothing to contribute to *détente* in the East–West conflict (see pp. 35–45).

The protagonists of the first phase of the Sino-Soviet conflict, Khrushchev and Mao, are dead. The conflict continued to grow in proportions, however, and showed that it was not linked to particular persons. After 1976 when the 'Gang of Four' had been sentenced, greater chances for a *rapprochement* seemed to exist again. Nevertheless, a number of points of conflict remained unsettled. Soviet publicists see these are relating to the following areas:

1   The concentration of Chinese troops at the border.
2   Conflicts about old allies (Mongolia) and new allies (Vietnam) of Moscow, particularly after the Chinese attack on Vietnam in 1979.
3   The *rapprochement* between China and the USA, which sparked off new fears of encirclement in the makers of Soviet foreign policy. The encirclement plan was attributed primarily to American foreign policy, first as a 'Kissinger' and then as a 'Brzezinski' strategy. Peking, however, had equally justified

fears of encirclement in view of the fact that Moscow had drastically expanded its influence in South-East Asia.[86]

4   Chinese support for the 'counter-revolution' in Afghanistan.
5   The upholding of territorial claims by the People's Republic of China, under the formula of 'disputed areas'.[87]

The official literature, such as the standard work published by Gromyko and Ponomarev, has become notably cautious in the tone of its portrayal of Sino-Soviet relations. Up to 1982, however, scientific publications from the advisory institutes (see pp. 24–7) were still geared to a tone of confrontation which was much sharper than the ideological confrontation with the West. In the 1970s the Chinese government upheld the theory that the Soviet Union was the more dangerous of the two superpowers.[88] The Soviet Union, by contrast, generally refrains from direct moral comparisons with Western nations and only denounces China's intensified co-operation with the NATO countries.

Soviet publications also make reference to further points of conflict with China:

1   China is accused of adhering to the *inevitability of war*, and even of regarding war as the prime instrument of achieving foreign policy aims (pressure at the borders with the Soviet Union, Vietnam and India).[89] As late as 1982, when efforts to achieve a renewed *rapprochement* were in full swing, one of the best known Soviet experts on China maintained that China was the most aggressive military state in the world — ranking 125th in the world order of per capita income but third in armaments expenditure and being constantly guilty of indulgence in great power politics, hegemonism and a territorial requisitioning policy and militarism against its neighbours.[90]

2   China is accused of pursuing an *aggressive nationality policy*, particularly against those peoples with kindred in the Soviet Union (the Mongolians, Uighurs).[91] Some of these minorities along the border with the Soviet Union seem to orientate themselves more towards the neighbouring populations, even if only because of the higher standard of living on the other side of the border. By having the border open on both sides (no natural barriers, unreliable population groups along the borders), a feature which is fervently promoted by Soviet Union for propaganda purposes, Soviet foreign policy actually provokes part of those same Chinese military efforts which she then uses as a reason for feeling threatened.

3   The focal point of conflict today, however, still remains the disturbance that the Soviets believe the People's Republic of China to be causing in the reshaping of the comparative strength

of forces in the *Third World*. The accusation of hegemony, however, is exaggerated in view of the limited successes that the Chinese have scored.[92] China is criticised for trying to slacken the ties between Moscow and the Third World countries — where China itself is not strong enough to apply such a policy, it is the capitalist countries that move in.[93] In such areas where China does feel strong enough, such as in South-East Asia, Soviet criticism accuses China of engaging in export offensives at dumping prices, although even Soviet publications cannot escape the fact[94] that China has secured no more than 2 per cent of foreign trade in this area, whilst Japan commands 26 per cent, the USA 16 per cent, Great Britain 6 per cent and even the Federal Republic of Germany 5 per cent of the foreign trade of the countries in question as suppliers. Although Chinese development aid has frequently been regarded as embodying less self-interest than Soviet aid,[95] China is still subject to the same accusations as those levelled against the 'neo-colonialist powers' (see pp. 118–23). It is claimed that Chinese aid does not help the Third World countries to help themselves but promotes Chinese raw materials and export interests instead. There are even certain contradictions in the line of argument — on the one hand, Chinese development aid is claimed to place an 'irresponsible' emphasis on the light goods and consumer goods industry, which does not produce very high returns, yet on the other hand, China is unjustifiably accused of supporting expensive prestige items for purposes of propaganda. The railway in Tanzania is usually the sole example cited here.[96]

4   The final point of complaint upheld by Soviet publicists is China's *support for liberation movements* that are fighting allies of Moscow, such as in Afghanistan, Cambodia and Angola.[97] Although the Soviet Union had been in favour of China's admission to the UN even in periods of conflict, once China joined the forum the Soviet Union frequently found herself subject to sharper criticism from China of all countries than from the USA.[98] This too has served to intensify the conflict about influence in the Third World up to the present.

Chinese official sources in early 1984 saw mainly three obstacles which should be removed by the Soviet Union to achieve better Soviet–Chinese relations: a reduction of Soviet troops along the Sino-Soviet and Sino-Mongolian borders; withdrawal of Soviet troops from Afghanistan; and withdrawal of Vietnamese troops from Kampuchea.[99]

The latest positions to emerge from Moscow signal a willingness to talk and also tone down the accusation.[100] The sole progress achieved so far, however, is that China is endeavouring to maintain an equal distance

Table 6.6
Conflicts in the socialist world

	Countries involved	Solution
1948–55	USSR–Yugoslavia	Agreement, interrupted by recurrent tensions in 1956, 1958–62, 1969, 1978–80
1948–to date	Albania–Yugoslavia	No solution so far, many incidents at the borders
1956	USSR–Poland	Agreement
1956	USSR–Hungary	Military intervention
1961–to date	USSR–Albania	No solution
1960–to date	USSR–China	No solution, military conflict in 1968/69
1968	USSR–Czechoslovakia	Military intervention
1975–78	Vietnam–Cambodia	Military intervention
1975–to date	China–Vietnam	Military intervention in 1979, no solution
1980/81	USSR–Poland	Solution postponed after introduction of martial law

Source: A. Bebler: 'Konflikte zwischen sozialistischen Ländern', *Österreichische Militärische Zeitschrift*, 1984, No. 2 (112–120), p. 115.

from Moscow and Washington. At the XXV Party Congress the principle of peaceful coexistence was extended to take in China.[101] At the XXVI Party Congress, Brezhnev began to broach the subject of China hesitatingly: 'China needs to be talked about separately'. He felt that the designation of 'feudal, fascist dictatorship' used by the present Chinese government to describe the cultural revolution supplied an ex post justification for the attitude adopted by the Soviets at the time, and he placed his hopes for the future in the Chinese people.[102] The overall tone revealed a considerably greater readiness to come to an understanding than at the XXV Party Congress in 1976, where the talk had still been of an 'in principle, irreconcilable struggle against Maoism'.[103]

Accusations that China is being isolated by the Soviet Union are rejected.[104] Enough attempts have, however, been made at isolation by both sides, and the Soviet Union has remained more successful. At the start of the conflict, outside observers were frequently inclined to attribute greater blame to the Soviets for intensifying the confrontation. More recent analyses, however, reveal a more positive picture of the Soviet attitude. Soviet foreign policy took great care not to escalate the conflict, whilst the People's Republic of China proceeded with the inconsiderateness of a sectarian.[105] Whatever the Soviet Union did to the People's Republic of China (and the Soviet Union did not pay sufficient attention to the sensitivity of a Third World country such as China in the 1950s), China more than got her own back on the smaller socialist countries in the vicinity — as the 'educational war' against Vietnam in 1979 showed.

No socialist world system has developed. Not even the promise that socialism would guarantee *per se* peaceful conflict resolution has been fulfilled. A Yugoslav scholar recently counted at least 11 conflicts (among more than 50) which involved military threats within the socialist camp (see Table 6.6).

Theories of a socialist world system are more popular among Western theoreticians (such as Wallerstein) than among Soviet scholars. Long-term socialist goals envisage a world state which plans the totality of international processes and secures peace. The 'anarchy of the world of states' left behind by the age of capitalism is to be overcome. Soviet publicists now make increasingly rare reference to these long-term goals.[106] Surprisingly enough, those Western socialists who still orientate themselves by these goals are not placing their hopes for the qualitative changes, which will bring this goal one step nearer, on the Soviet Union in the near future. Instead, they set greater store by Utopian changes that are expected to come about in the Western world.[107]

7 The Soviet Union and the Third World

The Soviet conception of the Third World

The expression 'Third World' is generally only used in quotation marks in Soviet literature and preference is given instead to the phrase 'developing countries'.

The beginnings of the Soviet Union's dealings with the Third World were linked to Soviet policy endeavours to win back the earlier Islamic regions of the Tsarist Realm. On 3 December 1917 the Council of People's Commissars issued a declaration to all 'working Muslims in Russia and the Orient' in which they were promised freedom from colonial dependence. In the period following the October Revolution Russia was still interested in partner-like relations. The young Soviet power was not sufficiently well-established to pursue great power politics and took her ideological claim more seriously during this period than after the Second World War.

The Soviet government had no elaborate strategy worked out for the Orient. Comintern activities were directed predominantly towards Europe.[1] An initial attempt at ideological expansion southwards came in September 1920 at a congress of the Eastern peoples in Baku, which was organised by Zinov'ev and Radek. At this highly improvised congress a 'holy war' was declared against 'British imperialism'. Since the congress did not achieve any continuity in its propagandist mobilisation, this initial attempt at gaining influence in the Third World remained largely without consequence.

The Soviet Union could only hope to establish good relations with a national revolutionary regime, such as that of Turkey under Atatürk, in spite of the century-old conflicts between the Sublime Porte and the Tsars. Mustafa Kemal, however, made no secret of the fact that his model was the Western democracies and not the Soviet concept. It was only after the Second World War, with Turkey's accession to NATO, that the tolerably good relations that had existed with Turkey until then deteriorated. The Soviet Union bore part of the blame for this deterioration through her territorial claims and the demand for special rights of passage through the Dardanelles (see pp. 35–41).[2] Most other Third World countries still had colonial status up until the Second World War or had close ties with a number of colonial powers.

It was only after the Second World War, in the age of decolonialisation, that the Soviet Union was able to play a part in shaping relationships within the Third World. She attempted this successfully in Korea and China, and less successfully in Iran, from which she withdrew under the pressure of the Western powers in 1946. Prior to 1945 Mongolia had been the only state in the world that regarded the Soviet Union as a model. Even after the Second World War, however, there was no theory on the development of Third World countries to socialism. All the statements made on this subject were based on analogies with the experience of the Central Asian republics under Soviet rule.[3]

The socialist camp, in the Soviet view, only expanded into what is pompously termed the socialist world system today with the accession of a number of Third World countries into Comecon (Mongolia 1962, Cuba 1972, Vietnam 1978). Since then a more attractive and flexible theory of development has been called for than that supplied by the Mongolian copy of the Soviet system. In the case of Cuba, it could not be assumed from the outset that the Soviet path of development would be the path that this country would follow. As late as 1962, therefore, the Soviet Union was still hesitating about designating Cuba 'socialist' and would presumably have hesitated even longer had not Cuba offered itself as a useful point for bringing influence to bear at the gateway to America. In the Soviet opinion, one of the chief features of socialist countries was the leading role of the party.[4] This was lacking in Cuba. Whilst the dominance of the military over the disintegrating party was branded as a type of 'barracks socialism' in the polemics against China,[5] Soviet publicists condemned the insignificance of the party in Cuba in much milder terms. In the classification of systems of government, the Cuban system was rated as a 'special type of socialism', characterised by forms of 'direct democracy'.[6]

The appraisals of the first countries that turned towards socialism still showed a degree of uncertainty at the outset in the Soviet literature. Many socialist leaders had not overcome the European perspective they had held since the second International and adhered dogmatically to the fact that capitalism constituted an inevitable transitional step towards socialism.[7] This dogmatism, to which Stalin also adhered, had negative consequences for Soviet foreign policy in the Third World. Communists were repeatedly recommended to enter into alliances with corrupt bourgeois governments, ranging from the Kuomintang through to the Batista government in Cuba, prior to Castro's take-over of power. Trotsky had already attempted to unmask this 'stage-by-stage dogmatism' in his theory of permanent revolution as a pretext for not pursuing any further revolutionary politics.[8]

It was not until the 1961 party programme that a theory of non-capitalist development emerged in concrete form. After the war, reference was generally made to 'national democracy'. This was taken to mean a type of rule that was not exercised by a particular party or class but by alliances of popular fronts (which only excluded the imperialists and the comprador bourgeoisie) but was not yet under the hegemony of the Communist party.[9] The Soviet doctrine used the designation of 'socialist' sparingly — with the European People's Democracies as well to begin with. Faced with the continuing rise in the number of Third World countries which denoted themselves 'socialist', however, the Soviet doctrine found itself unable to maintain the stringent rules for the definition of socialism. Even in India under Nehru, a non-aligned country that was totally non-Marxist, there was scarcely a party that did not claim to be following 'socialist goals'.[10]

'Third route' theories, which sought a path between socialism and capitalism and frequently began with great outbursts of social mobilisation, generally ended in typical middle-class politics, such as Kemalism, Nasserism, Latin American populism or the Ujamaa socialism of Tanzania.[11] Soviet publicists thus registered certain success with their claims that all these indigenous versions of socialism were doomed to fail. On the other hand, however, they still had to react to this rapid increase in socialism in the Third World and allow the developing countries a certain ideological autonomy.[12] Soviet doctrine thus had to steer a course between the two extremes. The overemphasis on the Soviet model led to accusations that the Soviet Union was thinking in ethnocentric terms,[13] yet at the same time the claim to be a centre of ideological guidance for the Third World as well was not to be completely renounced. Emphasis was thus placed on the birthright of Soviet socialism, and the national variants of socialism were acknowledged to have future prospects in so far as they secured their existence and ideological substance through an alliance with the socialist camp.

In the mid-1960s there were two countries in Asia (Syria and Burma) and five in Africa (Algeria, Ghana, Guinea, Mali and United Arab Republic) which, in the Soviet view, were on a non-capitalist course of development. Most of these forfeited this claim very soon afterwards.

Initially they were showered with sharp polemics for this. The recent literature, however, has come to appreciate the 'pioneer role' of the renegades like Egypt to a greater extent again.[14] Burma was frequently suspected of pro-Chinese leanings and contacts with the socialist camp remained at a low level. All the same, Burma was still included in the list of countries that were following a non-capitalist course of development. In other cases former attachment turned into hate — Soviet literature saw Numeiri's policy in the Sudan as being marked by 'anti-Communist hysteria' once the previously close relationship with Moscow had been abandoned.[15] The Soviet Union was not always over-particular about the countries to which she granted such honorary titles and even Idi Amin's regime temporarily received the designation 'non-capitalist'.[16] Where there were no spectacular clashes with Soviet interests and no changes of alliance the Soviet publicists were sparing in their subsequent criticism of countries. This was so after Nkrumah's fall in 1966 and following the break between the Ivory Coast and Moscow in May 1969. In zones that were prone to *putsches*, allowance had to be made for a certain ideological risk. The Soviet literature has become more cautious of late in its use of the designation 'country of socialist orientation', as in the case of Nicaragua.[17]

There was still a fairly wide spread in the terminology of Soviet publications in the 1970s. A number of authors used expressions such as 'non-capitalist course of development' and 'socialist orientation' synonymously. Other authors prefer the term 'socialist orientation', since it introduces a positive aim and not simply a negative criterion into the classification of Third World countries. A clear distinction was drawn between national–democratic and people's–democratic state power.[18]

Despite the greater care taken in ideological calculations, Soviet theory still has difficulty in admitting to setbacks in socialist development. As a rule, no mention is made of the further development of countries that were once of socialist orientation. Only recent publications have started openly admitting that, contrary to the case in Europe, the course of development is not irreversible. Ghana, Mali, Egypt and Somalia are listed as examples showing that non-capitalist development can also fail due to social contradictions.[19] The Soviet Union found herself in a particularly awkward situation when she granted the two neighbouring countries of Ethiopia and Somalia the designation 'of socialist orientation'. When a conflict developed between the two over Ogaden, Moscow sided with Ethiopia and withdrew Somalia's designation on account of its 'chauvinist and expansionist endeavours'.[20]

The preferred usage of the expression 'countries of socialist orientation' has taken on more than an academic significance in the meantime, with the Brezhnev doctrine being applied to a country of socialist orientation for the first time in Afghanistan (see pp. 75–7). The case of

Afghanistan obviously provides no more of a basis than the Soviet literature has so far done on which to conclude that all attempts at changing a regime would be defended with the same effort on the part of the Soviet Union. The immense scatter of the countries of socialist orientation throughout the world in itself would seem to exclude this. This group is today regarded as taking in Algeria, Burma, the Congo, Guinea, Syria, Tanzania, Yemen, Angola, Ethiopia, Madagascar, Mozambique and its latest member — Afghanistan.[21] A number of authors' justifications of the term socialist orientation make it sound as though only development towards socialism is irreversible and hence to be defended at all costs. The transitional stage of socialist orientation was introduced into the classification, however, to save having to make committing forecasts about future development in concrete cases. Countries of socialist orientation are still exposed to the influence of the 'capitalist world market', and the revolutionary movement is not led by Marxists but by 'revolutionary democrats'.[22] They are thus still exposed to the danger of 'petty bourgeois retrograde development', which generally takes the form of a return to a 'mixed economy' and the calling off of the class war. Even the activism of left extremists can constitute a danger for democratic revolutionary movements. Only in cases where the national revolution assumed 'forms of People's Democracy' (such as in North Korea and North Vietnam) did it lead without setback to socialism.[23]

Soviet social scientists are making increasing efforts to define the category 'countries of socialist orientation' in terms of the substance of development so as to have something to set against the Western modernisation theories that they reject.[24] A number of authors have divided the countries of socialist orientation into sub-groups:

1   Countries pursuing the route to revolutionary change through mass organisations (since true parties have not emerged everywhere);
2   Countries with revolutionary change by military élites. This breakdown is justified with the distinction that Lenin drew between 'form' and 'content' of a dictatorship. If the content of a regime's doctrine is 'socialist', then with this subtle differentiation, the 'form' of military exercise of power seems less offensive.[25]

The most desirable form of regime still remains the exercise of power by a vanguard party.[26] A military dictatorship can only be regarded as progressive in the Soviet doctrine if it tries to mobilise the masses for socialism, as was the case with the Peruvian military in the failed Sinamos organisation.[27] Even if the 'movement' has developed into a 'party' this will not yet be the party of a 'class vanguard' but generally a 'national front', which forms the vanguard of the class. Which class this is is left in semi-obscurity, since most of these countries scarcely have a proletariat in the European sense.[28]

Only a few of the countries of socialist orientation rank among the systems that have developed democratic revolutionary parties of a vanguard nature. In the Soviet view, such parties exist in Afghanistan, Angola, Benin, the Congo, Ethiopia, Mozambique and Yemen. Other countries of socialist orientation such as Burma, with less vanguard-conscious democratic revolutionary parties, have been classified under a second heading along with Algeria, Syria and Tanzania.[29] The sole decisive difference is the degree of dependence on the Soviet Union.

A number of Soviet authors today openly admit that the countries of socialist orientation are not defined by objective criteria alone. If the level of nationalised industry were to be taken as an indicator, then Tunisia would be more socialist than the Congo. It is thus necessary to look for additional, more pronouncedly political criteria in the Third World, such as the strength of the 'progressive forces', the breaking of the supremacy of foreign capital and the activity and level of literacy of the masses. Reference is made to these political characteristics in warning against an extension of the designation of socialist orientation to countries which have not proved worthy of it in terms of their structure, such as Bangladesh, Indonesia or Zambia.[30]

When it comes to *de facto* policy, there is one political criterion which constitutes the deciding factor for the terminology used: the degree to which the countries concerned are orientated towards the Soviet Union. Soviet foreign policy has never been afraid of maintaining good relations even with countries that have suppressed Communists, such as Egypt, Iraq and, at the outset, Sudan. The 'progressive forces' are thus not always identical with the strength of the Communist party. Countries suspected of pro-Chinese inclinations, as was Burma for a number of years, were judged much more negatively than other countries, even though Burma appeared much more socialist measured in terms of objective criteria than did some of the African states that the Soviet Union was out to win, which were overhastily designated as being of socialist orientation. The internal Soviet discussion, however, is becoming much more objective on this point as well. As a rule, blanket negative judgements are only passed on countries which once seemed to have a national revolutionary character but which have now broken away, such as Egypt and Somalia.[31] The Soviet Union has moderated its tone towards other countries no longer recognised as systems of socialist orientation in so far as they do not pursue a pronounced anti-Soviet and pro-American policy.

This classificatory pettifoggery in itself suggests that the socialist countries' theory on the Third World scarcely plays any role in the development of strategies to furnish an alternative to mere copies of Eastern or Western development models. The theory of autocentred development is portrayed as being Chinese self-sufficiency chauvinism, ignoring the advantages of the socialist division of labour. The basic needs strategies, discussed chiefly in the group of 77 developing countries, are similary rejected. In Manila in 1979 Cuba put in an application on behalf of the group of 77 for the concept of basic needs to be rejected, claiming that it was a 'Morgenthau Plan for poor countries', designed to cut them off from any chances of industrialisation. Collective self-reliance, or the formation of cartels by countries exporting raw materials, is not subject to head-on attack. In individual cases, verbal agreement with this strategy makes the theoretical point that even this strategy will not be able to abolish the workings of the law of value on the capitalist-dominated world market.[32] In the Soviet view, only a policy of socialist orientation and non-capitalist development can be successful here. Soviet theoreticians do not accept a general North–South conflict and their support for developing countries has become much more differentiated than during the initial period.[33]

Diplomatic offensives in the world of non-aligned states

Although it is really economic problems that constitute the most pressing problems for Third World countries, Soviet foreign policy is frequently focused on security matters even in cases where Third World countries do not feel themselves to be threatened. Diplomatic offensives have been aimed primarily at the dissolution of pro-West alliances, such as SEATO, ANZUS and CENTO. The ASEAN group, however, was increasingly welcomed by Soviet propaganda as a step in the direction of 'neutrality' — even though its membership was in part identical to that of SEATO.[34] The Soviet Union endeavoured to promote the belief in Asia that one-sided dependence on the USA would not pay off, as the relinquishing of South Vietnam had shown. The Soviet Union rated the practical dissolution of SEATO in 1974 as a success. The CENTO Pact countries (dissolved in 1979) then became the focal point of Soviet attentions in South-West Asia.

The successes of Soviet diplomacy in Asia, however, were not as great as portrayed in the Soviet Union's own accounts. The idea of an institution of 'collective security in Asia', which was repeatedly launched in different variants by Moscow, met with little favourable response. The danger of an organisation dominated by the Soviets appeared greater than the security benefit to those countries caught up in the triangle of American, Chinese and Soviet influence.[35] This mistrust on the part of the smaller Asian countries stemmed from historical experiences. The

1954 treaty between China and India swore profusely to peaceful coexistence but did nothing to prevent the long years of border war between these two biggest Asian countries.[36] The Soviet Union was unable to dispel the suspicion that the new pact was ultimately directed against China, despite many assertions to the contrary in the Soviet literature.[37] Since the Bandung conference China has commanded a certain respect as a fully-Asian power, whilst the Soviet Union has scarcely succeeded in gaining any recognition as an Asian power. Despite certain failures in her diplomatic offensive, however, the Soviet Union has still registered a certain territorial gain, since many Asian countries have come to accept her as holding joint responsibility for peace and security in Asia.

In the 1970s Soviet policy on Asia also became more differentiated and flexible. As early as 1965 Moscow revised its exclusively pro-Indian attitude in the Kashmir conflict so as to prevent Pakistan from falling completely under Chinese influence.[38] Soviet courting became less selective — at the end of the 1970s the Soviet Union even courted a country like Saudi Arabia, which had previously been apostrophised as reactionary and feudalistic. Soviet publicists acknowledged that the Saudis had a partially progressive role in the Middle East conflict of 1979.[39] Despite this, the Soviet Union was unable to make up all the prestige that she lost in South-West Asia as well following the previous Arab–Israeli war of 1973 (see pp. 114–16). Nevertheless, Soviet publicists proudly maintain that no peace settlement is possible in South-West Asia without the involvement of the Soviet Union[40] — an assertion that has, in fact, been proved wrong by the attempted Israeli–Egyptian *rapprochement* through American mediation. At times it has been suggested that the Soviet Union is trying to achieve her right to participate in a peace settlement in the Middle East through better relations with the more conservative states such as Saudi Arabia and Jordan (which has recently even started importing weapons from the Soviet Union), following the failure of her attempts to achieve this through the formation of support points in friendly nations like Syria and Iraq. There are doubtless certain points on which the Fahd Plan for peace in the Middle East, submitted to the UN in October 1981, coincides with the Soviet proposals for a peace settlement.[41] The Saudi press has recently still been accusing the Soviet Union of a 'contradictory policy in South-West Asia' but has not excluded the right of the Soviet Union to play a part in the region. At this point in time, however, there were not even diplomatic relations between Riad and Moscow.[42]

None of the at times spectacular territorial gains by the USSR in the Middle East has so far proved to be lasting. Iraq, which for a long time was virtually regarded as a satellite of Moscow, disclaimed Soviet policy towards Somalia. The hostility between the two Baath parties in Syria and

Iraq had a negative influence on Moscow's relations with both countries. The intervention in Afghanistan was not welcomed by previously friendly Arab countries. In Iraq relations with the Soviet Union cooled down to such an extent that France began to replace the Soviet Union as an arms supplier.[43] Even the attempt at appearing strictly neutral in the Iraq–Iran conflict met with failure. Soviet influence did not make any significant progress in Iran either, although Moscow lent strong propagandist support to Teheran's anti-American policy. Conflicts repeatedly developed with the Khomeini regime on account of the alleged support that the Soviet Union was giving to Iraq and the rebel Kurds.[44]

Non-aligned Asian countries such as Burma, Indonesia and India constituted the chief targets of Soviet soliciting. These endeavours proved least successful in Burma, since despite the crisis in Sino–Burmese relationships between 1967 and 1971, China proved more successful in expanding trade relations and in handling the obstinate quality of Burmese neutrality and isolationism.[45] There is scarcely a country which meets up so well to Soviet conceptions when measured in terms of the objective criteria for socialist orientation. Burma's close co-operation with China and a number of capitalist countries has, however, repeatedly been a source of irritation to Soviet publicists.[46]

For a time Soviet foreign policy seemed to be registering greatest success in India. Critics at home and abroad almost suspected that Nehru's concept of non-alignment had been abandoned when the treaty of friendship was signed with the Soviet Union in 1971. Despite all their criticism of India, American politicans had to recognise that they had been partly responsible for this success on the part of Moscow through their over-hasty *rapprochement* with China. Kissinger admitted to erroneous judgements: 'It was not easy to imagine Nehru's daughter consciously steering non-aligned India into a *de facto* alliance with the Soviet Union'.[47] In the period that followed this Soviet diplomatic success the USSR has been likened to a pyromaniac who first starts a fire and then wants to be praised for calling in the fire brigade for assistance.[48] The Soviet Union doubtlessly encouraged India to intervene in East Pakistan, humiliated China unnecessarily and demonstrated to the Americans just how limited their scope was in Southern Asia.

Even this success on the part of Soviet foreign policy turned out to be more limited than the West had initially feared. The paradoxical consequence was that India became so dominant in the sub-continent with the aid of Soviet weapons that it was less dependent on the Soviet Union for the future. The Soviet Union had won itself out of the alliance, as it were. India again began to operate on the principle of equidistance that had been the basis for Nehru's concept of non-alignment, particularly during the period of the interregnum of the Desai government (1977–79). When the first Indian atomic explosion took place (in 1974) the Soviet Union no doubt began to wonder how she could dispel the spirits that this conjured up. When Indira Gandhi returned to power she adopted a line of conflict against the Communists in the country and the honeymoon of 1971 was also over on the foreign policy front.[49]

Soviet foreign policy scored its greatest successes amongst non-aligned countries in the international organisations. An increasing number of developing countries came to vote with the Soviet Union and the socialist bloc in the UN. Only a minority of countries, such as Sierra Leone, Kuwait and Tunisia, credibly maintained their principle of non-alignment through their voting behaviour in the UN as well.[50] The Eastern bloc developed into the most disciplined group in the UN as far as voting behaviour was concerned, although this was at the cost of a lack of flexibility in the forming of coalitions over the long term.[51]

The Soviet Union was able to exert less direct influence in the non-aligned nations' movement. The help of her allies was of great value here, particularly the activities of Cuba and Vietnam. The movement of non-aligned nations was increasingly committed to a 'positive concept' of non-alignment, giving up the search for equidistance between the two blocks in favour of close friendship with the socialist camp.[52]

When the non-aligned nations began to gather together in 1961 their main aim was to avoid warlike confrontations. By 1979 the movement was orientated more towards decolonisation and a new world economic movement and small-scale armed conflicts were permitted, if need be, in order to pursue these aims. In 1961 only 25 states met together in Belgrade, in 1979 virtually the whole of the Third World was represented with 94 delegations. The chairmanship, which was held by the Cubans up to 1982, was of great benefit to the makers of Soviet foreign policy. Cuba, one of the founder members of the organisation had always followed a very anti-imperialist line in its propaganda. The pro-Soviet note, however, was something new which had been completely lacking at the Belgrade and Cairo conferences. In the early phase, Cuba still held reservations *vis-à-vis* the Soviet Union, accusing her of not engaging in enough activities to establish the internationalism that figured prominently in Soviet propaganda. In Havana, Tito became Castro's biggest opponent. Cuba was unable to have all its own way in the question of the exclusion of Egypt and the admission of the Samrin Vietnamese puppet government in Cambodia, which had pushed out the Pol-Pot regime. Cuba also had to enter into compromises with the moderates so as to avoid splitting the movement. The feeling spread in Havana that Castro had overdone adherence to a party line within this movement.[53] Cuba's support of the Soviet intervention in Afghanistan reduced the credibility of the Cuban position even further in the eyes of a large number of non-aligned states. The majority of non-aligned nations have not so far approved of this intervention. In the UN 104 delegations voted in favour of a resolution condemning the Soviet attack on Afghanistan. Of these, 57 were from the group of non-aligned nations and an additional 9 votes came from countries holding observer status in the non-aligned movement. Other countries only abstained because they feared the stigma of voting openly with the USA.[54] At the summit conference of the heads of state and government of the nonaligned countries held in New Delhi in March 1983, Indira Gandhi endeavoured to achieve a more moderate line for the movement. Singapore maintained at the conference that the Soviet Union was about to take the movement into her hands with the aid of its pro-Soviet members. Even in New Delhi, however, these were estimated only to number 15 to 20. Since the West has started paying greater attention to the non-aligned movement again, Soviet power no longer seems to be increasing in linear proportions within the movement.

The Soviet Union's economic relations and development aid in the Third World

The Soviet Union has retained a certain attraction as a development model for a large number of Third World countries,[55] particularly due to the development successes in the Central Asian republics. It has not, however, proved possible to translate this prestige of the Soviet Union into fitting successes in foreign trade and development aid policy.

The share of developing countries in the trade of the Soviet Union and the Comecon countries is relatively small. The Soviet Union dominates these trade relations but her share is on the decline. In 1970, 60 per cent of all Comecon exports to the Third World came from the USSR. In 1980, the figure was only about half as high. Measured as a percentage of total Comecon foreign trade, the Soviet Union, with her 18 per cent, still holds the greatest share of trade with Third World countries (see Table 7.1).

One of the slogans applied by Western market economists to the Third World stresses 'trade not aid'. The Soviet Union acts more or less on the reverse principle, since the Comecon countries have only a few goods to offer that cannot be obtained in better quality in the West and since better politics can be pursued with development and arms aid than with trade, which has become increasingly dissociated from political fluctuations (see Chapter 5).[56] Such an order of priorities is obviously not spelt out in the Soviet literature. This literature criticises the capitalist countries for their policy which, it is maintained, is helping to reduce the developing countries' share of world trade.[57] For Comecon, by contrast, absolute figures for growth are given (in roubles). It can be seen from Comecon statistical data, however, that the percentage share of Third World trade

Table 7.1
Level of Soviet foreign trade with developing countries (1981)

	% turnover	in million roubles
Bulgaria	11.6	1 957
Cuba	3.6	344
Czechoslovakia	6.4	1 518
GDR	6.4	1 978
Hungary	11.8	2 924
Poland	10.0	2 672
USSR	14.1	16 883

Source: *Statisticheskii ezhegodnik stran-chlenov. SEV. 1983.* Moscow, Finansy i statistika 1982, p. 315.

has only risen in the case of the Soviet Union for some recent years (1980: 12.7 per cent, 1981: 15 per cent, 1982: 14.1 per cent) and went down occasionally. Viewed over the medium term, the Soviet Union's trade with the developing countries has fallen on many occasions — there have been years when it was as high as 16 per cent. These fluctuations cannot, however, be rated as the outcome of a conscious policy of discrimination. East–South trade is particularly prone to fluctuations from year to year, as a function of the situation on the world market and the hard currency problems of the Comecon countries.

The product structure of Soviet trade with the developing countries deviates from the pattern that has been established for East–West trade (see pp. 79–89). In her trade with the Third World the Soviet Union is not primarily an exporter concentrating on raw materials and semi-finished products. The share of machines and complete factory installations in trade with the Third World amounts to about one-third of Comecon exports and one-fifth of Soviet exports. Soviet data reveals the focal points of trade as being the neighbouring countries in Asia — India, Turkey, Iraq, Iran — see Table 7.2.

Argentina deviates from this pattern. It does, however, constitute a special case on account of the Soviet Union's grain purchases. Comparing different years (1984 and 1976), it can be seen that the cooling down of relations (Iraq) or the development of close ties (Argentina) does indeed affect the development of trade with the Soviet Union.

When it comes to development aid as well, the Soviet Union's performance does not live up to the claims made in the literature. In the eyes of the Soviets, the development aid provided by the capitalist countries marks an insufficient attempt to make good the damage caused by colonialism and post-colonialism (price declines and unstable terms of trade). The Soviet Union does not feel a share of the blame for this damage, since she does not consider herself an ex-colonial power and regards the damage of the decolonisation period as being exclusively the

Table 7.2

Share of chief trading partners in the Third World in Soviet foreign trade (turnover in %)

	1984	1976
India	2.0	1.5
Libya	0.9	n.a.
Argentina	0.8	n.a.
Iraq	0.7	1.3
Afghanistan	0.6	0.3
Iran	0.4	0.8
Egypt	0.4	0.8
Syria	0.3	0.4
Brazil	0.3	0.5
Turkey	0.2	0.2
Algeria	0.2	0.3
Malaysia	0.2	0.2

Source: *Vneshnyaya torgovlya SSSR v 1985 g* Moscow, Finansy i statistika, 1985, p. 15 and earlier issues.

product of the capitalist-dominated world economic order.[58] Charles Bohlen once remarked mockingly that colonialism in the Soviet view was linked to the one-sided idea of 'you get there by sea'.[59] The regions adjacent to Russia, which were formerly virtual colonies and now belong to the Union, are today rated as showpieces of Soviet development aid — and not entirely without good reason.

Part of Soviet development aid can also be summed up under normal economic relations. Certain projects were declared to be gifts in the initial phase of Soviet engagement in the Third World, although Western economists were always able to find something that had been supplied in return.[60] A stricter definition of development aid only recognises goods and services that are provided to the developing countries on favourable terms. Three-quarters of such resources come from the Western industrial states and one-fifth from the OPEC countries. Only 5 per cent comes from Comecon countries. At the beginning of the 1970s the Comecon countries had a much higher share, which then fell during the 1970s. According to OECD calculations, the development aid provided by the whole of the socialist camp in 1979 accounted for only about 55 per cent of the aid supplied by a Western nation such as the Federal Republic of Germany.[61] All the same, the Soviet Union increased the percentage of development aid in her national income from 0.10 per cent (in 1978) to 0.14 per cent (1980), representing twice the average for the People's Democracies but still only a fraction of the aid supplied by Western democracies (see Table 7.3).

In all fairness, it must be pointed out that the Soviet Union finds it particularly difficult to increase her development aid, since this often has

Table 7.3
Comparison of Comecon countries' development aid (1980)

	million $ US	% GNP
USSR	1 580	0.14
Total Comecon	1 817	0.12
People's Democracies	237	0.06
OPEC countries	6 999	1.45
Western industrial countries	26 708	0.37
of which: USA	7 091	0.27
France	4 041	0.62
FRG	3 518	0.43
Japan	3 304	0.32
Great Britain	1 785	0.34

Sources: *OECD Press A* (81) 26 dated 15.6.1981; H. Machowski and S. Schulz: *RGW-Staaten und Dritte Welt. Wirtschaftsbeziehungen und Entwicklungshilfe*, Bonn, Europa Union Verlag, 1981, p. 46.

to be funded with hard currency — particularly the additional grain purchases for Cuba, Cambodia and Vietnam and the special purchases of Cuban sugar, which then has a negative impact on the Soviet balance of payments.[62] Nevertheless, contrary to the case with trade, the Soviet Union has increased her share of net Comecon outpayments from 80 per cent (1979) to almost 90 per cent (1980). Almost three-quarters of Soviet development aid is focused on the chief allies in the Third World, Cuba and Vietnam. Of the non-socialist countries, India figured top of the list with pledges to a value of 800 US $. Amongst the countries of socialist orientation Afghanistan and Ethiopia are the chief recipients of Soviet aid.[63]

These countries, which are doubtlessly given preference for political reasons, receive subsidies and credit on favourable terms. The share of such subsidies in the sum total of pledges is estimated at 36 per cent for 1980. Project credits to countries within the Western sphere of influence (Turkey, Latin America), by contrast, are granted under much less favourable conditions (see Table 7.4).

Alongside the political motives for aid, such as the intensification of the socialist orientation of a number of developing countries, economic interests are coming to play an increasing role for the Soviet decision-makers. The stepping-up of exports and the securing of a number of important raw materials for the Soviet Union are playing a part in the expansion of economic and development aid relations with a number of countries, such as with Afghanistan and Iran (natural gas), Iraq (oil), Bolivia and India (coal), Guinea (bauxite), Algeria (aluminium) and Morocco (phosphate).[64]

Table 7.4
The instruments of Comecon countries' development aid

	USSR 1978	1979	1980	Eastern European countries 1978	1979	1980
Total gross outpayments (in million $ US)	1419	1811	2031	486	513	401
of which to:						
Cuba, Dem. People's Rep. of Korea, Vietnam	800	1160	1160	170	142	142
Afghanistan, Cambodia, Laos	107	149	449	23	27	21
Repayments (in million $ US)	465	408	451	149	155	164
Total net outpayments (in million $ US)	954	1403	1580	337	358	237
% of GNP	0.10	0.13	0.14	0.09	0.09	0.06
Percentage share of subsidies in pledges	32	30	34		27	16
of which to (% of total pledges):						
Subsidies to Cuba, Dem. People's Rep. of Korea, Vietnam	20	19	15	4	n.a.	n.a.
Subsidies to Afghanistan, Cambodia, Laos	6	7	16	3	3	4
Subsidy component of credit to:						
Cuba, Dem. People's Rep. of Korea, Vietnam	(74)	(74)	(74)	(67)	(67)	(67)
Other countries	40	31	46	39	30	31
Global subsidy component (%)	77	69	74	58	57	54

A marked specialisation has developed in the sectoral distribution of Comecon development aid. Food aid has only been granted on rare occasions. Ideological consistency has meant that the Soviet Union has not supported any projects that would inevitably strengthen small farmers or industrial undertakings. In Western estimates technical aid takes in 33 000 Soviet development helpers (plus 48 000 from the Eastern European People's Democracies and 13 000 from Cuba). The percentage of scholarships and contributions to multilateral offices serving development policy is very small in Soviet aid (see Table 7.5). Armaments aid is occasionally camouflaged as development aid (as in Western countries). This plays a particular role in Soviet relations (see pp. 71–7). According to Western estimates in a NATO study, however, economic aid has increased, by contrast to armaments aid. The latter still accounted for approximately 1.23 billion dollars in 1980.[65]

All the figures listed so far are based on Western estimates, which differ

Table 7.5

Estimated sums of development aid paid out by the Eastern European countries to developing countries and multilateral agencies 1970–80 (in million $ US)

	1970	1971	1972	1973	1974	1975	1976	1977	1978	1979	1980
Project and programme aid	276	324	286	289	298	322	362	344	397	370	350
of which to: 1 Cuba, Vietnam	150	150	125	150	125	125	182	142	170[a]	142	142
2 Afghanistan, Cambodia, Laos	1	—	3	—	2	1	3	8	23	27	21
3 Other developing countries	125	174	158	139	171	196	177	194	204	201	187
Catastrophe aid and humanitarian aid	2	x	5	21	6	x	14	11	49	102	9
Scholarships	14	14	15	16	16	17	25	30	35	35	35
Contributions to multilateral agencies	2	2	3	3	4	5	5	5	5	6	7
Total gross outpayments	294	340	309	329	324	344	406	390	486	513	401
Repayments	78	86	95	103	113	119	126	140	149	155	164
Total net outpayments	216	254	214	226	211	225	280	250	337	358	237
% of GNP	0.10	0.11	0.09	0.08	0.07	0.07	0.08	0.07	0.09	0.09	0.06
Total net outpayments without countries under 1 and 2	66	103	88	77	86	100	97	102	146	190	74
% of GNP	0.03	0.04	0.03	0.03	0.03	0.03	0.03	0.04	0.04	0.05	0.02
GNP (billion $)	214	230	250	273	299	331	349	369	384	393	(398)

a Including a subsidy from the GDR to Vietnam for the sum of 28 million US $
— no aid or insignificant aid
x less than half the smallest unit given in the table
() fully or partially estimated

Source: 'Die Entwicklungshilfe der COMECON-Länder im Jahre 1980', *Handbuch für internationale Zusammenarbeit, 188* May 1982 (1–8), pp. 4, 8.

widely from each other (e.g. OECD and NATO). Soviet and Comecon offices publish virtually no figures on development aid and the few that they do publish provide little information — such as the number of projects promised and completed in Third World countries. Although these figures seem to provide little information at first sight, since they are not specified according to content, a comparison of projects under contract with those that have already been brought into operation does allow certain conclusions to be drawn about shifts in the trends within Soviet development aid. If the most recent figures are compared with earlier data (see Table 7.6), then certain shifts do emerge in the Soviet commitment in the Third World. In Iran and Iraq the number of projects

Table 7.6

Number of development projects built in the Third World with Soviet aid in recent years (in key countries)

	No. under contract	In operation	Credit and donation pledges in million $ US 1954–79
Comecon developing countries			
Mongolia	810	438	
Cuba	440	206	
Vietnam	278	192	
Other socialist countries			
China	256	256	
North Korea	70	58	
Laos	43	4	
Countries of 'socialist orientation'			
Afghanistan	157	75	1290
Algeria	107	63	715
Syria	62	34	770
Ethiopia	40	4	225
South Yemen	33	14	205
Guinea	31	25	
Other developing countries			
Iran	119	74	1165
Egypt	107	94	1440
Iraq	98	70	705
India	90	55	2280
Turkey	15	8	3330

Sources: *Narodnoe khozyaistvo SSSR v 1980 g*, Moscow, Finansy i statistika, 1981, p. 541; National Foreign Assessment Center: *Communist Aid Activities in Non-Communist Less Developed Countries*, Washington DC, 1980, pp. 18ff; H. Hubel: *Die sowjetische Nah- und Mittelostpolitik*, Bonn, Europa Union Verlag, 1982, p. 18.

supported by the Soviet Union has declined. Even for India, 174 projects were still listed for 1978, whilst the figure for 1980 was only 90. The youngest countries of socialist orientation, such as Ethiopia, Laos and Afghanistan, have moved sharply into the foreground.

Given the Soviet Union's growing obligations, the scarcity of foreign exchange and the development of the Comecon countries' balance of payments (see pp. 97–108), the Soviet Union is reaching the limits on the expansion of her development aid. In publications the Soviet Union and the developing countries still continue to make the Western democracies responsible for the decline in economic relations and development aid. In the meantime, criticism from the Third World countries has ceased to spare the Soviet Union as well. Since the 4th UNCTAD conference in Nairobi in 1976 the Soviet Union has come under increasing attack for her practice of counter-trading, her price formation with industrial goods and her passiveness in the reshaping of the world economy.[66]

Armaments aid and military consultation in the Third World

Of all the instruments of Soviet foreign policy that are designed to strengthen the influence of the socialist camp in the Third World it is the Soviet Union's armaments aid that has attracted the most attention from Western publicists, since this is where Moscow's successes have been most clear to see. Soviet publicists accuse the Western powers of pursuing an armament policy for profit interests in the Third World.[67] The increase in arms expenditure in Third World countries which stems from co-operation with socialist countries, however, is regarded as a completely different policy in qualitative terms. Economic interests in arms trading are not now excluded but the primacy of political considerations still applies to this area as well.

It was in the Korean war that the Soviet Union first emerged as a large-scale supplier of arms. Nevertheless, it was not suggested that the Soviet Union had consciously wanted to stir up the war, since she had tried to curb North Korea's claims on the diplomatic front. Kim il Sung in North Korea had often spoken of the possibility of a second Korean war. The Soviet Union (North Korea's biggest supplier of arms), however, doubtlessly had a moderating influence in Pjungjang.[68]

At the outset — in the 1950s — the Soviet Union was not completely happy about the supplies. She made a number of efforts to camouflage her arms trade through Czechoslovakian and Polish firms. Today Soviet arms trading has reached proportions that can no longer be concealed. Soviet figures on arms trading are even harder to come by than figures for development aid. Here again we have to rely on estimates from the Secret Service and from scientific institutes engaged in strategic research.

Initially Soviet arms trading was difficult to monitor because it was concentrated essentially on countries with a socialist structure (China, North Korea, North Vietnam). After 1955 this concentration was gradually abandoned. The first non-socialist countries to receive Soviet arms were in South-West Asia. By about 1972 the Soviet Union had already overtaken the USA in the trade of a number of heavy weapon systems.[69] From 1977 to 1980 the Soviet Union, holding 27.4 per cent of the world's arms trade, ranked second to the USA (43.4 per cent) but above France (10.8 per cent), which occupied third place (see Table 7.7).[70] The Soviet Union has far fewer customers on the arms market than the USA and, as with her other aid, concentrates her supplies on specific

Table 7.7

Rank order of the biggest arms exporting countries 1977–80 (in million $ US and in terms of fixed prices, 1975)*

	Overall value	% of total exports	% of total value to Third World	Biggest importing country per exporting country
1 USA	24 893	43.3	60.8	Iran
2 USSR	15 755	27.4	79.5	Syria
3 France	6 213	10.8	76.5	Morocco
4 Italy	2 273	4.0	76.6	South Africa
5 Great Britain	2 141	3.7	81.7	India
6 FRG	1 712	3.0	37.6	Italy
7 Third World	1 271	2.2	98.0	—
8 Norway	724	1.3	—	Sweden
9 Netherlands	536	0.9	87.0	Peru
10 Brazil[b]	421	0.7	97.2	Chile
11 Israel[b]	367	0.6	100.0	South Africa
12 Australia	361	0.6	63.7	Philippines
13 China	333	0.6	95.0	Pakistan
14 Sweden	277	0.5	50.9	Great Britain
15 Switzerland	240	0.4	27.1	Canada
16 Canada	177	0.3	98.3	Ivory Coast
17 South Africa	116	0.2	100.0	Zimbabwe
18 Finland	112	0.2	—	USSR
19 Czechoslovakia	107	0.2	43.9	Bulgaria
20 Libya[bc]	98	0.2	96.0	Syria
Others	334	0.6	80.8	—
World total	57 459	100.0	68.7	

* Figures are the SIPRI trend-indicator values.
a Values include licence sales for the production of heavy weapons.
b Also included in the Third World export group.
c Figures for Libya do not represent a trend on account of the resale of aircraft and tanks.
Source: SIPRI–Computer–Datenbank: *SIPRI Rüstungsjahrbuch '81/82*, Reinbek, Rowohlt, 1982, p. 184f.

regions. In the 1960s India and Indonesia were given particular preferential treatment to strengthen them against the pact countries of SEATO and CENTO. Checking Chinese influence also played a role in the distribution of arms aid within Asia.

At the start of the 1980s 90 per cent of all arms exports went to the Arab countries and, in particular, to Iraq, Syria, Libya, Algeria and South Yemen. Central America marks a further focal point due to the large-scale weapon deliveries to Cuba. The selective principles underlying the allocation of arms were subsequently further abandoned and every country that sought arms supplies from the Soviet Union (generally because a number of wishes had not been fulfilled by the Western countries) actually received them. The Soviet Union prefers direct deliveries — production under licence was only permitted in exceptional cases, such as in India.

How can this rapid advance of the Soviet Union on the world's arms market be explained? There are a number of factors which have been decisive in the success of Soviet foreign relations:

1   The USSR frequently offered *better terms of payment* than the West. Prices were often lower. World market prices were only charged to Third World countries that could afford them, such as Libya. Financially weak countries, such as Ethiopia, were given the opportunity to counter-trade: raw materials in exchange for Soviet arms.[71]

2   The USSR has drastically expanded her *infrastructure* for arms exports over the past few years, in particular by expanding her fleet and introducing long-distance air freight.

3   Western competitors have felt themselves more strongly bound by restrictions imposed on deliveries into zones of tension and on the supply of heavy arms than has the Soviet Union. Arms purchases in the Soviet Union have been *less dependent upon fluctuations in the political climate* than supplies from the USA. The requirement for approval by Congress means that additional (internal American) restrictions are also involved. The Soviet Union has thus stepped in to fill many of the gaps in the field of heavy weapons that the Western powers have not wished to fill. For tanks, surface-to-air missiles and heavy artillery the Comecon countries hold the lead. For armoured vehicles, helicopters and aircraft, the Americans were still in the lead at the end of the 1970s (see Table 7.9).[72]

4   The Soviet Union's arms policy led to the accumulation of rapidly-ageing arms stores which are kept primarily for politically motivated 'clearance sales'.[73]

5   Soviet deliveries are generally *not assumed to embody any economic profit motives*.[74] Secondary, political intentions are not so easily

Table 7.8
The biggest arms importing countries in the Third World from 1977–80 (in million $ US)

	Overall value	% share in overall value for Third World	Biggest exporter per importing country
Iran	3 446	8.7	USA
Saudi Arabia	3 133	8.0	USA
Jordan	2 558	6.5	USA
Syria	2 311	5.9	USSR
Iraq	2 172	5.5	USSR
Libya	2 107	5.4	USSR
South Korea	1 987	5.0	USA
India	1 931	4.9	USSR
Israel	1 778	4.5	USA
Vietnam	1 220	3.1	USSR
Morocco	1 121	2.9	France
Ethiopia	1 086	2.7	USSR
Peru	995	2.5	USSR
South Yemen	964	2.4	USSR
South Africa	950	2.4	Italy
Algeria	882	2.2	USSR
Taiwan	737	1.9	USA
Kuwait	664	1.7	USSR
Argentina	642	1.6	FRG
Brazil	641	1.6	Great Britain
Egypt	594	1.5	USA
Indonesia	522	1.3	USA
Pakistan	512	1.3	France
Chile	482	1.2	France
Thailand	412	1.0	USA
Others	5 657	14.3	—
Total	39 504	100.0	

Source: *SIPRI Yearbook of World Armaments and Disarmament*, Stockholm, 1981, p. 198.

recognised by the Third World countries and only lead to differences of opinion in the long term. The economic aspect of arms sales is assuming increasing interest for Soviet planners. It is estimated that 10 per cent of all Soviet foreign exchange comes from arms trading.[75]

6   *National liberation movements* enjoy a high ranking as a medium of Soviet policy, which they only possess for Western countries in exceptional cases. The FLN in Algeria and the Pathet Lao in Laos thus received Soviet weapons at an early stage. Later the African liberation movements were equipped against the Portuguese colonial power with the aid of Moscow. The PLO in the Middle East was an important arms customer of the Soviet Union. Only occasionally did governments that were fighting against revolu-

Table 7.9
Weapon types supplied by the great powers

	USA	USSR	Western Europe
Tanks and machine guns	6 110	8 570	2 090
Artillery	3 715	6 310	955
Armoured cars and troop transporters	9 735	6 975	2 430
Submarines	24	9	20
Supersonic fighter aircraft	11 160	1 990	355
Subsonic fighter aircraft	925	390	35
Helicopters	1 730	575	1 180
Other aircraft	1 520	260	855
SAM	6 240	15 745	1 065

Source: US Congress, Senate, Committee on Foreign Relations: *Prospects for Multilateral Arms Export Restraint*, Staff Report, 96th Congress, 1st Session, Apr. 1979, p. 11.

tionary movements receive Soviet armaments aid, such as Ceylon in 1971 against the 'Guevarist' guerrilla movement, which Moscow regarded as an 'adventure'.[76] Voluntaristic left-wing groups in the Western world have always been verbally rejected in Soviet publications. As far as support for a number of movements such as the 'red brigades' and the 'Red Army Faction' is concerned, there are only suppositions to work on so far. All that can be established here is that wherever the Soviet Union co-operates actively with Third World liberation movements, she takes a milder view of Western European terrorism. The American struggle against 'international terrorism' is increasingly being pilloried as a campaign against national liberation movements and particularly against the PLO.[77] In judging individual terrorist movements the Soviet publicists align themselves fairly extensively to alliance partners in the terrorists' country. The 'red brigades' are thus assessed with quotations from and through the eyes of the Communist Party newspaper *Unità*. The condemnation of groups in the Federal Republic of Germany which bore pro-Chinese traits is even harsher.[78] In a number of commentaries the leading role in the struggle against extremism is ascribed to the Communist Party of the country.[79] This, however, is an exaggeration, in view of the comparative strength of forces within the countries concerned, particularly since it is maintained at the same time that extremism and terrorism in a large number of Western democracies primarily serve 'reaction'.

Although arms trading and the supply of spare parts have bound Third World countries more closely to the Soviet Union, not all the close co-operation has been of a lasting nature. Changes of alliance have occasionally taken place on both sides (see Table 7.10).

Table 7.10
Bloc changes in arms trading since 1968

	Supplier New	Old	Time of change	Underlying reason
Cambodia	China	USA	1973	Change of regime
Laos	USSR	USA	1973	Change of regime
Ethiopia	USSR	USA	1977	Change of regime
Somalia	West	USSR	1977	Change in Soviet policy
Egypt	West	USSR	1974	Reduced dependence
Sudan	West	USSR	1974	Reduced dependence
Iraq	various	USSR	1975	Reduced dependence
Peru	various	West	1973	Reduced dependence
Libya	various	West	1970	Oil money
North Yemen	West	USSR	1974	Policy change
Zambia	various	West	1971	Non-alignment policy
Congo	East	France	1978	Change in regime policy

Source: St. G. Neumann and R. E. Harkavay (eds): *Arms Transfers in the Modern World*, New York, Praeger, 1979, p. 73.

'Concerted action' — Soviet–Cuban co-operation in armed conflicts in the Third World

It was only in the era of coexistence that the Third World became the focus of the Soviet Union's strategical thinking. One of the unpleasant side-effects of *détente* policy for the West was that the calm on the East–West front allowed the Soviet Union to engage in more intense North–South activities. It thus became possible to work out concepts for a low-cost military engagement at the lowest potential level of confrontation.[80]

Her increased arms trade led to the Soviet Union becoming involved *de facto* in ever more conflicts throughout the world. In ideological terms the propaganda in favour of aid to national liberation movements even came to be accorded constitutional status in 1977 (Article 30). Much to the disappointment of some of these national liberation movements, however, the Soviet Union never let herself be committed on the prerequisites for this support or the proportions it would assume. The Soviet decision-makers decided on their engagement as a function of the individual case, in highly pragmatic fashion. Soviet publications deny any 'export of revolution' and counter-arguments from the West with claims about the 'export of counter-revolution'.[81] In the Soviet view, American behaviour in the Third World amounts to a call for an eternal guarantee of the status quo — a guarantee that no one can provide given the dynamic nature of the process.[82]

Although the doctrine acknowledges the struggle between two

principles in the support for national liberation movements (the Soviet Union versus the export of counter-revolution), the Soviet Union has taken care only to intervene in conflicts that can be pursued on a regional basis and has avoided any direct confrontation with the other super-power. The latter has only been possible on a more frequent basis since America began to place less emphasis on her world policing role in the 1970s. The danger of direct confrontation with the USA was most to be feared in the Middle East conflicts. The Soviet Union showed notable restraint here as well, however, and only supported the Arab countries to the extent required to put them in a position to ward off an attack. There is no indication that the Soviet Union ever encouraged Arab attacks on Israel. In the Middle East wars the Soviet Union supported the Arab side politically but her military commitment was kept at a low level, much to the disappointment of the radicals in the Arab countries and in the PLO. The consequence of this moderation was a loss of political influence. Egypt turned towards America again and terminated the 1971 Treaty of Friendship with the Soviet Union in 1976. Syria once threw Soviet warnings to the winds and intervened in Lebanon.

According to Soviet accounts, the Soviet Union has never sought 'any advantage or possessions' in the Middle East — neither military bases nor rights on the removal of raw materials — and neither has she ever sought to influence the internal development of Middle East countries.[83] Much of this is true, but not quite everything. The Soviet Union has at times functioned as a middle-man in raw materials trading and has sold at a profit materials obtained on favourable terms from friendly nations.[84]

Even these dealings, however, were more of a by-product of political relations. There is little evidence to suggest that the Soviet Union engages in planned ring trading in order to improve her foreign exchange situation. Only occasionally has the Soviet Union obtained rights to extract raw materials and although her quest for military bases increased again as she gained greater world standing — after renouncing her bases from Finland to China — she has had less success here than American endeavours to date. Even military aid has not always produced fitting benefits. At the Camp David negotiations to secure peace with Israel and during the Israeli intervention in the Lebanon in 1982, the Soviet Union was relegated to the role of spectator.[85] The strategy of American territorial gain, which Kissinger introduced in order to win back the positions formerly lost under Dulles in 1955, brought regional success for the USA.[86]

As with America's policy on India, the American policy on the Middle East and its successes actually provoked the counter-successes scored by Soviet foreign policy in other areas. The rebuff in the Middle East undermined the Soviet Union's self-confidence. It was thus no wonder that she strove for territorial gains in other locations, starting in the mid

1970s with a region from which the Americans were beginning to stand back following the Vietnam trauma, namely with Africa. Although there was no fear of the Americans launching a counter-intervention in Angola and Ethiopia, the Soviet Union learned from the sensitivity that had surrounded her previous attempts at penetrating Africa and tried to reduce the appearance of Soviet intervention by deploying Cuba. Cuba seemed particularly suitable for conducting proxy interventions on behalf of the Soviet Union since it was able to provide large numbers of black-skinned soldiers and could better pass itself off as a non-aligned state at that time than at the end of the 1970s. Nevertheless, the support provided by the Soviet Union and Cuba did not produce unlimited success for Soviet foreign policy. Despite this aid the MPLA was unable to bring the whole country under control even though the South African aid for the counter groups remained relatively ineffective. The FNLA, which had not orginally been anti-Soviet, was driven into an alliance with China and the West through the Cuban–Soviet presence. The action sparked off deep mistrust in the neighbouring countries and did nothing to promote African unity.[87]

The Soviet Union had to choose between two allies in the conflict in the Horn of Africa and hence could never achieve more than 50 per cent success right from the start. In November 1977 Somalia broke off relations with the Soviet Union. Once again the Western powers did not intervene, despite fervent diplomacy on the part of the conservative Arab states for support for Somalia. Soviet portrayals lay the blame for this conflict exclusively on Somalia, spurred on by 'reactionary circles in the West and a number of Arab countries'.[88]

The Soviet Union expanded her influence in the West and South of Africa and also in the Horn of Africa through her concerted action with Cuba. Even today, however, it cannot be said for certain that the use of military power was worthwhile overall. The Soviet Union did not achieve reliable allies or stable positions in any of the regions. Either the internal situation of the Moscow-orientated regime remained unstable, as in Angola and Ethiopia, or one-sided dependence on the socialist camp was increasingly abandoned as the regime became consolidated, as was the case in India. Even in Angola and Mozambique there are endeavours to balance out the one-sided orientation towards Moscow through greater contact with the Western world. Both countries want to participate in the negotiations for Lome III and accepted for this purpose a Berlin clause which no socialist country would accept.[89] It is also difficult to assess the drawbacks of Soviet participation in terms of the growing mistrust of countries that have become neighbours to Soviet systems of socialist orientation. In the Soviet understanding intervention in the Third World constitutes 'brotherly help', whilst even humanitarian action by the West, such as in Zaire in 1978, has been held up to be 'intervention'.[90]

Originally, many African states reacted more allergically to American attempts at intervention than to Soviet attempts. Since the Soviet Union has had to be taken more seriously in this part of the world, however, there has been an increase in harsh counter-reactions by the African élites.

The role of Cuba in Soviet policy on Africa is also disputed. Is Cuba acting as a Soviet satellite or in its own interests? It is difficult to reach any conclusions on this from the Soviet literature. The country's exposed position means that Cuban publications stress friendship with the Red Army much more than do statements from other Comecon countries.[91] The relationship between Cuba and the Soviet Union is portrayed as having been harmonious since Castro's take-over of power, as though there had never been any differences of opinion.[92]

No Latin American country has such a high military budget as Cuba. The reduction in troops from some 300 000, at the start of the 1960s to some 100 000 in the mid-1970s, however, shows that whilst Cuba's military efforts were indeed a response to the perception of an internal and external threat to the country, it cannot be concluded that there were plans for large-scale campaigns outside the country, on account of the troop reductions.[93] When it came to supporting revolutionary movements in the Third World, co-operation with the Soviet Union was far less conflict-free than portrayed in the Soviet literature. In the 1960s Cuba was still pursuing its own policy of support for guerrilla movements in Latin America, a policy towards which the Soviet Union remained sceptical. Castro's attempts to create a regional guidance centre for liberation movements in the Western hemisphere were more of a thorn in the flesh for the Soviet Union. In the opinion of a number of scientists, Soviet military aid to Cuba was sharply reduced from 1966 to 1969 because of these differences in opinion.[94] Even in the late 1960s the two countries' policy on Africa was by no means identical. Cuba set greater store by ideological affinity, and the Soviet Union by strategical and geopolitical considerations.[95]

Whilst the partnership with Cuba counts as asymmetrical today, Cuba is still not rated as a satellite of Moscow that has no will of its own.[96] The co-operation is based on a division of labour, with the Soviet Union supplying equipment and financial aid and Cuba providing the man-power to furnish Soviet deliveries with the necessary know-how (see Table 7.11). Only in Angola and Ethiopia did the military forces supplied by Cuba run into thousands. In most cases, no more than a couple of hundred military advisors are sent. The OECD has estimated the number of Cuban development workers at 13 000 (see Table 7.11). It has been concluded from Soviet influence to moderate Cuban intervention zeal — such as in campaigns against Namibia that would have been bound to lead to direct confrontation with South Africa — that Cuba has attempted to

Table 7.11
Cuban troops, military and civil advisors in Africa (1980)

	Military		Civil advisors
Algeria	10–20		6 000–9 000
Angola	19 000		
Benin	10–20		
Congo-Brazzaville	300		200–275
Equatorial Guinea	10–20		50–100
Ethiopia	13–15 000		500–600
Guinea–Bissau	50		40–50
Iraq	10–20		1 000
Libya	200	(1979)	
Madagascar	650–750	(1977)	
Mozambique	200–300		400–500
Sierra Leone	10–20		
Somalia	500	(1976)	
South Yemen	300–400		100–200
Tanzania	50	(1979)	80
Uganda	60	(1978)	
Zambia	100		

Source: M. L. LeoGrande: *Cuba's Policy in Africa, 1959–1980*, Berkeley, Institute of International Studies, 1980, pp. 66 f., 69.

pursue politics on its own account in Africa.[97] In 1972 Cuba received some 4.5 per cent of total Soviet development aid, which still placed it behind more developed Comecon countries, such as Bulgaria (12.2 per cent) or the GDR (7.3 per cent).[98] At the start of the 1980s it became the chief recipient of Soviet aid, along with Vietnam, and in view of Cuba's payment difficulties it has at times been suggested that Cuba is paying off the three billion or so dollars that flowed into the country in 1980 to the Soviet Union with its manpower.

Only very biased right-wing or left-wing critics[99] see a type of 'overall strategy' behind the concerted action between Cuba and the Soviet Union. Rivalry with the USA and China, regional considerations and favourable opportunities have no doubt provided a much more limited scale for Soviet interventions. Soviet politics in the Third World has been predominantly opportunist and reactive.

8 The Communist World Movement as an Instrument of Transnational Politics

Transnational politics through Communist parties

Whilst the bourgeois parties were traditionally confined to a national level and only began to pursue effective transnational politics after the Second World War, socialist and Communist parties laid emphasis on the international aspect right from the start, seeing their strength in transnational co-operation. In the first two Internationals there was no socialist state power that could have used the international co-operation as an instrument of national politics. It was only the Third Communist International which produced an international organisation that has been an instrument at the service of one specific country right from the start.

After the October Revolution Trotsky had still hoped that it would soon be possible to replace the traditional style of foreign politics by a transnational revolutionary policy of the party and army. Today, Soviet foreign relations have been 'nationalised' to such an extent that semi-official documents from the Ministry of Foreign Affairs, destined for publication abroad, make no reference at all to co-operation with the Communist movements and special publications on international activities of the party stress common actions between Soviet government and the Communist party.[1] All the more emphasis is then placed on this aspect in the Secretary General's speeches to the Party Congresses. Transnational party relations have their fixed position here, coming after the reference to co-operation with other socialist states and the Third World and prior to the handling of relations with the capitalist countries. At the XXVI Party Congress in 1976, Brezhnev outlined the party's functions in this field as the following activities: reception of party delegations from abroad; attendance of and participation in foreign party congresses; and regular exchange of information with brother parties.[2]

By way of conclusion, Lenin's sentence that all nations are progressing towards socialism is repeated — 'this is inevitable', wrote Brezhnev, but added that the development was taking place under various forms of democracy and dictatorship of the proletariat.[3] To support this he cited the different forms prevailing from Yugoslavia (the sole non-full member of Comecon mentioned) through to the GDR. In Brezhnev's view, given such large-scale differences within the Communist world movement and the complexity of its tasks, differences of opinion are inevitable. Compromises are recommended, although not with 'reformists', dogmatic sectarians or 'left-wing adventurers'. It was a long path with many schisms that led up to the point where the Communist world movement was acknowledged to be no longer a monolith. At the XXVI Party Congress, Brezhnev counted 94 active parties worldwide. If one takes the global figures given in the Soviet party statistics (see Table 8.1) then, at first sight, the triumphant advance of Communism would seem to be unstoppable.

Table 8.1
Growth in the world's Communist parties

	No. of parties	Worldwide membership
1917	1	400 000
1928	46	1 700 000
1939	69	4 200 000
1946	78	20 000 000
1960	87	35 000 000
1969	88	50 000 000
1980	92	over 75 000 000

Source: V. V. Zagladin *et al.* (ed.): *Dvizhushchie sily mirogo revolyutsionnogo protsessa*, Moscow, Politizdat, 1981, p. 320.

Global growth figures of this type are used to conceal the setbacks and regional failures that have occurred, particularly in Europe — in some cases as a reaction to aggressive acts of Soviet foreign policy. Of the 75 million Communists in the world (some Western sources put the figure at only 56 million), 94 per cent belong to established state parties. Three-quarters of these do not profess unconditional loyalty to Moscow orthodoxy today but can be rated as 'Eurocommunists' instead.[4] In large areas of the Third World the overall balance of the expansion of Communism tends to be rather minimal (see Tables 8.2 and 8.3). Exceedingly global growth rates are cited here as a way round this fact:

Asia — 600 000, twice as many Communists as in 1970, Latin America — 400 000.[5]

All the same, progress has in fact been achieved by comparison with the limited beginnings of the Communist world movement. Not all this progress, however, has directly benefitted the strength of the Soviet Union in the world. At the time when Comintern was founded there was no true Communist party outside Soviet Russia apart from the German Communist Party (KPD). The founding congress of Comintern in Moscow in March 1919 was only attended by representatives of small revolutionary groups. Even the KPD hesitated before joining. Hugo Eberlein had been instructed to vote against the founding of a Third International because the party feared isolation of the Communists in Germany and patronising treatment from the Bolsheviks. It was only the murder of Rosa Luxemburg, the chief opponent to the new founding, that cleared the way to the KPD's accession to Comintern.[6] Comintern's doctrinaire policy split a series of socialist parties which were willing to join (Italy, France). Only in France did the majority join the Communists temporarily. The Norwegian workers' party left Comintern again in 1923.[7] Further mistakes committed by the CPSU and Comintern, which was dependent upon it, served to weaken the Communist movement in the world:

1   The narrow-minded *struggle against* the '*social fascists*' up to 1935 made alliances with socialists and social democrats difficult and made it easier for Fascist groups, whose strength had been wrongly estimated, to gain power.
2   Purges and *Gleichschaltung* lowered the prestige of the Communist parties.
3   The *Hitler–Stalin Pact* and the change of direction of many Communist parties between 1939 and 1941 cost additional public confidence, which could only be won back in a few countries, such as France and Italy, through resolute resistance movements after 1941.

When luck began to turn to the Soviet side in the Second World War, Stalin had Comintern dissolved for tactical reasons in 1943. The Communist parties were instructed by the last Secretary General, Dimitrov, to introduce a 'national front' policy in their respective countries. The new alliance policy facilitated the Communist party's seizure of power in large areas of Eastern Europe and the Communist parties' participation in the first post-war coalitions in Western Europe. These coalitions broke down, however, in 1947. Ramadier dismissed the Communists from his government in France after they had voted with the opposition on a question of confidence. Whilst the dissolution of the coalition with the Communists in France can be explained more in terms

Table 8.2
The world's Communist parties and their ideological orientation

Eastern Europe and the Soviet Union	Mid-1982 population	Communist party membership	Party leader	Congress, if any	Orientation/legal status	Percentage of vote; seats in legislature
Albania (PPSh)	2 792 000	146 363 claim	Enver Hoxha	—	IR/*	99.9 (1979); all 250 to Democratic Front
Bulgaria	8 940 000	825 876 claim	Todor Zhivkov	—	M/*	99.99 (1981); all 400 to Communist-approved slate
Czechoslovakia	15 369 000	1 584 011 claim	Gustáv Husák	—	M/*	99.0 (1981); all 350 to National Front
East Germany (SED)	16 738 000	2 202 277 claim	Erich Honecker	—	M/*	99.9 (1981); all 500 to National Front
Hungary (MSzMP)	10 714 000	811 833 claim	János Kádár	—	M/*	99.3 (1980); all 352 to Patriotic People's Front
Poland (PZPR)	36 229 000	2 488 000 claim	Wojciech Jaruzelski	—	M/*	99.5 (1980); all 460 to National Unity Front
Romania	22 510 000	3 150 000 claim	Nicolae Ceauşescu	—	M/*	98.5 (1980); all 369 to Socialistic Democracy and Unity Front
USSR	269 876 000	17 800 000 claim	Yuriy Andropov	—	M/*	99.9 (1979); all 1,500
Yugoslavia (SKJ)	22 689 000	2 200 000 claim	Nikola Stojanovic	12 June 26–30	IM/*	— (1978); all 308 to Socialist Alliance

Western Europe	Mid-1982 population	Communist party membership	Party leader	Congress, if any	Orientation/legal status	Percentage of vote; seats in legislature
Austria	7 510 000	15 000 est.	Franz Muhri	Extraord. Jan 30	M/+	0.96 (1979); none
Belgium	9 881 000	14 000 est.	Louis Van Geyt	24 Mar. 24–28 Ext. Dec. 19	IM/+	2.13 (1981); 2 of 212
Cyprus (AKEL)	642 000	12 000 est.	Ezekias Papaioannou	15 May 13–16	M/+	32.8 (1981); 12 of 35 Greek Cypriot seats

Country	Population	Membership	Leader	Congress	Type	Electoral
Denmark	5 125 000	10 900 est.	Jorgen Jensen	—	M/+	1.1 (1981); none
Finland	4 816 000	50 000 claim	Jouko Kajanoja	20 May. 14–15	M/+	17.9 (1979); 35 of 200[bb]
France	54 174 000	710 000 claim	Georges Marchais	24 Feb. 3–7	M/+	16.2 (1981); 44 of 491
Greece	9 743 000	73 000 claim	Kharilaos Florakis	11 Dec. 15–18	M/+	10.9 (1981); 13 of 300
Iceland (AB)	233 000	2 200 est.	Svavar Gestsson	—	IM/+	19.7 (1979); 11 of 60
Ireland	3 533 000	500 est.	Andrew Barr	18 May 14–16	M/+	— (1982); none
Italy	57 353 000	1 720 000 claim	Enrico Berlinguer	—	IM/+	30.4 (1979); 201 of 630
Luxembourg	366 000	600 est.	René Urbany	—	M/+	5.0 (1979); 2 of 59
Malta	376 000	150 est.	Anthony Baldacchino	—	M/+	— (1981); none
Netherlands	14 349 000	15 000 est.	Elli Izeboud	28 Nov. 26–28	IM/+	1.8 (1982); 3 of 150
Norway (AKP)	4 113 000	Under 1 000 est.	Paal Steigan	—	B/+	0.7 (1981); none
(NKP)		Under 600 est.	Hans Kleven	—	M/+	0.3 (1981); none
Portugal	10 056 000	187 000 claim	Alvaro Cunhal	—	M/+	16.7 (1980); 41 of 250
San Marino	22 000	300 est.	Ermengildo Gasperoni	—	IM/+	25.0 (1978); 16 of 60
Spain	37 940 000	Under 100 000 est.	Gerardo Iglesias	—	IM/+	3.8 (1982); 4 of 350
Sweden (VPK)	8 331 000	17 000	Lars Werner	—	IM/+	5.6 (1982); 20 of 349
Switzerland (PdA)	6 407 000	5 000 est.	Armand Magnin	—	M/+	1.5 (1979); 3 of 200
Turkey	48 105 000	Negligible	Ismail Bilen	—	M/O	
UK (CPGB)	56 095 000	18 500 claim	Gordon McLennan	—	M/+	1.1 (1979); none
West Germany (DKP)	61 697 000	48 856 claim	Herbert Miles	—	M/+	0.2 (1980); none
West Berlin (SEW)[cc]	1 900 000	7 000 est.	Horst Schmitt	—	M/+	0.7 (1981); none

Source: R. Wesson: Checklist of Communist Parties, 1982, *PoC*, 1983 (94–102), p. 98.

Table 8.3
International Communist 'front organisations'

	Headquarters	Claimed membership	Branches	Countries
Afro-Asian People's Solidarity Organisation	Cairo	no data	87	
Christian Peace Conference	Prague	no data		at least 80
International Association of Democratic Lawyers	Brussels	approx. 25 000	approx. 80	approx. 120
International Organisation of Journalists	Prague	over 180 000		
International Union of Students	Prague	over 10 000 000	approx. 118	
Women's International Democratic Federation	East Berlin	over 200 000 000	129	114
World Federation of Democratic Youth	Budapest	over 150 000 000	over 250	approx. 100
World Federation of Scientific Workers	Paris	approx. 450 000	approx. 33	
World Federation of Trade Unions	Prague	approx. 200 000 000	approx. 71	
World Peace Council	Helsinki	no data	over 135	

of domestic policy, the withdrawal of the Communists from Gasperi's government in Italy can also be attributed to foreign policy influences. The American government without doubt exerted a certain pressure here.[8]

Although Stalin had not pushed the Western Communists on to a path of revolutionary campaigns and mass strikes and had advised them instead to co-operate with non-Communist parties,[9] the USA became increasingly alarmed at the growing tension and the civil war situations that had developed on the periphery of Europe. The Truman Doctrine and the Marshall Plan for the reconstruction of Europe (the latter was by no means aimed directly against the Soviet Union, since it was open to the People's Democracies of Eastern Europe as well) caused Stalin to change his tactics. The Communist movement was to be more strongly co-ordinated again, the instrument for this being Cominform. The founding conference in September 1947 can scarcely be referred to as a meeting of the Communist world movement. Invitations were sent out to the parties on a very selective basis. The Communists from the Soviet-occupied zone were missing from the Est and only the French and Italian parties were invited from the West. There were no non-European parties present, not even the Communist party of China, which was on the point of gaining a definitive victory over the Kuomintang regime. During preliminary talks, Stalin made no secret of his contempt for the old Comintern in the presence of Dimitrov, its last Secretary General.[10] In Stalin's view, the tasks of Cominform were twofold: it was to exert stronger control over the Eastern European countries and was to direct the Western European countries on to more of a line of conflict within their countries. Mass strikes, breaks of coalition and splits in a large number of trade unions dominated by the Communists (CGT, CGIL, SAK) were the result.[11] Of the Eastern European parties only Gomulka seems to have opposed this new institution at the time.[12] The new unity of the world movement did not last long. The break in relations between Tito and Stalin meant that the Cominform headquarters had to be moved from Belgrade. In 1956 Cominform was dissolved. Since then the Communist parties have only had one joint institution — a central information office in Prague, which publishes the periodical *Peace and Socialism* in a large number of languages. It remains to the present a guardian of orthodoxy, which strongly propagates the Soviet model.[13]

The dissolution of Cominform in April 1956 further weakened the means available to the Soviets to control the individual Communist parties. The Polish resistance and Hungarian uprising in Autumn 1956 were further instances that promoted alienation between Western European parties and the CPSU. In Denmark, in 1959, the majority of the Communist party leadership broke away from the Moscow-orientated party for the first time ever and followed its own path of democratic socialism under Aksel Larsen. The Italian party became the vanguard of an individual path to socialism in Western Europe with Togliatti's theses on polycentrism and his memorandum on 'The Question of the International Workers' Movement and its Unity' (1964), which later came to be designated Togliatti's testament. The crushing of the Prague Spring in 1968 causes further severe damage to the standing and influence of the CPSU.

Since then it has proved difficult for the CPSU to gather the 'brother parties' round a single table for a world conference. The European conference of Communist parties in East Berlin in June 1976 provided the first tangible evidence for Eastern bloc populations as well of the new orientation prevailing in many Communist parties in the West. A name was put to this orientation in 1975 with the term 'Eurocommunism'. This was a misleading designation, as the periodical *Novoe vremya* quite rightly noted in a polemic against Carrillo, since the Communist parties of Europe have no uniform concept and the common features that they do share, extend beyond the boundaries of Europe. Furthermore, this concept provides an invitation to exaggerate the anti-Soviet stand of Western European parties.[14] The Eurocommunists orientated themselves against the concept of 'proletarian internationalism' and unconditional solidarity with the Soviet Union. In addition, they rejected any kind of ideological leadership centre and refused binding resolutions taken by the world movement. International solidarity was to replace the over-exclusive proletarian internationalism. Despite pressure from the Soviet side, the final document of the East Berlin conference contained no reference to Marxism–Leninism as the uniform doctrine and no condemnation of Maoism. Emphasis was placed on the sovereignty and independence of the parties. Moscow did not even succeed in having a condemnation of so-called 'anti-Sovietism' included in the document. Fundamental rights and political freedoms were highlighted more sharply than in any earlier declaration and the Western parties succeeded in making the party organ of the host country, *Neues Deutschland*, reproduce the wording of the declaration in full.[15]

All the same, the various schisms only curtailed the dominant position of the CPSU in the Communist world movement to a limited extent.

Yugoslavia's liberal experiment enjoyed considerable sympathy from left-wing socialist groups in the West and a number of Third World countries (e.g. Algeria). Despite this a worldwide 'Titoism' did not come into being. Yugoslavia's impact in the world was due less to its self-governing socialism and more to its policy of non-alignment (see pp. 124–7). In the Eastern bloc Titoism had only a limited influence during the Cominform era, since relentless purges were conducted in all the People's Democracies. From 1948 to 1952, 8500 Communists are said to have fled from the Eastern European coutries to Yugoslavia.[16] In the West Titoistic groups remained insignificant. The influence of the Federation of Yugoslav Communists was only expanded by intensive party contacts, particularly with Italy. Once again, this influence centred less on the self-governing model and more on specific common features in foreign and security policy.[17] Stalin tried to force Yugoslavia to its knees with wide-ranging pressures. He employed instruments of economic warfare, the non-observation of reparation obligations from Hungary, political pressure with the cancellation of all friendship and mutual assistance pacts, and subversive activity through the founding of a 'Political Committee of Yugoslavs in Exile'.[18] Only after Stalin's death did an improvement come about once again in relations between the CPSU and the Yugoslav party. Khrushchev's pragmatism was able to put together some of the pieces that Stalin's dogmatism had smashed in the communist world movement.

China too only succeeded in achieving a limited degree of influence on Communist parties in South-East Asia (see pp. 109–17). When the Third International Consultation of Communist and Workers' Parties was held in Moscow in June 1969 following lengthy insistence by the CPSU, it was intended that this meeting should make clear *inter alia* the isolation of the Communist party of China. Of the 75 delegations that attended, the majority were following the Soviet line. Fourteen parties failed to turn up. Only seven of these could be designated pro-Chinese. With the exception of Albania, they were concentrated in the South-East Asian and Pacific regions (Cambodia, Thailand, Burma, Malaysia, Indonesia, New Zealand). Important parties, such as those of North Korea and North Vietnam, which were operating between the blocs, were similarly missing.[19]

In the meantime the CPSU has achieved further territorial gains in Vietnam and Laos at the expense of China. In India, rivalry developed between two parties, which Indira Gandhi skillfully played off against each other. At the start of the 1980s the factions moved closer together again under pressure of harsher confrontation with the government.[20] The predominance of the English language and culture amongst the Indian élites always kept the influence of the CPSU at a relatively limited level, despite verbal adoption of programme points.[21] Rival Chinese influence also comes up against the same restrictions, however, and hence this conflict in India's Communist subculture ended in stalemate.

In Japan, the Sinophile Communists similarly only gained the upper hand for a short period. The 'revisionists' faithful to Moscow were excluded in 1964 and the party acknowledged its adherence to the Chinese model. As early as 1966, however, the party was looking for means of coexistence with the CPSU again. The party gradually build up a stand that rejected both the Soviet and the Chinese model for Japan and was orientated towards Western European Communist concepts.[22]

China attempted to form splinter parties in a large number of developing countries, in which the parties faithful to Moscow also led a pitiful existence. These included Africa, the Gulf region and Latin America. Castro had not held this to be a sensible strategy even prior to his split with Peking in 1965, although he was inwardly closer to Mao than to Khrushchev on many ideas regarding the revolutionary liberation of the Third World. This was because the Moscow-orientated leadership cadres from the towns and cities, which formed the mainstay of the Moscow-orientated Communists, did not correspond to his leadership ideal. Moscow occasionally attempted to split Peking-orientated parties by way of a response to Chinese offensives (e.g. in Indonesia). Overall, however, Moscow was less dependent upon a splitting strategy than Peking, and hence Peking's initiatives often appeared more offensive than the activities of the Moscow-orientated Communists.

The CPSU showed moderation in its rivalry with Chinese influence as far as the Palestine liberation movement was concerned. The CPSU never let itself be committed to radical aims such as the total destruction of Israel under pressure from Sinophile wings.[23] Relations between the Communist party of China and the Eurocommunist parties improved, although they did not become close. One spectacular *rapprochement* was that between the Communist party of China and the Federation of Yugoslav Communists. After the Soviet Union's intervention in Czechoslovakia in 1968, the previous hateful attacks on Yugoslav revisionism were stopped for reason of state.[24] Even China was not able to draw Yugoslavia towards her, however, and did not prevent the development of close co-operation between Yugoslavia and Comecon. Moscow was successful in warding off Chinese offensives on most fronts but never achieved a victory at which the CPSU could have wholeheartedly rejoiced. From Japan and India, through to Europe and Latin America, the Sino-Soviet party conflict served primarily to highlight the particular features of national and regional endeavours.

Cuba created a special problem for the CPSU, which proved difficult to handle. Differences of opinion could not be thrashed out between the parties to begin with since the Cuban party was no more than a rather inefficient club of veterans at the outset. Soviet influence was considerable but not as dominant in questions of the initial development strategy as the American literature has at times assumed.[25] Soviet publicists welcomed in particular Cuba's rejection of self-sufficiency concepts (along the lines of the Chinese motto of 'building up on ones own strengths') and the acceptance of the socialist division of labour.[26] All the remaining differences of opinion, however, can scarcely be interpreted as an inter-party conflict.

The inter-party conflict, which influenced the Communist world movement, only developed with Cuba at the end of the 1960s when the

Soviet Union became more cautious than before in her support of Latin American guerrilla movements. With Cuba it was seen that the Soviet Union and the Communist parties inclined towards her did not regard the guerrilla movements as a strategic instrument which they believed would be successful, despite the lip service that they paid to them.[27] Castro now adopted some of the stands that had once caused Guevara to clash with the Soviet advisors in Cuba. During this period Castro was not afraid to brusquely snub the Communist parties of Latin America, which hardly acted without Moscow's approval: 'If the alleged Communists in any country cannot fulfil their task, then we shall support those who, without calling themselves Communists, appear as true Communists in their struggle and action'.[28] This amounted to fraternisation with revolutionaries such as Douglas Bravo, who had been declared 'party enemies' by the orthodox party, and undermined the hierarchical structures of the Communist parties. This criticism did not even stop when it came to the Soviet Union, on account of her co-operation with oligarchic dictatorships in Latin America.

It was only after the decline of the guerrilla movement (which Moscow had assessed more realistically) that Castro moved closer to the Soviet stand again for lack of any alternative. During his visit to Chile in 1971, solidarity with the Eastern bloc was made the focus of his speeches in a very conspicuous manner.[29] Havana did not become a regional centre of leadership for world Communism,[30] however, and Moscow, with its flexible policy towards Cuba, was much better able to maintain its leadership role and make use of Cuba in concerted action than in the conflict with the Chinese (see pp. 109–17).

Eurocommunism constitutes an abstraction of a wide range of liberalisation trends. Its ideological unity has often been overestimated. The striving for ideological pluralism largely evades any new categorisation of its perspectives in a transnational comparison. Despite this, a number of common trends can be pinpointed within the liberal Western European Communist parties:[31]

1   Rejection of the exemplary role of the Soviet line.
2   Acceptance of party pluralism and the parliamentary system. The abandoning of the 'dictatorship of the proletariat' in a number of programmes, even by the French Communist party, which has never become completely Eurocommunist.
3   Independence of the trade union movement, renunciation of the concept of 'transmission belt'.
4   Normalisation of relations with the church.
5   Moves away from the ideology of nationalisation and from the central planning of all conditions of production and reproduction.

6   Co-operation with all parties of the 'constitutional spectrum', extending beyond the old popular front concepts.

The CPSU was able to make concessions on all these points of domestic policy. The truly irreconcilable differences of opinion lay in the realm of foreign policy perspectives and also have direct bearing on the comparative strength of forces in the world:

1   Proclamation of a new (non-proletarian) internationalism.
2   Rejection of an ideological leadership centre.
3   Rejection of unconditional support for the Soviet Union and open criticism when Soviet foreign policy has engaged in repression (Hungary, Czechoslovakia, Poland, Afghanistan).
4   Acceptance of NATO until such time as it becomes possible to dissolve the military blocs.
5   Recognition of the European Community.
6.   Only co-operation with the CPSU 'as with every other party', as once proclaimed by Carrillo, has not yet become the prevailing doctrine in Western European Communism.

The Soviet Union has not accepted a large number of these ideological stands. Despite a number of harsh reactions at the outset, however, she has made an effort not to let the conflict escalate over the past few years. The nearer a party is to power, the more transnational party contacts have been surrounded by the rites of international politics. The Soviet ambassador, for instance, was frequently present at negotiations between the CPSU and the Italian Communist party.[32] In Third World countries the CPSU has frequently turned its back on brother parties in favour of contact with revolutionary liberation movements.[33]

Despite increasing flexibility, the CPSU still holds instruments for disciplining dissenting brother parties. The CPSU has made more than just a few mistakes here, which have served to reduce willingness to co-operate even further:

1   The CPSU did not take up proposals to organise *joint conferences* to resolve conflicts that had not emanated from the Soviet Union (like the proposals that Togliatti had already made in 1964). Instead, the CPSU always tried to be the party that issued the invitation, even when the conference was to be held outside the Soviet Union.
2   The CPSU failed to *consult* or even just to inform brother parties before taking decisive steps. Prior to the invasion of Czechoslovakia, questions from Communist leaders about rumours of an imminent intervention were all met with evasive denials.[34]
3   The last joint institution, 'The Problems of Peace and Socialism' in Prague, is heavily dominated by Soviet commentators and

functionaries, a facet which has increasingly annoyed the Eurocommunists.[35] Editor-in-chief, Zaradov, (who died in April 1982) ranked alongside Ponomarev (the Head of the International Department of the CPSU Central Committee) as one of the most vehement critics of the trends towards independence in Western Communism.

Brezhnev commented optimistically on these differences of opinion at the XXVI Party Congress. Despite all the varying opinions it would still be possible to develop co-operation to counter the 'general class adversary'. He maintained that the CPSU was no longer setting itself up as a judge of the different opinions, projecting the role of arbitrator on to the future — 'the chief arbitrator in deciding upon outstanding problems will be time and practical experience'.[36] The CPSU was not, however, in the habit of leaving the world movement to develop entirely by itself. The Soviet Union may hold fewer instruments of discipline today than in the Stalin era, but communication, on the other hand, has become more difficult. In the party's early years foreign parties at times attempted to play off the factions within the Soviet party against each other.[37]

Despite this, the CPSU still uses a number of instruments of transnational politics to maintain discipline:

1   The mildest form of attempts at disciplining is *polemics*. This was employed in an extensive campaign against Carrillo's concept of Eurocommunism. For the rest, the Soviet literature generally remains totally silent on Eurocommunism. A picture is painted of an intact world of internationalism and specific features of individual parties are not generalised to cover a whole region.[38] Criticism spares the parties as a whole and personalises the conflict in terms of individual figures (Carrillo, Elleinstein or Paietta). Where it proves impossible to reach a consensus (such as on the internationalism question) a steady flow of formula compromises is put forward. It is acknowledged to the Western Communists that the problems can all be solved in highly differing fashions. In the final instance, however, they will only be resolvable by the 'international working class'.[39] Although the contentious word 'proletarian' is omitted, a less committing term is used to put forward what is essentially the same thesis.

At times relief mechanisms are also applied to explain the ideological deviation of Western parties. 'Imperialist doings' are highlighted — now that it has proved impossible to keep the Communists away from power any longer, attempts are underway to make them renounce their close ties with the CPSU through bringing psychological pressure to bear. In response to these softening-up tactics it is stressed that the Soviet Union does not need to force internationalism on any of its brother parties, since internationalism is founded on 'objective' principles which are evident to all. The Soviet Union is defended against defamation to the effect that she herself has given up internationalism in favour of good relations with bourgeois governments, and it is asserted that the Soviet Union will adhere to internationalism, irrespective of whether it brings her advantages or drawbacks.[40]

2   A harsher form of disciplining is the 'deprival of affection' and *discrimination in international communication*. The CPSU put up with much criticism from the Communist party of Italy without reducing intensive contacts. It was only after the Italian party had been suspected of being the centre of leadership of Eurocommunism and after this had become a familiar catchword worldwide that the CPSU curtailed contacts around 1977.[41] At the XXVI Party Congress in Moscow in 1981, Paietta as the Head of the Italian Communist party delegation was no longer even allowed to read his message of greeting.

3   The most dangerous sanction is *CPSU interference in internal party affairs*. Lower and middle cadres frequently proved to be more orthodox than their leadership. The CPSU has at times successfully attempted to mobilise these cadres against their leadership (Austria 1969/70, Norway 1975). Although the formation of factions (*krugovchina*) and splitting go against the principles of 'democratic centralism' (also since condition of accession No. 12 of the Comintern statutes no longer applies), the CPSU has made use of this instrument to keep a party on course. Official splittings have only been attempted with small parties (Australia 1971, Sweden 1977). In the case of large parties it was feared that the orthodox minority might become isolated (e.g. in Finland).[42] In Spain, Lister was even restrained from founding an opposing party to Carrillo's party in 1970.[43]

4   It is suspected that *rewards* have been made in the form of *financial support*. Since indirect party financing has taken on increasing significance in comparison to direct subsidies (apart from in the Federal German Communist party)[44] and societies that enjoy the sympathy of the Communists have been preferentially involved in East–West trade, this could be taken as a sanction through the threat of a withdrawal of means. Given the obscurity that surrounds financing, however, there are only more or less well-founded assumptions here.[45]

The success of all these means of disciplining is doubtful. Even in the allegedly so 'Finlandised' Finland (see pp. 46–50), the majority of Cómmunists have reacted defiantly to CPSU attempts to bring pressure to bear. The Communist parties of the Western world can no longer simply be presented as the fifth column[46] and the countries of socialist orientation have frequently not remained as docile as Moscow had hoped. Even where relatively good relations were maintained with the Soviet Union, such as in Algeria, no Communist country emerged. The

Soviet model has lost some of its attractiveness, yet Soviet power has increased to such an extent that the CPSU still retains an indirect influence even where parties are inwardly distanced. The spectacular breaks with the CPSU that the West had hoped for have not come about. The CPSU's capacity to engage the services of all Communist parties in the pursuit of her world policy aims, however, has also diminished.

A number of Eurocommunists such as Giorgio Napolitano have thus even maintained that one can no longer speak of an 'international Communist movement',[47] an assumption which would seem to be exaggerated. Western strategies that attempted to counter the advance of the European Communists with quarantine measures (such as in Portugal in the mid 1970s),[48] proved to be just as one-sided. This experience meant that the entry of the French Communist party into Mitterrand's government in 1981 was registered more calmly in America as well. If France follows the pattern of smaller countries (Iceland, Finland), whereby Communists not only enter government but also leave it again in line with the rules of the constitution, then further relaxation will come about in the relationship between Communist parties and the upholding forces of Western democracies. It is not yet possible to estimate the consequences that this will have for the CPSU's transnational politics.

The less important Communist parties have become as an instrument of transnational politics, the greater the significance of the social organisations has become as a point of departure for Soviet foreign policy, although the time is long since past when international federations of social organisations frequently constituted the sole channel between the Soviet Union and a large number of other countries.[49]

Transnational politics through social organisations

In the light of the growing significance being assumed by progressive movements in the restructuring of the international order (see Chapter 1), the social organisations are coming to hold a higher status in foreign policy according to the Soviet doctrine, even if they can no longer be placed in the setting of the Communist world movement.[50] As they become stronger, however, the social organisations are less prepared today than they have been in the past to accept the primacy of leadership by the party. In the First International the trade unions were still included as equal-status members alongside the parties.[51] In the Second International the division of labour between party and trade unions was established under the dominating influence of the German Social Democratic Party, SPD, concealed in ever new formula compromises from Kautsky. Lenin intensified the priority of the party even further within the Communist world movement. The realisation of this leadership by the party, however, frequently led to the Communists being carried into isolation. Not only were national trade union movements split (Finland, France, Italy) but the social democratic and labour-orientated trade unions withdrew from the World Federation of Trade Unions with its head office in Prague and, in December 1949, founded the International Confederation of Free Trade Unions (ICFTU), which was to become considerably more influential in the Western European workers' movement. The American umbrella organisations AFL and CIO provided support in the building up of an anti-Communist counter-organisation in Europe. The Communist world movement's attempt to use its own strength to defeat the non-Communists by a majority of votes backfired.[52] Much to the distress of Soviet observers, the efforts to achieve reunification served the interests of the reformist majority, which also controlled the European Federation of Trade Unions founded in 1973. The biggest predominantly Communist-orientated trade union in the West, namely the Italian CGIL, loosened its ties with the head office in Prague and joined the European Federation. Only France's CGT hung between the blocs for a while, although becoming increasingly inwardly distanced from the Eastern bloc trade unions.[53]

The Soviet Union made allowance for this development by building up her relations with the non-Communist Western trade unions — relations which are strongly emphasised in the new Soviet trade union literature.[54] The Soviet literature is becoming increasingly more cautious with its recommendations to Western trade unions. It frequently treats the 'class struggles', which are still discovered everywhere in the West, in a purely immanent fashion. There is no profession of solidarity with the Eastern trade unions in these confrontations. Only the 'exemplary role of socialism' for the workers' movement fighting in the West is still emphasised.[55] Up to the 1970s the Soviet trade union movement came up against a powerful opponent in its efforts to bring influence to bear — namely the American trade union umbrella association, AFL-CIO. Although the relations between state and trade unions are unusually loose particularly in America, the umbrella association under George Meany constituted such a heavy counterweight in the world trade union movement that it can be doubted as to whether Lenin's concept of trade unions being transmission belts for the will of the party produced maximum success at international level. The Soviet literature has always contained harsh criticism of the influence of the American trade unions with their acute anti-Communism and their dislike of unilateral disarmament proposals. Even the American trade unions, however, were not defined in the Soviet transnational politics strategy as belonging to the 'reactionary camp' and hopes were placed on the progressive circles of a large number of individual trade unions in America.[56]

Since the mid-1970s the Soviet Union has gained increasing influence in a number of international organisations in which trade unions are represented, with the help of a growing number of (at least verbally) radical organisations. The American trade unions even stepped back temporarily within the International Labour Organisation when the PLO gained entry in 1975.[57] In this sphere as well, however, Soviet successes led to the Americans wrongly assessing the situation. Expansion of Soviet influence did not continue within the ILO either. The Soviet trade unions increasingly found themselves in the dock due to the absence of free working conditions in the Soviet Union. When the harsh anti-Communist line of the AFL-CIO was revised following Meany's departure, the mistakes that had led a number of Western trade unions to leave the ground to the socialist countries' trade unions unchallenged were also put right.[58]

Conclusion

After 1917 the Soviet system was not sufficiently prepared for the continued existence of foreign policy in a socialist society. Trotsky, the first Foreign Commissar, had hoped that he would be able to 'shut up shop' after a few revolutionary speeches and, as organiser of the Red Army, preferred to devote himself to the politics of revolution. The fact that the system was confined to socialism in one country, however, made a return to traditional foreign politics necessary. Instead of classical diplomacy dying out in the Soviet Union, the country went on to develop the most powerful foreign policy machinery of the world.

There was no foreign policy theory available for a world in which, contrary to all forecasts, capitalism remained dominant. Lenin's imperialism theory was at best a sectoral substitute and was not easy to translate into concrete foreign policy action. This shortfall on the theory side only came to be balanced out to some extent when the Soviet Union developed into a world power and scientific political consultation was expanded. The 'relative strength of forces in the world' and the 'reshaping of international relations' figure at the centre of the Soviet doctrine today. The makers of foreign policy in Moscow are increasingly trimming the horizon of their expectations. Although the party programme, the constitution and the Party Congress speeches still contain ideological statements about the further development of world society, and the ideology by no means serves simply to cloak purely national power interests, as has frequently been assumed in the West, practical politics is becoming increasingly orientated towards individual analyses involving a high level of expertise and fundamental concepts that are becoming increasingly capable of generating consensus between East and West (see Chapter 1).

The foreign policy decision-making process has become more pluralist than earlier totalitarianism theoreticians held to be possible. This is at most a consultative pluralism, however, at the top echelons of an authoritarian regime, in which only a few élite sectors are involved with any influence. The foreign policy machinery and its top leadership gained increasing weight during the 1970s. The institutional seat of sovereignty, however, remained the Politburo of the party. The quality of Soviet diplomats has risen. Western negotiators acknowledge a growing competence on the part of their Soviet opponents. The technical, scientific revolution, which is playing a growing role in Soviet portrayals of the driving forces behind socialism, is reflected in clear improvements to cadre training and political consultation through scientific expertise (see Chapter 2).

The East–West conflict enjoys a lesser rating in Soviet systematics than in the Western literature. Although the terminology is different, the same exaggerated bipolar thinking as in Western systems emerges. The image presented of the Western world is becoming more differentiated. Despite a fair number of propaganda campaigns, the image that the population holds of Western countries is more positive on many points than the attitude of Western populations to the Soviet Union. In the 1970s there was a far-reaching change in the assessment of the USA's allies in the Soviet literature, particularly as far as the Federal Republic of Germany was concerned (see Chapter 3).

The Soviet concern for security, which stems from her historical experiences and the fear of threat from four potential enemies (USA, Western Europe, China, Japan), would appear to be exaggerated in objective terms, although it is understandable from a subjective viewpoint. The more differentiated view of 'balance' is new to Moscow. Instances of sectoral imbalance are no longer denied in such a blanket fashion as previously.

In view of the substantial increase in Soviet initiatives on disarmament policy it is frequently not easy to distinguish between tactical propagandist proposals and proposals that are meant to be taken seriously. Those proposals from the Soviet Union that are designed to be taken seriously still show a lack of sensitivity on the part of Moscow for the pluralism of the Western world and for the different security interests of the USA's allies, although the Soviet Union frequently tries to create divisions in the Western camp by holding up national interests. The vicious circle of the arms spiral, which has hardly been made any more transparent by the contradictory information from quantitative research into military potential in East and West, will presumably only be broken in the long term if the West accepts the sufficiency principle (see Chapter 4).

East–West relations in the economic sphere — and a both short-sighted and unsuccessful embargo policy pursued against the socialist countries by the USA — shows that not all the Soviet Union's feelings of inferiority are unfounded. Apart from in the military field, the Soviet Union has not been able to catch up on the West's lead in either the economic sphere or in culture and its role as a social model. The negative influence that this has had on the exaggerated endeavours in the sole area in which equal status has been more or less achieved, does not suggest a conflict strategy for the West (see Chapter 5).

The expansion of the socialist camp has been bought at the cost of growing differences of opinion with 'real socialism'. The Soviet Union can no longer demonstrate her hegemonial position within the Council for Mutual Economic Aid and the Warsaw Pact in the same way as previously. Despite (or, indeed, because of) the Soviet Union's preponderance of military and economic power, there are more limited boundaries on the integration of socialist countries than in regional groupings in the West — boundaries that are made even more rigid by the specific nature of socialist planned economies (see Chapter 6).

Today Soviet foreign policy is focusing its greatest efforts to expand the power of the socialist camp on relations with the Third World. The Soviet Union has only been able to gain a regional controlling influence in military aid. Progress in economic relations and development aid is limited and problems with foreign exchange on a world scale mean that there is little prospect of the Soviet Union achieving sizeable breakthroughs. Soviet diplomacy has achieved major successes in some regions of the Third World (South-East Asia, India, Africa) but these successes have generally been helped on by serious errors in American foreign policy and have frequently proved not to be lasting once the Americans have revised their policy. More lasting successes have often been downgraded for the Soviets through losses in adjacent regions. The Soviet Union has avoided becoming engaged in a direct confrontation with American military power in any region of the world (see Chapter 7).

Even the additional potential of Communist parties in the West and the Third World, which was intended to serve the Soviet Union as a lever to achieve advantages for Moscow through transnational politics, has not worked out to be so favourable for the 'Fatherland of Socialism' as the West had once feared. Centrifugal tendencies and specific, national endeavours within Communist parties have contributed towards a growing criticism of the Soviet Union. It would seem doubtful whether a Communist world movement, in the sense of an institution securely steered from Moscow, can still be held to exist (see Chapter 8).

All in all, the West has reason to be alert in the face of Soviet initiatives but no justification for panicky over-reactions to each and every Soviet move. A clear-cut definition of the West's own vital interests is necessary in order to avoid conflict, and these have generally been respected by Soviet actors in the past. In the case of the stealthy penetration of Afghanistan, which was underway even prior to the socialist coup at the end of the 1970s, this was not the case — to the detriment of world peace (see Chapter 4, pp. 51–77).

The rise of a new power, which calls for equal status within the circle of great powers, was scarcely ever achieved without warlike confrontations up to the Second World War in the classic system of balance. Given the nuclear threat that hangs over the existence of the whole world, opposite numbers in the West will have to accept the equalising moves of the new Soviet world power in a loosely-knit bipolar world system with greater tolerance than has been the custom in the history of states to date. It is just before and just after the equalising move by a new world power that the danger of armed conflict is greatest. It was not without a willingness on the part of the Soviets to make concessions in the four large crises which led to the brink of war that the first era has already been mastered (see Chapter 3, pp. 35–50). The challenges of the second great era of crises still await the world.

Notes

Introduction

1 U. Schmiederer: *Die Außenpolitik der Sowjetunion*, Stuttgart, Kohlhammer, 1980.

2 On the immanent approach, V. Gransow: *Konzeptionelle Wandlungen der Kommunismusforschung. Vom Totalitarismus zur Immanenz*, Frankfurt, Campus, 1980, p. 160f.

3 On the methodology of these comparisons, J. Hough: 'The Comparative Approach and the Study of the Soviet Union', in J. Hough *The Soviet Union and Social Science Theory*, Cambridge/ Mass., Harvard UP, 1977, pp. 222–239; K. von Beyme: *Economics and Politics within Socialist Systems. A Comparative and Developmental Approach*, New York, Praeger, 1982, pp. 4ff.

Chapter 1

1 W. Zimmerman: *Soviet Perspectives on International Relations 1956–1967*, Princeton UP, 1969, p. 203

2 E. A. Pozdnjakov: *Sistemnoi podchod i mezhdunarodnye otnosheniya* Moscow, Nauka, 1976.

3 D. V. Ermolenko: *Sotsiologiya i problemy mezhdunarodnykh otnoshenii*, Moscow, MO, 1977, p. 18.

4 V. V. Kravcenko: *Obshchestvennye organizatsii SSSR na mezhdunarodnoj arene*, Moscow, MO, 1969, p. 98.

5   D. Geyer (ed.): *Osteuropa-Handbuch. Sowjetunion. Außenpolitik*, Cologne; Böhlau, 1972, vol. 1, p. 51.

6   H. Ticktin: in E. Jahn (ed.), *Sozioökonomische Bedingungen der sowjetischen Außenpolitik*, Frankfurt, Campus, 1975, pp. 66ff.

7   H. Adomeit and R. Boardman (eds): *Foreign Policy Making in Communist Countries*, Westmead, Saxon House, 1979, p. 21.

8   G. F. Kennan: in C. J. Friedrich (ed.) *Totalitarianism*, New York, Grosset & Dunlap, 1964, p. 35; R. C. Tucker: *The Soviet Political Mind: Studies in Stalinism and Post-Stalin Change*, New York, Norton, 1963.

9   M. D. Shulman: *Stalin's Foreign Policy Reappraised*, Cambridge/Mass., Harvard UP, 1963, p. 3.

10   B. Meissner: Triebkräfte und Faktoren der sowjetischen Außenpolitik', in B. Meissner and G. Rhode (eds), *Grundfragen sowjetischer Außenpolitik*, Stuttgart, Kohlhammer, 1970 (9–40), p. 30.

11   D. Geyer: 'Voraussetzungen sowjetischer Außenpolitik in der Zwischenkriegszeit', in *idem* (ed.): *Sowjetunion. Außenpolitik 1917–1955*, Cologne, Böhlau, 1972 (1–85), p. 51.

12   J. L. Nogee and R. H. Donaldson: *Soviet Foreign Policy since World War II*, Oxford, Pergamon Press, 1981, p. 5.

13   S. I. Ploss: 'Studying the Domestic Determinants of Soviet Foreign Policy', in P. Hoffmann and F. J. Fleron (eds), *The Conduct of Soviet Foreign Policy*, New York, Aldine, 1980 (76–90), p. 78.

14   I. P. Blischenko: *Vneshnie funktsii sotsialisticheskogo gosudarstva*, Moscow, Jurlit, 1971, pp. 63ff.

15   cf. *Sowjetunion 1978/79. Herausgegeben vom Bundesinstitut für ostwissenschaftliche und internationale Studien*, Munich, Hanser, 1979, p. 198.

16   B. Meissner and G. Rhode (eds): *Grundfragen sowjetischer Außenpolitik*, Stuttgart, Kohlhammer, 1970, p. 16.

17   J. Krassin: *Revolution und sozialer Fortschritt*, Moscow, Progress, 1980, p. 289.

18   E. A. Pozdnjakov: *Sistemnoi podchod i mezhdunarodnye otnosheniya*, Moscow, Nauka, 1976, p. 155.

19   F. Burlatzky: 'The Modelling of International Relations' in Soviet Political Sciences Association, *International Relations: Trends and Prospects*, Moscow, USSR Academy of Sciences, 1982 (78–88), p. 79.

20   P. Fridesh: *Sotsialisticheskaya vneshnyaya politika*, Moscow, Progress, 1978, p. 10 (Translation from Hungarian); Yuzef Kukulka: *Problemy teorii mezhdunarodnykh otnoshenii*. Moscow, Progress, 1980 (Translation from Polish).

21   B. N. Ponomarev (ed.): *Konstitutsiya SSSR. Politiko-pravovoi kommentarii*, Moscow, Politizdat, 1982, p. 110.

22   Krassin, op. cit. (note 17), p. 286.

23   *MEW* Vol. 13, p. 640.
24   Krassin, op. cit. (note 17), p. 287 f.
25   W. Geierhos: *Das Kräfteverhältnis. Die neue Globalstrategie der Sowjetunion*, Lüneburg, Ost-Akademie, 1980, p. 13.
26   W. Zimmerman, op. cit. (note 1), p. 159f.
27   G. Shachnazarov: 'K probleme sootnosheniya sil vo mire', *Kommunist*, 1974, No. 3, pp. 77–89; G. Shachnazarov: 'Neue Faktoren in der Politik von heute', *Gesellschaftswissenschaften* 1977, No. 1, pp. 43–56. Shortened version in *Osteuropa-Archiv*, Sep 1977, pp. 501–506.
28   St. Tiedtke: *Rüstungskontrolle aus sowjetischer Sicht*, Frankfurt, Campus, 1980, p. 35.
29   G. Shachnazarov: 'Matematicheskie metody izucheniya mezhdunarodnykh otnoshenii', *SI*, 1981, No. 1, p. 102f; J. M. Baturin: 'Problemy modelirovaniya mezhdunarodnykh otnoshenii, *SI*, 1981, (103–110), p. 108.
30   G. Shachnazarov: *Futurology Fiasco. A Critical Study of Non-Marxist Concepts of How Society Develops.* Moscow, Progress, 1982, p. 128; idem: *Sotsializm i budushchee*, Moscow, Nauka, 1983.
31   G. Shachnazarov: 'Peace and Mankind's vital needs', op. cit. (note 19) (28–49), p. 35.
32   A. A. Gromyko (ed.): *Diplomatiya stran sotsializma*, Moscow, MO, 1980, p. 178.
33   'Liefert Moskau Argentinien informationen über den britischen Flottenverband?' *FAZ* 15. 4. 1982, p. 1.
34   G. Shachnazarov: *Gradushchii miroporyadok*, Moscow, Politizdat, 1981, p. 9.
35   Shachnazarov, op. cit. (note 34), p. 32f.
36   Shachnazarov, op. cit. (note 30), p. 60ff.
37   Burlatzsky, op. cit. (note 19), 1982, p. 86.
38   cf. A. Dallin: 'The Domestic Sources of Soviet Foreign Policy' in S. Bialer (ed.), *The Domestic Context of Soviet Foreign Policy*, London, Croom Helm, 1981 (335–408), p. 337.
39   V. Aleksandrov: 'Fundamental'nye printsipy vneshnej politiki sotsializma', *Mezhdunarodnaya zhizn'*, 1980, No. 4 (13–22), p. 22.
40   cf. A. Ulam: 'Russian Nationalism', in Bialer, op. cit. (note 38), 1981 (3–17), p. 7.
41   Meissner, op. cit. (note 10), 1970, p. 16.
42   cf. 'Triebkraft', in *Kleines Wörterbuch der Marxistisch-Leninistischen Philosophie*, Berlin, Dietz, 1974, p. 282f.
43   S. N. Morozov (ed.): *Gegemonizm: s epochoi v konflikte*, Moscow, Progress, 1982, p. 5.
44   F. Griffiths: 'Ideological Development and Foreign Policy', in Bialer, op. cit. (note 38), 1981 (19–48), p. 37.

45   G. A. Arbatow: *Der sowjetische Standpunkt. Über die Westpolitik der UdSSR*, Munich, Rogner & Bernhard, 1981, p. 120.
46   G. A. Arbatov: *Ideologicheskaya bor'ba v sovremennykh mezhdunarodnykh otnosheniyakh*, Moscow, Politizdat, 1970, *passim*.
47   B. N. Ponomarev: Izbrannoe. Rechi i stat'i, Moscow, Politizdat, 1977.
48   Griffiths, op. cit. (note 44), p. 20.
49   B. Meissner: 'Außenpolitik auf dem Parteitag der KPdSU', *Außenpolitik*, 1981, No. 2 (129–144), p. 131.
50   Meissner op. cit. (note 49), p. 132.
51   R. Axelrodt and W. Zimmerman: 'The Soviet Press on Soviet Foreign Policy: A Usually Reliable Source', *BJPolS*, 1981 (183–200), p. 200.
52   C. H. Lüders: 'Ideologie und Machtdenken in der sowjetischen Außenpolitik', *APuZG*, B 37/1981 (3–38), p. 37.
53   D. V. Ermolenko: *Sotsiologiya i problemy mezhdunarodnykh otnoshenii*, Moscow, MO, 1977, pp. 88, 109.
54   H. Adomeit: *Die Sowjetmacht in internationalen Krisen und Konflikten*, Baden-Baden, Nomos, 1983, p. 446.
55   J. L. Nogee and R. H. Donaldson: *Soviet Foreign Policy since World War II*, New York, Pergamon, 1981, p. 38.

Chapter 2

1   E. Krippendorff: in E. Jahn (ed.), *Sozioökonomische Bendingungen der sowjetischen Außenpolitik*, Frankfurt, Campus, 1975, p. 49.
2   Ticktin: in Jahn, op. cit. (note 1), 1975, p. 66.
3   M. Voslensky: *Nomenklatura. Die herrschende Klasse der Sowjetunion*, Vienna, Molden, 1980, p. 411.
4   E. Schneider: 'Die zentrale politische Führungselite der UdSSR', part 1, *BioSt* 14/1982, pp. 15ff.
5   J. F. Hough: *Soviet Leadership in Transition*, Washington, Brookings, 1980, p. 110.
6   B. Meissner: 'Parteiführung, Parteiorganisation und soziale Struktur der KPdSU', *OE*, 1981 (732–768), p. 758.
7   I. I. Pronin: *Rukovodashchie kadry: Podbor, rasstanovka i vospitanie*, Moscow, Mysl', 1981, pp. 158ff; *Partinoe stroitel'stvo*. Moscow, Politizdat, 1981, pp. 272ff.
8   Willy Brandt: 'Breschnew: Vertrauensvolle Gegnerschaft', *Der Spiegel*, 46/1982, p. 148f; H. Kissinger: *White House Years*, Boston, Little Brown, 1979, p. 113.
9   B. Meissner: 'Der auswärtige Dienst der UdSSR', *Außenpolitik*, 1977, No. 1 (49–64), p. 48.

10 V. A. Zorin: *Osnovy diplomaticheskoi sluzhby*, Moscow, MO, 1977, 2. ed., p. 126.

11 Meissner, op. cit. (note 10), p. 55f; B. Meissner: Das aussen- und sicherheitspolitische Entscheidungssystem der Sowjetunion', *APuZG*, B 43, 1983, pp. 31–45.

12 Zorin, op. cit. (note 10), 1977, p. 107.

13 cf. K. von Beyme: *Der sowjetische Föderalismus*, Heidelberg, Quelle & Meyer, 1964, p. 40f.

14 Legal sources in N. V. Mironov: *Pravovoe regulirovanie vneshnikh snoshenii SSSR 1917–1970 gg*, Moscow, MO, 1971, pp. 231ff.

15 R. Bernhardt: *Der Abschluß völkerrechtlicher Verträge im Bundesstaat*, Cologne, Kiepenheuer & Witsch, 1957, p. 20.

16 S. R. Vikharev: 'Soyuznaya respublika kak sub"ekt mezhdunarodnogo prava', *SGiP*, 1960, No. 6, pp. 65–73.

17 *Dokumenty vneshnei politiki SSSR*, Moscow, Politizdat, Vol. 1, 1957, p. 345 f.

18 op. cit. (note 17), Vol. 7, 1963, p. 397.

19 Leon Trotsky: *Mein Leben*, Berlin, Fischer, 1930, p. 282f.

20 G. V. Chicherin: *Stat"i i reci po voprosam mezhdunarodnoi politiki*, Moscow, Izdatel'stvo sotsial'no-ekonomicheskoi literatury, 1961, p. 276.

21 V. I. Lenin: '*Wie wir die Arbeiter- und Bauerninspektion reorganisieren sollen*', *Ausgewählte Werke*, Berlin, Dietz, Vol. 3, p. 468.

22 Quoted in I. Gorochow *et al.*: *G. W. Tschitscherin. Ein Diplomat Leninscher Schule*, Berlin, Deutscher Verlag der Wissenschaften, 1976, p. 143.

23 R. M. Slusser: 'The Role of the Foreign Ministry', in I. J. Lederer (ed.), *Russian Foreign Policy*, New Haven, Yale UP, 1962 (197–239), p. 227.

24 Geyer, op. cit., 1972, p. 15.

25 T. J. Uldricks: 'The Impact of the Great Purges on the People's Commisariat of Foreign Affairs', *Slavic Review*, June 1977 (187–203), p. 188f.

26 I. Ehrenburg: *The Post-War Years 1945–1954*, London, McCosh, 1967, p. 277.

27 T. J. Uldricks: The Soviet Diplomatic Corps in the Chicherin Era. *Jahrbücher für die Geschichte Osteuropas*, 1975, 213–224.

28 V. Mićunović: *Moscow Diary*, London, Chatto & Windus, 1980, p. 23.

29 cf. M. Schwartz: *The Foreign Policy of the USSR: Domestic Factors*, Encina/Ca., Dickenson, 1975, p. 172f.

30 Sir W. Hayter: *The Diplomacy of the Great Powers*, New York, Macmillan, 1961, p. 23f.

31   J. D. Beam: *Multiple Exposure: An American Ambassador's Unique Perspective on East–West-Issues*, New York, Norton, 1978, p. 228.

32   H. Kroll: *Lebenserinnerungen eines Botschafters*, Cologne, Kiepenheuer & Witsch, 1967, pp. 363–75.

33   G. A. Craig: 'Techniques of Negotiation', in I. Lederer (ed.), *Russian Foreign Policy*, New Haven, Yale UP, 1966 (351–373), p. 372.

34   Soviet Diplomacy, op. cit., 1979, p. 498.

35   Leon Trotsky: *Mein Leben*, Berlin, Fischer, 1930, p. 354.

36   Clark, op. cit., p. 229.

37   H. Allardt: *Politik vor und hinter den Kulissen. Erfahrungen eines Diplomaten zwischen Ost und West*, Düsseldorf, Econ, 1979, p. 269.

38   Allardt, op. cit. (note 37), p. 274.

39   R. Axelrodt and W. Zimmerman: 'The Soviet Press on Soviet Foreign Policy: A Usually Reliable Source', *BJPolS*, 1981, pp. 183–200.

40   cf. T. Kirstein: 'Die Konsultation Außenstehender' durch die politischen Entscheidungsgremien in der Sowjetunion' in B. Meissner and G. Brunner (eds.) *Gruppeninteressen und Entscheidungsprozeß in der Sowjetunion*, Cologne, Wissenschaft und Politik, 1975 (61–77), p. 75f.

41   A. Z. Rubinstein: *The Soviets in International Organizations*, Princeton UP, 1964, pp. 262ff.

42   S. A. Kuznetsov: *Predstaviteli gosudarstv v mezhdunarodnykh organizatsiyakh*, Moscow, MO, 1980, p. 87; M. V. Mitrofanov: *Sluzhashchie mezhdunarodnykh organizatsii*. Moscow, MO, 1981, pp. 79ff.

43   E. Clark: *Corps Diplomatique*, London, Allen Lane, 1973, p. 232.

44   Ju. Kashlev: *Massovaya informatsiya i mezhdunarodnye otnosheniya*, Moscow, MO, 1981, p. 201.

45   P. Hübner: Prioritäten der sowjetischen kulturellen Außenpolitik heute', *BioSt*, 1982, No. 21, pp. 15ff.

46   Bogomolov, op. cit. 1977, p. 250.

47   Beam, op. cit. (note 31), 1978, p. 233f.

48   F. C. Barghoorn: *The Soviet Culture Offensive. The Role of Cultural Diplomacy in Soviet Foreign Policy*, Princeton UP, 1960, p. 336.

49   Chruschtschow, op. cit., 1971, p. 522.

50   Hübner op. cit. (note 45), 1982, p. 29f.

51   Quoted in Gorochow, op. cit. (note 22), 1976, p. 138.

52   Meissner and Brunner, op. cit. (note 40) p. 62f.

53   J. H. Barton and L. D. Weiler (ed.): *International Arms Control*, Stanford University Press, 1976, p. 92.

54   *Lenin Werke*, Vol. 31, p. 66.
55   K. von Beyme: *Die politische Elite in der BRD*, Munich, Piper, ²1974, pp. 162ff.
56   S. L. Tichvinski *et al* (ed.): *Vneshnyaya politika i diplomatiya zarubezhnykh stran*, Moscow, MO, 1981, p. 6.
57   D. V. Ermolenko: *Sotsiologiya i problemy mezhdunarodnykh otnoshenii*. Moscow, MO, 1977, p. 88.
58   V. Petrov: *Formation of Soviet Foreign Policy*, Orbis, Fall, 1973 (819–850), p. 841. Soviet Diplomacy, op. cit., 1979, p. 404f.
59   cf. K. Meyer: 'Wissenschaftspolitik', in O. Anweiler and K. H. Ruffmann (eds.), *Kulturpolitik der Sowjetunion*, Stuttgart, Kröner, 1973 (145–189), p. 160.
60   cf. R. Hill: *Soviet Politics, Political Science and Reform*, London, M. Robertson, 1980, pp. 168 ff.
61   G. Ch. Shachnazarov (ed.): *Sovremennaya burzhuaznaya politicheskaya nauka: Problemy gosudarstva i demokratii*, Moscow, Nauka, 1982.
62   Hough, op. cit. (note 5), 1980, p. 118.
63   *XX s"ezda Kommunisticheskoi partii Sovetskogo Soyuza Stenograficheskii otchet*, Moscow, Politizdat, 1956, 1, p. 323.
64   W. Zimmerman: *Soviet Perspectives on International Relations 1956–1967*, Princeton UP, 1969, pp. 38, 57.
65   'Deyatel'nost' nauchnykh uchrezhdenii Akademii Nauk SSSR v oblasti issledovanii problem mira i razoruzheniya', in *Mir i razoruzhenie*, Moscow, Nauka, 1980, pp. 174–205.
66   H. G. Brauch: *Abrüstungsamt oder Ministerium? Ausländische Modelle der Abrüstungsplanung*, Frankfurt, Haag & Herchen, 1981, p. 295.
67   Hough, op. cit. (note 5), 1980, p. 123.
68   E. Clark: *Corps Diplomatique*, London, Allen Lane, 1973, pp. 184, 192.
69   O. Eran: *Mezhdunarodniki. An Assessment of Professional Expertise in the Making of Soviet Foreign Policy*, Tel Aviv, Turtledove Publishing, 1979, p. 238f.
70   *MEiMO*, No. 5, 1971, p. 24.
71   R. V. Daniels: *Das Gewissen der Revolution. Kommunistische Opposition*, Cologne, Kiepenheuer & Witsch, 1962, pp. 470ff.
72   A. Dallin: 'Soviet Foreign Policy and Domestic Politics: A Framework for Analysis', in E. P. Hoffmann and F. J. Fleron (eds), *The Conduct of Soviet Foreign Policy*, New York, Aldine, 1980 (36–49), p. 45.
73   C. G. Pendill: 'Bipartisanship' in Soviet Foreign Policy-Making', in: Hoffmann and Fleron, op. cit. (note 72), (61–75), p. 74.

74   K. von Beyme: 'Gesellschaftliche Organisationen und Interessen-pluralismus in der Sowjetunion', in R. Löwenthal and B. Meissner (eds), *Sowjetische Innenpolitik. Triebkräfte und Tendenzen*, Stuttgart, Kohlhammer, 1968, pp. 39–48.

75   N. S. Khruschev: *Für dauerhaften Frieden und friedliche Koexistenz*, Berlin, 1959, p. 56.

76   *FAZ*, 30. 10. 1964; B. Meissner: 'Der Entscheidungsprozeß in der Kreml-Führung unter Stalin und seinen Nachfolgern und die Rolle der Parteibürokratie', in Meissner and Brunner (eds), op. cit. (note 40), (21–60), p. 40f.

77   *UPI* 15.6.1973, cf. Meissner and Brunner, op. cit. (note 40), p. 49.

78   Meissner and Brunner (eds), op. cit. (note 40), p. 53.

79   R. Rotermundt *et al. Die Sowjetunion und Europa. Gesellschaftsform und Außenpolitik der UdSSR*, Frankfurt, Campus, 1979, p. 107.

80   G. Józs: 'Politische Seilschaften in der Sowjetunion', *BioSt*, 1981, No. 31.

81   J. Löwenhardt: *Decision Making in Soviet Politics*, London, Macmillan, 1981, pp. 86, 91; H. G. Skilling and F. Griffiths: *Interest groups in Soviet Politics*, Princeton UP, 1971, pp. 27ff.

82   H. Nolte: *Gruppeninteressen und Außenpolitik*, Göttingen, Musterschmidt, 1979, p. 120.

83   *Pravda*, 10.3.1963, cf. Meissner and Brunner, op. cit. (note 40), p. 39.

84   H. Adomeit: 'Soviet Foreign Policy Making: The Internal Mechanism of Global Commitment', in H. Adomeit and P. Boardman (eds), *Foreign Policy Making in Communist Countries*, Westmead, Saxon House, 1979 (15–48), p. 34.

85   cf. A. von Borcke: 'Wie expansionistisch ist das Sowjetregime? Westliche Perzeptionen und östliche Realitäten', *BioSt*, 1981, No. 6, p. v.

86   G. Brunner: *Politische Soziologie der UdSSR*, Wiesbaden, Akademische Verlagsanstalt, 1977, Part 2, p. 154.

87   K. F. Spielmann: 'Defense Industrialists in the USSR', in D. R. Herspring and I. Volgyes (eds): *Civil-Military Relations in Communist Systems*, Boulder, Westview, 1978 (105–122), p. 108; E. L. Warner III: *The Military in Contemporary Soviet Politics. An Institutional Analysis*. New York, Praeger, 1977, pp. 20ff.

88   J. Valenta: 'Soviet Decisionmaking and the Czechoslovak Crisis of 1968', *StiCC*, 1975 (147–180), p. 168.

89   A. von Borcke: 'Die sowjetische Interventionsentscheidung: Eine Fallstudie zum Verhältnis sowjetischer Außen- und Innenpolitik', in H. Vogel (ed.), *Die sowjetische Intervention in Afghanistan*, Baden-Baden, Nomos, 1980 (119–180), p. 155.

90 M. Checinski: 'Die Militärelite im sowjetischen Entscheidung-sprozeß'. *BioSt*, 1981, No. 3, p. 11ff.

91 Kolkowicz: In: Skilling and Griffith, op. cit., 1971, p. 151.

92 *XXII S"ezd Kommunisticheskoi Partii Sovetskogo Soyuza*, Moscow Politizdat, 1962, Vol. 3, p. 67.

93 T. J. Colton: *Commissars, Commanders, and Civilian Authority. The Structure of Soviet Military Politics*, Cambridge/Mass., Harvard UP, 1979, p. 178f.

94 R. Kolkowicz: *The Soviet Military and the Communist Party*, Princeton UP, 1967, p. 27.

95 W. E. Odom: 'The Party–Military Connection' in D. R. Herspring and I. Volgyes (eds), *Civil–Military Relations in Communist Systems*, Boulder, Westview, 1978, pp. 27–52. idem, op. cit., 1979, p. 279.

96 K. von Beyme: *Ökonomie und Politik im Sozialismus*, Munich, Piper, 1975, 1977, pp. 342ff.

97 V. Bunce: *Do New Leaders Make a Difference? Executive Succession and Public Policy under Capitalism and Socialism*, Princeton UP, 1981, pp. 146ff.

98 Borcke, op. cit. (note 89), 1980, p. 130

99 M. Morozov: *Die Falken des Kreml. Die sowjetische Militärmacht von 1917 bis heute*, Munich, Langen-Müller, 1982, p. 393.

100 Checinski, op. cit. (note 90), 1981, p. 18.

101 Kissinger, op. cit. (note 8), 1979, p. 1139.

102 *Chruschtschow erinnert sich*, Reinbek, Rowohlt, 1971, p. 520.

103 F. C. Barghoorn: 'Die Sicherheitspolizei', In Skilling and Griffith, op. cit., 1974, (95–127), p. 114.

Chapter 3

1 W. Geierhos: *Das Kräfteverhältnis. Die neue Globalstrategie der Sowjetunion*. Lüneburg, Ost–Akademie, 1980, p. 36.

2 N. V. Sivachev and N. N. Yakovlev: *Russia and the United States. US–Soviet Relations from the Soviet Point of View*, Chicago UP, 1979, p. 255.

3 O. Bykov *et al: The Priorities of Soviet Foreign Policy Today*, Moscow, Progress, 1981, p. 20.

4 A. Z. Rubinstein: *Soviet Foreign Policy since World War II*, Cambridge/Mass., Winthrop, 1981, p. 272.

5 V. A. Zorin: *Osnovy diplomaticheskoi sluzhby*, Moscow, MO, 1977, p. 62.

6 Rubinstein, op. cit. (note 4), p. 272.

7 P. H. Nitze: 'Assuring Strategic Stability in an Era of Detente', *Foreign Affairs*, Jan. 1976, p. 217f.

8   H. S. Dinerstein: *Fifty Years of Soviet Foreign Policy*, Baltimore, J. Hopkins UP, 1968, p. 7.

9   V. Mastny: *Russia's Road to the Cold War. Diplomacy, Warfare and the Politics of Communism, 1941–1945*, New York, Columbia UP, 1979, *passim*.

10   I. M. Maiski: *Memoiren eines sowjetischen Botschafters*, Berlin Das europäische Buch, 1967, p. 807.

11   W. Link: *Der Ost–West-Konflikt*, Stuttgart, Kohlhammer, 1980, p. 104.

12   M. Djilas: *Gespräche mit Stalin*, Frankfurt, Fischer, 1962, p. 230.

13   E. M. Kennedy and H. O. Hatfield: *Freeze! How you can help prevent Nuclear War*, New York, Bantam Books, 1982, p. 99.

14   T. B. Millar: *The East–West Strategic Balance*, London, Allen & Unwin, 1981, p. 54.

15   W. Eichwede: *Revolution und internationale Politik, Zur kommunistischen Interpretation der kapitalistischen Welt, 1921–1925*, Cologne, Böhlau, 1971, p. 7.

16   E. Varga: *Die Krise des Kapitalismus und ihre politischen Folgen*, Frankfurt, EVA, 1969, pp. 426ff.

17   Ch. W. Kegley and P. McGowan (eds): *Foreign Policy USA–USSR*, London, Sage, 1982, p. 105.

18   A. L. George and R. Smoke: *Deterrence in American Foreign Policy*, New York, Columbia UP, 1974, pp. 504ff.

19   W. Korpi: 'Conflict, Power and Relative Deprivation', *APSR*, 1974, pp. 1569–1578.

20   Link, op. cit. (note 11), p. 161.

21   Th. B. Larson: *Soviet American Rivalry*, New York, Norton, 1978, p. 117.

22   G. Schweigler: 'Spannung und Entspannung: Reaktionen der Öffentlichkeit im Westen', in J. Füllenbach and E. Schulz (eds), *Entspannung am Ende?* Munich, Oldenbourg, 1980 (71–105), p. 93.

23   Schweigler, op. cit. (note 22), pp. 98, 103.

24   R. Inglehart and J.-R. Rabier. *Trust between Nationalities, Proximity, Projection, Historical Experience and Ease of Communication*, IPSA Congress, Rio, 1982, Appendix B.

25   *Chruschtschow erinnert sich*, Reinbek, Rowohlt, 1971, p. 520.

26   W. Brandt: 'Breschnew: Vertrauensvolle Gegnerschaft', *Der Spiegel*, 1982, No. 46, p. 149.

27   A. Dallin: 'Die Vereinigten Staaten aus der Perspektive der Sowjets' in Ch. Bertram et al. *Sowjetmacht der 80er Jahre*, Munich, Bernard & Graefe, 1981 (39–60), p. 43.

28   G. N. Bazenov: *SSSR – SShA: Delovoe sotrudnichestvo*, Moscow, MO, 1978; G. V. Ignatenko: *Razryadka i mezhdunarodnye dogovory*, Moscow, MO, 1978, pp. 51ff.

29   W. Zimmerman: *Soviet Perspectives on International Relations, 1956–1967*, Princeton UP, 1969, p. 215.

30   A. A. Kokoshin: *SShA: za fasadom global'noi politiki. Vnutrennie faktory formirovaniya vneshnei politiki amerikanskogo imperializma na poroge 80–kh godov*, Moscow, Politizdat, 1981.

31   I. M. Krasnov (ed.): *Sovetskii Soyuz glazami amerikantsev*, Moscow, Mysl', 1979, p. 36.

32   M. Schwartz: *Soviet Perceptions of the United States*, Berkeley, Univ. of California Press, 1978, p. 88f.

33   D. B. Petrov: *'Amerikanizm': ideologicheskii rakurs* Moscow, Mysl', 1980, p. 105.

34   G. A. Deborin *et al: Razryadka protiv antirazryadki*, Moscow, Politizdat, 1982, p. 147.

35   J. Laloy: 'Westeuropa aus der sowjetischen Perspektive', in Bertram *et al.*, op. cit. (note 27), 1981 (61–78), p. 61.

36   N. Lebedev: 'O klassovoj prirode mirnogo sosushchestvovaniya', *Kommunist*, 1975, No. 4 (52–62).

37   Ch. Royen: *Die sowjetische Koexistenzpolitik gegenüber Westeuropa*, Baden-Baden, Nomos, 1978, pp. 23ff.

38   B. P. Mirosnichenko *et al.* (ed.): *Vneshnyaya politika Sovetskogo Sojuza. Aktual'nye problemy*, Moscow, MO, 1967, p. 182f.

39   V. I. Popov *et al.* (ed.): *Vneshnyaya politika Sovetskogo Soyuza*, Moscow, Politizdat, 1978, pp. 201ff.

40   Popov, op. cit. (note 39), p. 243.

41   K. I. Spidchenko (ed.): *Politicheskaya i voennaya geografiya*, Moscow, Voennoe Izdatel'stvo, 1980, p. 171.

42   A. A. Gromyko and B. N. Ponomarev (ed.): *Soviet Foreign Policy, 1945–1980*, Moscow, Progress, 1981, p. 483.

43   G. A. Deborin *et al.*, op. cit. (note 34), p. 159; A. A. Kovalev: *Frantsiya na pereput'yakh mirovoi politiki*, Moscow, MO, 1983, pp. 149ff.

44   Spidchenko, op. cit. (note 41), pp. 155, 162, 222.

45   G. A. Vorontsov: *SShA zapadnaya Evropa*, Moscow, MO, 1979, p. 220.

46   N. N. Inozemtsev: *Leninskii kurs mezhdunarodnoi politiki KPSS*, Moscow Mysl', 1978, p. 111; V. G. Trukhanovskii and N. K. Kapitonova: *Sovetsko–Angliiskie otnosheniya, 1945–1978*, Moscow, MO, 1979, pp. 5–11.

47   V. A. Ryzikov: *SSSR — Velikobritanniya: razvitie otnoshenii 60–70e gody*, Moscow, MO, 1977, p. 78.

48   V. N. Cheklin: *SSSR — Velikobritanniya: razvitie delovykh svyazei*, Moscow, MO, 1979, p. 6.

49   Popov, op. cit. (note) pp. 277ff.

50   V. Belezki: *Die Politik der Sowjetunion in den deutschen Angele-*

genheiten in der Nachkriegszeit (1945–1976), Berlin, Staatsverlag der DDR, 1977, p. 129; P. F. Alekseev: *SSSR — FRG: proshloe nastoyashchee*, Moscow, Politizdat, 1980, p. 15.

51   Voroncov, op. cit. (note 45) p. 250.

52   *Chruschtschow*, op. cit. (note 25), p. 518.

53   G. Wettig: 'Die Beziehungen der Sowjetunion zur Bundesrepublik Deutschland', *BioSt*, 1982, No. 10.

54   Popov, op. cit., 1978, p. 252ff.

55   P. A. Abrasimov: *Zapadnyi Berlin, vchera i segodnya*, Moscow, MO, 1980, pp. 134.

56   R. Fritsch-Bournazel: *Die Sowjetunion und die deutsche Teilung*, Opladen, Westdeutscher Verlag, 1979, p. 158.

57   Belezki, op. cit. (note 50), p. 414.

58   G. Shachnazarov: *Gryadushchii miroporyadok*, Moscow, Politizdat, 1981, p. 33.

59   Vorončov, op. cit. (note 45), p. 253, 271.

60   Vorontsov, op. cit. (note 45), p. 272.

61   G. Ginsburg and A. Z. Rubinstein: 'Finlandization: Soviet strategy or geopolitical footnote?', in *idem (eds.): Soviet Foreign Policy Towards Western Europe*, New York, Praeger, 1978 (3–16), p. 9.

62   J. D. Beam: *Multiple Exposure. An American Ambassador's Unique Perspective in East–West Issues*, New York, Norton, 1978, p. 252.

63   Cf. W. Schütze: Rivalität im westeuropäischen Bereich', in Füllenbach and Schulz, op. cit. (note 27), (107–131), p. 119f.

64   C. F. Bergsten: 'Die amerikanische Europa–Politik angesichts der Stagnation des Gemeinsamen Marktes. Ein Plädoyer für Konzentration auf die Bundesrepublik', *EA*, 1974.

65   O. V. Sherstvova: *Islandiya Problemy vneshnei politiki*, Moscow, MO, 1983, p. 125; M. N. Os'mova: *Vneshnekonomicheskie svyazi SSSR so stranami severnoi Evropy*. Moscow, Izdatel'stvo Moskovskogo universiteta, 1983, pp. 132ff.

66   A. A. Gromyko and B. N. Ponomarev (eds): *Istoriya vneshnei politiki SSSR, vol. 2, 1945–1980*, Moscow, Nauka, 1981, p. 214.

67   M. Jakobson: 'Finnlandisierung — Rufmord durch ein Wort', *FAZ*, 12.7.1980, p. 6.

68   N. Ørvik: *Sicherheit auf finnisch. Finnland und die Sowjetunion*, Stuttgart, Seewald, 1972, p. 180.

69   M. Jakobson: *Finnish Neutrality*, London, Evelyn, 1968.

70   F. Singleton: 'The Myth of "Finlandization"', *International Affairs*, 1981 (270–285), p. 285.

71   Ginsburg and Rubinstein, op. cit. (note 61), p. 5.

72   Ginsburg and Rubinstein, op. cit. (note 61), p. 123.

73   S. I. Annatov: SShA i Evropa. *Obshchie problemy amerikanskoi kontinental'noi politiki*, Moscow, Mysl', 1979, p. 204.

74   Brandt, op. cit. (note 26), p. 148.

75   cf. K. E. Birnbaum: *The Politics of East–West Communication in Europe*, Westmead, Saxon House, 1979, p. 99ff.

76   R. Kylikov: *O mezhdunarodno–pravovoi otvetstvennosti za narushenie prav cheloveka*, Moscow, MO, 1979, p. 90; V.A. Mazov: *Principy Chel'sinki i mezhdunarodnoe pravo*, Moscow, Nauka, 1980, p. 216ff.

77   D. Mel'nikov et al. (ed.): *Mezhdunarodnye otnosheniya v zapadnoi Evrope*, Moscow, MO, 1974.

78   cf. Royen, op. cit. (note 37), p. 101.

79   I. D. Trotsenko: *Sel'skochozyaystvennaya politika 'obshchego rynka'*, Moscow, Mysl', 1979, pp. 267ff.

80   G. Schiavone: *The Institutions of Comecon*, London, Macmillan, 1981, pp. 101ff.

81   V. I. Kuznetsov: *SEV i 'obshchii rynok'*, Moscow, MO, 1978, p. 177.

82   W. von Bredow: *Vom Antagonismus zur Konvergenz? Studien zum Ost–West-Problem*, Frankfurt, Metzner, 1972, p. 188.

Chapter 4

1   R. Faramazyan: *Disarmament and the Economy*, Moscow, Progress, 1981, p. 42.

2   G. Wettig: *Die sowjetischen Sicherheitsvorstellungen und die Möglichkeiten eines Ost–West-Einvernehmens*, Baden-Baden, Nomos, 1981, p. 23.

3   *Sovetskii soyuz v bor'be za razoruzhenie. Sbornik dokumentov*, Moscow, Politizdat, 1977, pp. 8ff; Brezhnev, the 26th party convention, in *Materialy XXVI s" ezda KPSS*, Moscow, Politizdat, 1982, p. 21.

4   G. Arbatow: *Der sowjetische Standpunkt*, Munich: Rogner & Bernhard, 1981, p. 123.

5   G. A. Trofimenko: *SShA: politika, voina, ideologiya*, Moscow, MO, 1976, p. 246f; *Materialy*, op. cit. (note 3), p. 21; Arbatow, op. cit. (note 4), p. 128.

6   *Materialy*, op. cit. (note 3), p. 21.

7   op. cit. (note 3), p. 10.

8   Wettig, op. cit. (note 2), p. 84.

9   *Mir i razoruzhenie*, Moscow, Nauka, 1980, p. 132.

10   R. L. Garthoff: 'SALT and Soviet Military', *PoC*, Jan/Feb 1975; pp. 21–37; *idem* 'SALT I: An Evaluation. World Politics', *PoC*, Oct 1978, pp 1–25.

11 Wettig, op. cit. (note 2), p. 14.

12 M. Voslensky: *Nomenklatura. Die herrschende Klasse in der Sowjetunion* Vienna, Molden, 1980, p. 454.

13 *Der Spiegel*, No. 35, 1982, p. 136.

14 op. cit. (note 9), p. 133; *Nauchnii soviet po issledovaniyu problem mira i razoruzheniya. Evropa pered vyborom*, Moscow, Akademia nauka, 1980, p. 15.

15 Falin: Interview with *Der Spiegel*, 5.11.1979, p. 59.

16 *Frieden und Krieg*, Cologne, Pahl–Rugenstein, 1981, p. 49.

17 *Materialy*, op. cit. (note 3), p. 23.

18 Arbatow, op. cit. (note 4), p. 126.

19 R. Hutchings: *Soviet Defense Spending: Towards a Reconciliation of Different Approaches. Jahrbuch der Wirtschaft Osteuropas*, Munich, Olzog vol. 9, 2, 1981 pp. 207–244.

20 R. A. Faramazyan: *Razoruzhenie i ekonomika*, Moscow, Mysl', 1978, p. 22.

21 J. Critchley: *The North Atlantic Alliance and the Soviet Union in the 1980s*, London, Macmillan, 1982, p. 77.

22 C. Costoriadis: *Devant la guerre. Les réalités*, Paris, Fayard, 1981, p. 180; 11–13 % imputed in: *US Central Intelligence Agency: Estimated Soviet Defense Spending in Rubles 1970–1975*, Washington/DC, 1976, p. 16.

23 Faramazyan, op. cit. (note 1), p. 47.

24 H. Sonnenfeldt: 'Die Verschiebung des Gleichgewichts', in H. Kohl (ed.), *Der neue Realismus. Außenpolitik nach Iran und Afghanistan*, Düsseldorf, Erb, 1980 (22–36), p. 24.

25 *Soviet Military Power*, Washington US Government Printing Office, 1981. Criticism: L.H. Gelb: 'Hände weg von Zahlenvergleichen', *Der Spiegel*, 1981, No. 41, pp. 165–170.

26 E. L. Warner: *The Military in Contemporary Soviet Politics. An Institutional Analysis*, New York, Praeger, 1977, p. 153.

27 G. Krell: 'Das militärische Kräfteverhältnis bei den nuklear-strategischen Waffensystemen', in *DGFK-Jahrbuch 1979/80*, Baden-Baden, Nomos, 1980, p. 323–355; G. Krell and D. Lutz: *Nuklearrüstung im Ost–West-Konflikt*, Baden-Baden, Nomos, 1980; J. D. Douglass and A. M. Hoeber: *Soviet Strategy for Nuclear War*, Stanford, Hoover, 1979; R.W. Howe: *Weapons*, Garden City, Doubleday, 1980, pp. 30ff.

28 Krell, op. cit. (note 27), p. 334.

29 R. P. Berman: *Soviet Air Power in Transition*, Washington, Brookings, 1978, p. 75.

30 S. G. Gorshkov: *Morskaya moshch gosudarstva*, Moscow, Voennoe izdatel'stvo Ministerstva oborony SSSR, 1979, p. 414; For an aggressive interpretation cf. Critchley, op. cit. (note 21), p. 84.

31   W. Damm: 'Das militärische Kräfteverhältnis bei den Seestreit-kräften', in *DGFK-Jahrbuch*, op. cit. (note 27), (425–441), p. 430.
32   Caldwell and Diebold, op. cit., 1981, p. 33; E. L. Warner: *The Military in Contemporary Soviet Politics*, New York, Praeger, 1977, p. 156.
33   B. Dismukes and J. M. McConnell (eds): *Soviet Naval Diplomacy*, New York, Pergamon, 1979, p. 300.
34   D. S. Lutz: *Zur Methodologie militärischer Kräftevergleiche*, Hamburg, Institut für Friedensforschung und Sicherheitspolitik, 1981 (Xero), p. 5; and: *PVS*, 1982, H. 1 (6–26), pp. 17ff; More pessimistic: U. Nerlich (ed.): *Sowjetische Macht und westliche Verhandlungspolitik im Wandel militärischer Kräfteverhältnisse*, Baden-Baden, Nomos, 1982, pp. 49ff.
35   W. Perdelwitz: *Wollen die Russen Krieg?* Hamburg, Gruner & Jahr, 1980, pp. 250ff.
36   P. A. Kerber: *Sowjetische Macht und westliche Verhandlungspolitik im Wandel militärischer Kräfteverhältnisse*, Baden-Baden, Nomos, 1983; *FAZ*, 30.11.1982, p. 6.
37   St. Tiedtke: *Rüstungskontrolle aus sowjetischer Sicht*, Frankfurt, Campus, 1980, p. 10f; Th. W. Wolfe: *Sowjetische Militärstrategie*, Cologne, Westdeutscher Verlag, 1967, p. 197.
38   J. Critchley: *The North Atlantic Alliance and the Soviet Union in the 1980s*, London, Macmillan, 1982, p. 77.
39   *Narodnoe Khozyaystvo SSSR v 1980 g*, Moscow, Finansy i statistika, 1981, p. 357.
40   C. Costoriadis: *Devant la guerre. Les réalités*, Paris, Fayard, 1981, p. 179f.
41   R. K. Ashley: *The Political Economy of War and Peace*, London, Pinter/New York, Nichols, 1980, pp. 83ff.
42   R. Pipes: *US–Soviet Relations in the Era of Détente*, Boulder, Westview Press, 1981, p. 60.
43   *Nauchnii soviet po issledovaniyu problem mira i razoruzheniya: Evropa pered vyborom: Konfrontatsiya ili oslablenie voennoi napryazhennosti*, Moscow, Akademia Nauk SSSR, 1980, p. 9.
44   R. Faramazyan: *Disarmament and the Economy*, Moscow, Progress, 1981, p. 43.
45   A. J. Jefremov: *Die nukleare Abrüstung*, Moscow, Progress, 1981, p. 262.
46   R. A. Faramazyan: *Razoruzhenie i ekonomika*, Moscow, Mysl', 1978, p. 21.
47   Jefremov, op. cit. (note 45), p. 262; V. Basmanov: *Za voennuyu razryadku v Tsentral' noi Evrope*, Moscow, MO, 1978, pp. 107ff.
48   K. von Beyme: *Economics and Politics within Socialist Systems. A Comparative and Developmental Approach*, New York, Praeger, 1982, p. 177.

49 E. M. Kennedy and M. O. Hatfield: *Freeze! How you can help prevent Nuclear War*, New York, Bantam Books, 1982, p. 103.

50 G. Wettig: 'Instrumentarien der Entspannungspolitik', *BioSt*, 1981, No. 17.

51 D. S. Lutz (ed.): *Die Rüstung der Sowjetunion*, Baden-Baden, Nomos, 1979, p. 41; G. Fahl: *Salt II vor Start. Die strategische Grenznachbarschaft von USA und UdSSR*, Berlin, Berlin Verlag 1983.

52 Pipes, op. cit. (note 42), p. 60.

53 R. A. Faramazyan: *Razoruzhenie i ekonomika*, Moscow, Mysl', 1978, p. 44.

54 Gegen '"Ausrottungspolitik und Russifizierung" im Baltikum. Die Europäische Gemeinschaft will sich für das Selbstbestimmungsrecht der Balten einsetzen'. *FAZ*, 15. Jan. 1983, p. 5.

55 H. G. Skilling: 'CSCE in Madrid', *PoC*, Aug. 1981, pp. 1–16.

56 'Moskau an die Verpflichtungen erinnern', *FAZ*, 9.11.1982, p. 7.

57 V. I. Belov et al: *Socialist Policy of Peace. Theory and Practice*, Moscow, Progress, 1979, p. 276f; Basmanov, op. cit. (note 47), pp. 85ff.

58 cf. V. L. Israelyan: *Organitsiya ob"edinennykh natsii i razoruzhenie*, Moscow, MO, 1981, pp. 93ff.

59 G. Bluhm et al. *Abschreckung und Entspannung*, Berlin, Duncker & Humblot, 1977, pp. 683ff; A. V. Grishin and A. G. Baklanov: *Vneshnyaya politika SSSR i problemy evropeiskoi bezopaznosti*, in *Diplomatischeskii vestnik, god 1982*, Moscow, MO, 1983, pp. 97–104; S. L. Tichvinskij et al. (ed.): *Vneshnyaya politika kapitalisticheskikh stran*, Moscow, MO, 1983, pp. 230ff.

60 *Evropa pered vyborom*, op. cit. (note 14).

61 A. A. Gromyko and P. N. Ponomarev: *Soviet Foreign Policy. vol. 2, 1945–1980*, Moscow, Progress, 1981, p. 486.

62 *FAZ*, 23.12.1982, p. 5; Washington: Andropows Vorschlag unannehmbar, *FAZ*, 23.12.1982., p. 1.

63 G. Krell and D. Lutz: *Nuklearrüstung im Ost–West-Konflikt*, Baden-Baden, Nomos, 1980, p. 31.

64 J. Alford (ed.): *The Impact of New Military Technology*, Aldershot, Gower, 1981, p. 5.

65 Gromyko and Ponomarev, op. cit. (note 61), p. 486.

66 *Mir i razoruzhenie*, Moscow, Nauka, 1980, p. 131.

67 *Ministerstvo inostranykh del SSSR: Sovetskii Sojuz i bor'ba za razoruzhenie. Sbornik dokumentov*, Moscow, Politizdat, 1977, p. 10.

68 I. G. Usachev: *Sovetskii Soyuz i problema razoruzheniya*, Moscow, MO, 1976, p. 53.

69 R. L. Arnett. Soviet Attitudes Towards Nuclear War: Do they really think they can win? *The Journal of Strategic Studies*, Sept. 1979, pp. 172–191.

70   C. von Clausewitz: *Vom Kriege*, Berlin, Verlag des Ministeriums für nationale Verteidigung, 1957, p. 728; Lenin: 'Polnoe sobranie sočinenii'. 1969, vol. 26, p. 316.

71   R. Pipes: 'Why the Soviet Union Thinks it Could Fight and Win a Nuclear War', *Commentary*, July 1977, pp. 21–34. Reprinted in Pipes, op. cit. (note 42) pp. 135–170.

72   cf. R. S. Strode and C. S. Gray: 'The Imperial Dimension of Soviet Military Power', *PoC*, 1981, Nov/Dec (1–15), p. 2.

73   M. Bundy *et al.*: *Kernwaffen und das Atlantische Bündnis*, Europa–Archiv, 1982 (183–198), p. 197.

74   F. Krause: *Das konventionelle Kräftegleichgewicht in Europa*, Bonn, Friedrich Ebert-Stiftung, 1982; J. J. Mearsheimer: 'Why the Soviets Can't Win Quickly in Central Europa', *International Security*, 1982 (3–39), p. 7.

75   B. Rogers: 'Niemals eine Aggression gegen den Warschauer Pakt, aber für den Fall eines Angriffs auf die NATO alle Optionen offenhalten', *FAZ*, 24.6.1982, p. 5; 'Vier Deutsche antworten den vier Amerikanern. Der Verzicht auf den Ersteinsatz wäre eine Verminderung der amerikanischen Schutzgarantie', *FAZ*, 24.6.1982, p. 9; H. Rattinger: 'Strategieinterpretationen und Rüstungskontollkonzepte. Anmerkungen zum Nato-Doppelbeschluß', *APuZG*, 1981, B 28 (21–37), p. 24.

76   F. Barnaby (Director of SIPRI): 'Zum Stand der globalen Rüstung', APuZG, 1981, B 28, (11–19), p. 16.

77   Jefremov, op. cit. (note 45), p. 269.

78   J. H. Nun: *The Soviet First Strike Threat*, New York, Praeger, 1982.

79   W. Graf Baudissin: *nie wieder Sieg!* Munich, Piper, 1982, p. 193.

80   A. Riklin: 'Audiatur et altera pars. Dreifache militärische Lagebeurteilung', *APuZG*, 1981, B. 3 (3–22), p. 14.

81   R. Jervis: 'Why Nuclear Superiority Doesn't Matter', *Political Science Quarterly*, 1979/80, pp. 617–633.

82   A. Karenin: *Filosofiya politicheskogo nasiliya*. Moscow, MO, 1971, pp. 17ff.

83   B. M. Blechman and St. S. Kaplan: *Force without War. U.S. Armed Forces as a Political Instrument*, Washington, Brookings, 1978, p. IX.

84   St. S. Kaplan: *Diplomacy of Power. Soviet Armed Forces as a Political Instrument*, Washington, Brookings, 1981, p. 32; V. Matthies: *Kriege in der Dritten Welt*. Opladen, Leske, 1982, p. 28.

85   cf. F. Fukuyama: *Nuclear Shadowboxing: Soviet Intervention Threats in the Middle East*, London, Orbis, 1981 (579–605), p. 590f.

86   Kaplan, op. cit. (note 84), p. 39.

87   Kaplan, op. cit. (note 84), p. 42.

88   Ch. W. Kegley and P. McGowan (eds): *Foreign Policy USA–USSR*, London, Sage, 1982, p. 119.

89   K. I. Spidchenko (ed.): *Politicheskaya i voennaya geografiya*, Moscow, Voennoe izdatel'stvo, 1980, p. 296.

90   *Zaochnaya vysshaya partinaya shkola pri CK KPSS: Sovremennye mezhdunarodnye otnoshenya i vneshnyaya politika Sovetskogo Soyuza*, Moscow, Mysl', 1972, p. 217.

91   N. P. Newell and R. S. Newell: *The Struggle for Afghanistan*, Ithaca, Cornell UP, 1981, p. 108.

92   *The Undeclared War. Imperialism vs. Afghanistan.*, Moscow, Progress, 1980, p. 47.

93   Ch. Kushnik: *Afganistan glazami ochevida*, Moscow, Progress, 1982, p. 29f. (Kushnik was correspondent of the DKP newspaper *Unsere Zeit*).

94   op. cit. (note 93), pp. 79ff.

95   D. Frenzke: 'Die Einmischung als völkerrechtliches Problem der Ost–West-Beziehungen', *BioSt*, 1982, No. 2, p. 22.

96   A. V. Malashenko: 'Islam v ideologii natsional'no-demokraticheskoi partii (na primere FNO Alzhira)', in V. F. Lu (ed.): *Partii i revolutsionnyi protsess v stranakh Azii i Afriki*, Moscow, Nauka, 1983 (170–183), p. 175; A. B. Reznikov: *Iran: padenie Shakhskogo rezhima*, Moscow, Politizdat, 1983, pp. 132ff; E. G. Filimonov *et al.* (ed.): *Islam v SSSR*, Moscow, Mysl', 1983.

97   B. Meissner: 'Sowjetische Außenpolitik und Afghanistan', *Außenpolitik*, 1980 (260–283), p. 274.

98   W. Berner: 'Der Kampf um Kabul. Lehren und Perspektiven' in H. Vogel (ed.): *Die sowjetische Intervention in Afghanistan*, Baden-Baden, Nomos, 1980, p. 319–366.

99   Text in: Newell and Newell op. cit. (note 91;), pp. 217ff.

100   v. Borcke in: Vogel, op. cit. (note 98), pp. 169ff.

101   H. Dahm: 'Afghanistan als Lehrstück der politischen und militärischen Doktrin Sowjetrußlands', in Vogel, op. cit. (note 98), pp. 181–246. More differentiated: W. Wagner: *Das Ost–West-Verhältnis nach der sowjetischen Intervention in Afghanistan*, Europa-Archiv, 1980, pp. 135–146; H. Münkler: 'Afghanistan im Kontext', *Neue Politische Literatur*, 1982, 326–350.

102   V. M. Mazurov: *SShA, Kitai, Japoniya. Perestroika mezhgosudarstvennykh otnoshenii 1969–1979*, Moscow, Nauka, 1980, p. 82f.

Chapter 5

1   CIA: 'Wirtschaft der Sowjetunion nicht unterschätzen', *FAZ*, 10.1.1983, p. 4.

2   A. Bergson: *Productivity and the Social System. The USSR and the West*, Cambridge/Mass. Harvard UP, 1978, p. 169; K. von Beyme: *Economics and Politics within Socialist Systems*, New York, 1982, Praeger. pp. 178ff.

3   L. T. Caldwell and W. Diebold: *Soviet–American Relations in the 1980s. Superpower Politics and East–West Trade*, New York, McGraw-Hill, 1981, p. 57.

4   S. Bialer: *Stalin's Successors. Leadership, Stability, and Change in the Soviet Union*, Cambridge UP, 1980, pp. 158ff.

5   *Der ökonomische Wettbewerb zwischen der UdSSR und den USA*, Berlin, 1961, p. 77; A. Szymanski: 'The Socialist World-System', in Ch. K. Chase-Dunn (ed.), *Socialist States in the World-System*, London, Sage, 1982 (57–84), p. 82.

6   T. B. Larson: *Soviet–American Rivalry*, New York, Norton, 1978, p. 40.

7   P. J. D. Wiles: *Communist International Economics*, Oxford, Blackwell, 1968, p. 1.

8   A. A. Brown and E. Neuberger (eds): *International Trade and Central Planning*, Berkeley, University of California Press, 1968, p. 202.

9   B. S. Vaganov (ed.): *Vneshnyaya torgovlya v poslevoennoi period*, Moscow, MO, 1979, p. 3, 11.

10   V. I. Lenin: *Über die Außenwirtschaftsbeziehungen des Sowjetstaates*, Moscow, Progress, 1977, p. 143, and *LW*, vol. 8, pp. 170ff.

11   Lenin, op. cit. (note 10), p. 7.

12   E. Shershnev: *On the Principle of Mutual Advantage. Soviet–American Economic Relations*, Moscow, Progress, 1978.

13   V. P. Gruzinov: *Upravlenie v vneshnei torgovlei*, Moscow, MO, 1975, p. 223.

14   A. A. Goryachev: *Problemy prognoziorvaniya mirovykh tovarnykh rynkov*, Moscow, MO, 1981, pp. 6ff; Gruzinov, op. cit. (note 13), p. 223.

15   A. Nove: *The Soviet Economic System*, London, Allen & Unwin, 1978, p. 269.

16   B. Csikós–Nagy: *Socialist Economic Policy*, Budapest, Kaido, 1973, p. 223.

17   *Mezhdunarodnye raschety i finansirovanie vneshnei torgovli*, Moscow, MO, 1980, p. 285f.

18   J. Bethkenhagen and H. Machowski: *Integration im Rat für gegenseitige Wirtschaftshilfe*, Berlin, Berlin Verlag, 1976, p. 55.

19   Shershnev, op. cit. (note 12), p. 46.

20   B. S. Vaganov (ed.): *Vneshnyaya torgovlya SSSR v poslevoennii period*, Moscow, MO, 1979, p. 12.

21   O. T. Bogomolov (ed.): *Sotsializm i perestroika mezhdunar-odnykh ekonomicheskich otnoshenii*, Moscow, MO, 1982, p. 27.

22   I. A. Ornatskii: *Ekonomicheskaya diplomatiya*, Moscow, MO, 1980, p. 4.

23   A. A. Goryachev: *Problemy prognozirovaniya mirovykh tovarnykh rynkov*, Moscow MO, 1981, p. 6.

24   Vaganov, op. cit. (note 20), p. 11.

25   V. T. Zoloev: *Statistika vneshnei torgovli*, Moscow, Finansy i statistika, 1981, p. 3.

26   Vagnov, op. cit. (note 20), p. 13; Ørvik: *Sicherheit auf finnisch*, Stuttgart, Seewald 1972.

27   R. Swearingen: *The Soviet Union and Postwar Japan*, Stanford, Hoover, 1978, p. 155.

28   M. I. Krupyanko: *Sovetsko–yaponskie ekonomicheskie otnoshe-niya*, Moscow, Nauka, 1982, p. 176.

29   Y. Sazanami: 'Japan and the Development of East–West Trade' in G. Schiavone (ed.) *East–West Relations. Prospects for the 1980s*, London, Macmillan, 1982, (86–100), p. 95f.

30   J. Pinder in E. Schulz (ed.) *Die Ostbeziehungen der Europäischen Gemeinschaft*, Munich, Oldenbourg, 1977, p. 91f.

31   cf. M. Kreile: *Osthandel und Ostpolitik*, Baden-Baden, Nomos, 1978, pp. 131ff.

32   J. C. Brada: 'Technologietransfer zwischen West und Ost. Die Auswirkungen auf kommunistische Länder', *OE*, 1981, (943–956), p. 944.

33   H.-D. Jacobsen: *Die wirtschaftlichen Beziehungen zwischen West und Ost*, Reinbek, Rowohlt, 1975, p. 137.

34   *Vneshnyaya torgovlya SSSR v 1981 g*, Moscow, Finansy i statistika, 1982, pp. 187, 270f.

35   J. Bethkenhagen: 'Der Energie- und Rohstoffsektor der Sowjetun-ion und die Weltwirtschaft', in *Sowjetunion 1980/1981*, Munich, Hanser, 1981 (177–190), p. 178.

36   O. A. Sergienko: *Bor'ba za neft' i gaz Severnogo morya*, Moscow, MO, 1981, p. 135.

37   V. Gorsky: 'EEC–USA: The Transatlantic Duel', *International Affairs* (Moscow), 1982, No. 10 (24–32), p. 29.

38   op. cit. (note 17), p. 362.

39   M. Meshcheryakov *et al. SEV. Printsipy, problemy, perspektivy*, Moscow, Politizdat, 1975, p. 192.

40   Vaganov, op. cit. (note 20), p. 249.

41   J. J. Jeske: 'Umschuldungen: Die Wirklichkeit hat die Phantasie übertroffen', *FAZ*, 10.9.1982, p. 14; 'Ostblock tilgt Schulden am schnellsten', *FAZ*, 20.12.1983, p. 12.

42 'Kredite für die Sowjetunion nur noch zu Marktkonditionen', *FAZ*, 6.9.1982, p. 13; 'Die Banken handeln wie die Lemminge. Spiegel-Report über die bedrohliche Verschuldung der Entwicklungsländer und des Ostblocks', *Der Spiegel*, 1982, No. 36, pp. 129–139.

43 U. Stehr: *Wirtschaft und Politik in den sowjetischen Westbeziehungen*, Frankfurt, Campus, 1980, p. 11f.

44 cf. Sowjetunion, 1980/1981, op. cit. (note 35), p. 201.

45 G. Sokoloff: 'Western Participation in Soviet Development 1959–1979', in G. Schiavone (ed.), *East–West Relations. Prospects for the 1980s*, London, Macmillan, 1982 (73–85), p. 73.

46 L. H. Theriot and J. N. Matheson: 'Soviet Economic Relations with Non-European EMEA: Cuba, Vietnam and Mongolia', in Joint Economic Committee, *Soviet Economy in a Time of Change*, Washington, GPO, 1979, pp. 551–581.

47 H. Vogel: 'Die Wirtschaftskrise Polens — ein Dilemma sowjetischer Hegemonie', *OE*, 1981 (1037–1044), p. 1042.

48 M. Lavigne: *Les relations économiques est–ouest*, Paris, PUF, 1979, p. 75.

49 V. L. Mal'kevich: *Vostok — Zapad: ekonomicheskoe sotrudnichestvo, tekhnologicheskii obmen*, Moscow; *Obshchestvennye Nauki i sovremennost'*, 1981, p. 11.

50 A. Stent: *Technologie in den Osten? Zur Konzeption und Praxis des Consultative Group Coordinating Committee (Cocom)*, APuZG 1981, B 22 (38–46), p. 39.

51 'Reagan hebt die Sanktionen gegen Moskau auf', *FAZ*, 15.11.1982, p. 1.

52 Lavigne, op. cit. (note 48), p. 71.

53 'Wie sich der Osten Rüstungsgüter beschafft. Bonn: Transfer westlicher Technologie auf illegalen Wegen', *FAZ*, 17.8.1982, p. 2.

54 *Pravda*, 29.2.1980; A. A. Gromyko and B. N. Ponomarev (eds): *Istoriya vneshnei politiki SSSR. vol. 2, 1945–1980 gg.* Moscow, Nauka, 1981, p. 607.

55 K. P. Krause: Die Sowjetunion pokert am Getreidemarkt. Exportländer warten auf die Käufe', *FAZ*, 28.10.1982, p. 14.

56 G. W. Ball: *The Discipline of Power*, Boston, Little Brown, 1968, p. 278; Shershnev, op. cit. (note 12), p. 77.

57 G. Adler-Karlsson: *Western Economic Warfare. 1917–1967*, Stockholm, Almqvist & Wiksell, 1968, pp. 190, 200.

58 J. M. van Brabant: *Specialization and Trade Dependence in Eastern Europe. Jahrbuch der Wirtschaft Osteuropas*, Munich, Olzog, 1979, vol. 8, pp. 213–245.

59 Jacobsen, op. cit. (note 33), p. 157.

60 Ch. Levinson: *Wodka–Cola: Die gefährliche Kehrseite der wirtschaftlichen Zusammenarbeit zwischen Ost und West*, Reinbek, Rowohlt, 1978; Szymanski, op. cit. (note 5), pp. 60ff; D. Barclay: USSR: 'The Role of Compensation Agreements in Trade with the West', in US Congress, Joint Economic Committee, *Soviet Economy in a Time of Change*, Washington, GPO, 1979, vol. 2, pp. 462–481.

61 P. Hanson: *Trade and Technology in Soviet Western Relations*, London, Macmillan, 1981, p. 259.

62 *Syr'evoi krizis sovremennogo kapitalizma. Mirokhozyaystvennye aspekty*, Moscow, Mysl', 1980, pp. 286ff.

63 Wiles, op. cit. (note 7), p. 507.

64 S. L. Tikhvinskii *et al* (ed.): *Vneshnyaya politika i diplomatiya sotsialisticheskich stran*, Moscow, MO, 1981, p. 143.

65 *Geschichte der Partei der Arbeit Albaniens*, Tirana, Institut für Marxistisch–Leninistische Studien beim HK der PAA, 1971, p. 643.

66 A. J. Klinghoffer: *The Soviet Union and International Oil Politics*, New York, University Press, 1977, p. 296.

67 K. von Beyme: 'Détente and East–West Economic Relations', *Journal of Politics*, 1981, pp. 1192–1206.

68 V. P. Kolosov and L. I. Komlev: *Za ravnopravnye ekonomicheskie otnosheniya*, Moscow, MO, 1978, p. 17.

69 Wiles, op. cit. (note 7), p. 555.

70 S. G. Yurkov and G. P. Petrov (eds): *Vneshnepoliticheskie kontseptsii Maoizma*, Moscow, MO, 1975, p. 105; A. Eckstein: *China's Economic Revolution*, Cambridge UP, 1977, p. 254.

71 V. P. Fedorov: *Kapitalizm i mezhdunarodnye ekonomicheskie otnosheniya*, Moscow, MO, 1979, p. 130ff; A. P. Butenko *et al*: *Sotsializm i mezhdunarodnye otnosheniya*, Moscow, Nauka, 1975, pp. 352ff.

Chapter 6

1 A. A. Gromyko and P. N. Ponomarev (eds): *Soviet Foreign Policy. Vol. 2, 1945–1980*, Moscow, Progress, 1981, p. 538.

2 op. cit. (note 1), p. 521.

3 S. P. Sanakoev and N. I. Kaptsenko: *O teorii vneshneii politiki sotsializma*, Moscow, MO, 1977, p. 237.

4 J. K. Hoensch: 'Sowjetische Osteuropapolitik 1924–1955', in D. Geyer, *Sowjetunion. Außenpolitik 1917–1955*, Cologne, Böhlau, 1972 (382–447), p. 425.

5 J. Hacker: *Der Ostblock*, Baden-Baden, Nomos, 1983, pp. 57ff.

6 M. Djilas: *Gespräche mit Stalin*, Frankfurt, S. Fischer, 1962, p. 226; V. Dedijer: *The Battle Stalin Lost. Memoirs of Yugoslavia 1948–1953*, New York, Viking, 1971, p. 32f.

7 Hoensch, op. cit. (note 4), p. 427.

8 I. V. Dudinskii: *Sotsialisticheskoe sodruzhestvo: osnovnye tendentsii razvitiya*, Moscow, Mysl', 1976, pp. 43, 46.

9 M. Lentz: *Die Wirtschaftsbeziehungen DDR–Sowjetunion 1945–1961*, Opladen. Leske, 1979, p. 203.

10 Yu. I. Kandalov: *Mezhdunarodnye otnosheniya i ideologicheskoe sotrudnichestvo bratskikh sotsialisticheskikh stran*, Moscow, MO, 1981, p. 106.

11 J. K. Hoensch: *Sozialistische Osteuropa-Politik 1945–1975*, Kronberg/Düsseldorf, Athenäum/Droste, 1977, p. 64f.

12 M. V. Senin: *Sotsialisticheskaya intergratsiya*, Moscow, MO, 1969, p. 308.

13 J. Bethkenhagen and H. Machowski: *Integration im Rat für gegenseitige Wirtschaftshilfe*. Berlin, Berlin Verlag, 1976, p. 26.

14 M. Sénine: *L'intégration socialiste*, Moscow, Progress, 1974, p. 176. cf. A. Lebahn: 'Alternativen in den EG–RGW–Beziehungen', *Außenpolitik*, 1980 (147–166), p. 151.

15 P. Marer and J. M. Montias (eds): *East European Integration of East–West Trade*, Bloomington, Indiana UP, 1980, p. 32.

16 V. P. Sergeev: *Mezhdunarodnoe sotsialisticheskoe razdelenie truda: pokazateli i tendentsii razvitiya*. Moscow, Mysl', 1979, p. 187.

17 Marer and Montias, op. cit. (note 15), p. 381.

18 Ju. F. Kormov (ed.): *Agrarno–promyshlennaya integratsiya stran SEV*, Moscow, Nauka, 1976, pp. 6ff.

19 K. von Beyme: *Ökonomie und Politik im Sozialismus*, Munich, Piper, 1975, 1977, pp. 26ff.

20 E. L. Bondarenko: *Vyravnivanie urovnya ekonomicheskogo razvitiya stran-chlenov SEV v usloviyach integratsii*, Moscow, Izdatel'stvo Moskovskogo Universiteta, 1979, p. 93.

21 G. Schiavone: *The Institutions of COMECON*, London, Macmillan, 1981, p. 79.

22 Figures in C. Davaadorz and V. Cedenbal: *MNR. Itogi shestidesyatiletiya sotsial'no-ekomonicheskogo razvitiya*, Moscow, Progress, 1981, p. 107.

23 H. Bräker: 'Die Aufnahme Vietnams in den RGW und die Politik der Sowjetunion und der VR China in Südostasien', *BioSt*, 1979, No. 7, p. 9.

24 P. Summerscale: 'Is Eastern Europe a Liability to the Soviet Union?', *International Affairs*, 1981, p. 585–598.

25 P. Hanson: 'Soviet Trade with Eastern Europe', in K. Dawisha and P. Hanson (eds): *Soviet–East European Dilemmas. Coercion,*

Competition, and Consent, London, Heinemann, 1981 (90–107), p. 93; Yu. A. Konstantinov: *Mezhdunarodnaya valyutnaya sistema stran-chlenov SEV,* Moscow, Finansy i statistika, 1982, p. 5.

26 A. M. Alekseev *et al: Sotsialisticheskaya integratsia i ee preimushchestva pered kapitalisticheskoi,* Moscow, Nauka, 1975, p. 385.

27 J. Wilczynski: *The Economics and Politics of the East–West Trade,* London, 1969, p. 337; R. Damus: *RGW. Wirtschaftliche Zusammenarbeit in Osteuropa,* Opladen, Leske, 1979, pp. 61ff.

28 B. Meissner and P. Farkas: *Preisdiskriminierung innerhalb des RGW? Jahrbuch der Wirtschaft Osteuropas,* Munich, Olzog, 1973, vol. 4 (295–318), p. 316.

29 A. I. Levin: *Sotsialisticheskii vnutrennii rynok,* Moscow, Mysl', 1973, p. 20; V. E. Rybalkin: *Mezhdunarodnyi rynok SEV,* Moscow, Mysl', 1978, p. 35.

30 I. P. Oleinik and V. P. Sergeev (ed.): *Problemy sotsialisticheskaya ekonomicheskoi integratsii,* Moscow, Mysl', 1974, p. 243; M. F. Kovaleva and F. N. Shevyakov (ed.): *Sotsialisticheskaya integratsija: protsess razvitiya i sovershenstvovaniya,* Moscow, Mysl', 1976, p. 310.

31 Bethkenhagen and Machowski, op. cit. (note 13), p. 68.

32 G. Proft *et al. Planung in der sozialistischen ökonomischen Integration,* Berlin, (Ost) Staatsverlag der DDR, 1972, p. 154.

33 V. Meshcherakov, *et al. SEV. Printsipy, problemy, perspektivy,* Moscow, Politizdat, 1975, pp. 202ff.

34 P. Lorenz: *Multinationale Unternehmen sozialistischer Länder,* Baden-Baden, Nomos, 1978, p. 131; Lebahn, op. cit. (note 14), pp. 159, 166.

35 Proft, op. cit. (note 32), p. 152.

36 K. I. Mikul'skii (ed.): *Problemy proizvodstva v stranakh SEV,* Moscow, Ekonomika, 1974, p. 44.

37 B. Bracewell–Milnes: *Economic Integration in East and West,* London, Croom Helm, 1976, p. 184; Hacker, op. cit. (note 5), p. 886.

38 V.I. Kuznetsov: *SEV i 'Obshchii rynok',* Moscow, MO, 1978, p. 60.

39 Marer and Montias, op. cit. (note 15), p. 22.

40 A. K. Subbotin: *Mirovye ekonomicheskie problemy,* Moscow, MO, 1980, p. 120ff; B. G. Dyakin and B. G. Pankov: *SEV: Problemy integratsii,* Moscow, Molodaya gvardiya, 1978, p. 128.

41 V.I. Kuznetsov: *SEV i 'Obshchii rynok',* Moscow, MO, 1978, p. 177. A. Stent: *From Embargo to Ostpolitik.* Cambridge/Mass, Harvard UP 1981, Chapter 10.

42 M. Baumer: *Zur Multilateralisierung des Außenhandels der RGW–Mitgliedsstaaten,* Ebenhausen, Stiftung Wissenschaft und Politik, 1975, p. 159.

43   G. Schiavone: *The Institutions of COMECON*, London, Macmillan, 1981, p. 100.

44   W. C. Clemens: *The U.S.S.R and Global Interdependence. Alternative Futures*, Washington, American Enterprise Institute, 1978, p. 102.

45   Lebahn, op. cit. (note 14), p. 164.

46   A. Uschakow: *Der Rat für gegenseitige Wirtschaftshilfe*, Cologne Wissenschaft und Politik, 1962, p. 59.

47   I. O. Chlestova: *Arbitrazh vo vneshne-ekonomicheskikh otnosheniyakh stran-clenov SEV*, Moscow, Nauka, 1980, p. 9.

48   V. I. Zuev: *Mirovaya sistema sotsializma. Ekonomičeskie i politicheskie aspekty edinstva*, Moscow, MO, 1975, p. 161.

49   G. M. Charachaš" yan: *Sotsialisticheskaya integratsiya i mezhdunarodnoe razdelenie truda*, Moscow, Ekonomika, 1978, p. 174ff, Dyakin and Pankov, op. cit. (note 40), p. 128, V. Ya. Mastabei: *Razvitie nauchno–tekhnicheskoi integratsii stran–chlenov SEV*, Kiev, Naukova Dumka, 1981.

50   Ch. Coker: Adventurism and Pragmatism: The Soviet Union, Comecon, and Relations with African States', *International Affairs*, 1981, pp. 618–633. L. M. Kapitsa: *Vozdeistvie dvukh mirovykh sistem na osvobodivshiesya strany*. Moscow, MO, 1982, p. 212ff.

51   Yu. P. Zhuravlev: *Mezhdunarodnye svyazi SEV*, Moscow, MO, 1978, p. 54f.

52   I. I. Orlik: *Politika zapadnikh derzhav o otnoshenii vostochno-evropeiskikh sotsialisticheskikh gosudarstv*, Moscow, Nauka, 1979, p. 152.

53   Hanson, op. cit. (note 25), p. 96.

54   P. Wiles (ed.): *The New Communist Third World*, London, Croom Helm, 1982, p. 29.

55   cf. J. Russell: *Energy as a Factor in Soviet Foreign Policy*, Westmead, Saxon House/Lexington, Lexington Books, 1976, p. 138.

56   H. Fiedler: 'Bündnissystem und Vertragsbeziehungen', in D. Geyer and B. Meissner (eds): *Sowjetunion Außenpolitik III*, Cologne, Böhlau, 1976 (139–162), p. 139.

57   B. Meissner (ed.): *Der Warschauer Pakt. Dokumentensammlung.*, Cologne, Wissenschaft und Politik, 1962, p. 128.

58   *SSSR–GDR. 30 let otnoshenii 1949–1979*, Moscow, Politizdat, 1981.

59   G. Zieger: *Der Warschauer Pakt*, Hannover, Niedersächsische Landeszentrale für Politische Bildung, 1974, p. 108.

60   *Mezhdunarodnye organizatsii sotsialisticheskikh gosudarstv*, Moscow, MO, 1980, p. 29.

61   J. Hacker: 'Der Warschauer Pakt', in Geyer and Meissner op. cit. (note 56), p. 172.

62   J. Erickson: 'The Warsaw Pact — the Shape of Things to Come?', in K. Dawisha and P. Hanson (eds), *Soviet–East European Dilemmas*, London, Heinemann, 1981 (148–171), p. 168.

63   D. R. Herspring: 'The Warsaw Pact at 25', *PoC*, Sept/Oct 1980, pp. 1–15.

64   B. Meissner: *Die 'Breschnew–Doktrin'*, Cologne, Verlag Wissenschaft und Politik, 1969, pp. 25ff; Hacker, op. cit. (note 61), pp. 919ff.

65   Th. Schweisfurth: *Sozialistisches Völkerrecht? Darstellung, Analyse, Wertung der sowjetmarxistischen Theorie vom Völkerrecht 'neuen Typs'*, Berlin, Springer, 1979, pp. 568, 304ff.

66   B. N. Topornin: *Politicheskaya sistema sotsializma*, Moscow. MO, 1972, p. 9.

67   Quoted in Schweisfurth, op. cit. (note 65), p. 172; Hacker, op. cit. (note 61), pp. 909, 906.

68   M. A. Klochko: *Soviet Scientists in Red China*, New York, 1964, p. 49.

69   Djilas, op. cit. (note 6), p. 231.

70   J. Glaubitz: *China und die Sowjetunion. Aufbau und Zerfall einer Allianz*, Hannover, Landeszentrale für politische Bildung, 1973, pp. 5ff.

71   O. B. Borissow and B. T. Koloskow: *Sowjetisch–chinesische Beziehungen 1945–1970*, Berlin, Staatsverlag der DDR, 1973, p. 77.

72   D. S. Zagoria: *The Sino–Soviet Conflict 1956–1961*, Princeton UP, 1962, p. 47.

73   Z. K. Brzezinski: *The Soviet Bloc. Unity and Conflict*, New York, Praeger, 1961, pp. 409ff.

74   J. Lévesque: *The USSR and the Cuban Revolution*, New York, Praeger, 1978, p. 118.

75   Borissow and Koloskow, op. cit. (note 71), p. 251.

76   F. D. Holzman: *Foreign Trade under Central Planning*, Cambridge/Mass., Harvard UP, 1974, pp. 86ff.

77   R. O. Freedman: *Economic Warfare in the Communist Bloc. A Study of Soviet Economic Pressure Against Yugoslavia, Albania and Communist China*, New York, Praeger, 1970, p. 115; F. Schurmann: *Ideology and Organization in Communist China*, Berkeley, University of California Press, 1966, p. 241.

78   P. J. D. Wiles: *Communist International Economics*, Oxford, Blackwell, 1968, p. 513; F. H. Mah: *The Foreign Trade of Mainland China*, Edinburgh UP, 1972, pp. 180ff.

79   Figures on trade relations: *Otnosheniya Sovetskogo Soyuza s Narodnoi Korei 1945–1980. Dokumenty i materialy*, Moscow, Nauka, 1981, p. 400.

80   R. A. Scalapino and Ch.-S. Lee: *Communism in Korea*, Berkeley,

University of California Press, 1972, vol. 1, pp. 638ff; Ch. S. Lee: *Korean Workers' Party. A Short History*, Stanford, Hoover, 1978, pp. 96ff.

81 J. I. Domínguez: *Cuba. Order and Revolution*, Cambridge/ Mass., Belknap Press, 1978, p. 163f.

82 P. Van Ness: *Revolution and Chinese Foreign Policy. Peking's Support for Wars of National Liberation*, Berkeley, University of California Press, 1971.

83 G. Linde: 'Sowjetische Politik auf der arabischen Halbinsel', *BioSt*, 1978, No. 44, p. 7.

84 cf. Ch. S. Kang: *China in Waffen. Die Rüstungs- und Abrüstungspolitik der VR China von 1969 bis zum Tod Mao-Tse-Tungs*, Frankfurt, Haag & Herchen, 1979, p. 30; O. Weggel: *Die Außenpolitik der VR China*, Stuttgart, Kohlhammer, 1977, pp. 110ff.

85 Lévesque, op. cit. (note 74), p. 116.

86 V. B. Vorontsov: *Kitai i SShA: 60–70e gody*, Moscow, Nauka, 1979, pp. 120ff.; V. M. Mazurov: SShA, *Kitai, Japoniya. Perestroika mezhgosudarstvennkh otnoshenii 1969–1979*, Moscow, Nauka, 1980, p. 160.

87 Gromyko and Ponomarev, op. cit. (note 1), pp. 562–572.

88 J. D. Pollack: 'Chinese Global Strategy and Soviet Power', *PoC*, 1981, Jan–Feb (54–69), p. 58f.

89 S. G. Yurkov and G. P. Petrov: *Vneshnepoliticheskie kontseptsii Maoizma*, Moscow, MO, 1975, p. 105; H. J. Mayer: 'Zu den Ursachen des chinesisch-vietnamesischen Krieges von Februar–März 1979', *BioSt*, 1980, No. 16, pp. 39ff.

90 O. B. Borisov: *Vnutrennyaya i vneshnyaya politika Kitaya v 70e gody*, Moscow, Politizdat, 1982, p. 365f.

91 A. A. Moskalev: *Politika KNP v natsional'no yazykovom voprose*, Moscow, Nauka, 1981, pp. 137ff.

92 M. I. Sladkovskii (ed.): *Gegemonistskaya politika Kitaya ugroza narodam Azii, Afriki i Latinskoi Ameriki*, Moscow, Politizdat, 1981, p. 106.

93 P. Artem'ev: *Problemy razvivayushchikh stran i maoistskaya diplomatiya v OON*, Moscow, Nauka, 1978, p. 152.

94 S. A. Manezhev: *Ekonomicheskie otnosheniya KNR so stranami Yugo–vostochnoi Azii*, Moscow, Nauka, 1980, pp. 170, 172.

95 J. F. Copper: *China's Foreign Aid. An Instrument of Peking's Foreign Policy*, Lexington, Lexington Books, 1976; J. Horvath: *Chinese Technology Transfer to the Third World*, New York, Praeger, 1976.

96 N. S. Kulesov: *Pekin protiv natsional'no-osvoboditel'nogo dvizheniya*, Moscow, MO, 1981, pp. 36, 41.

97 Y. Vertzberger: 'Afghanistan in China's Policy', *PoC*, May/Jun 1982, pp. 1–23.

98   S. S. Kim: *China, the United Nations and World Order*, Princeton UP, 1979, p. 497.

99   H. Li: 'The Crux of the Sino–Soviet Boundary Question. China and the World', *Beijing Review Foreign Affairs Series, No. 1*, 1982, pp. 46–73; 'China looks for "solid progress" in talks with Soviets', *China Quarterly*, 16.2.1984, p. 1.

100   I. Alexandrov: 'On Soviet–Chinese Relations', *International Relations* (Moscow), 1982, No. 7, pp. 16–19.

101   S. Bialer (ed.): *The Domestic Context of Soviet Foreign Policy*, London, Croom Helm, 1981, p. 40.

102   *Materialy XXVI s"ezda KPSS*, Moscow, Politizdat, 1982, p. 10f.

103   *Materialy XXV s"ezda KPSS*, Moscow, Politizdat, 1976, p. 11.

104   *Vneshnyaya politika Sovetskogo Soyuza*, Moscow, Politizdat, 1978, p. 336.

105   R. C. Horn: 'The Soviet Union and Asian Security', in S. Chawla and D. R. Sardesai (eds), *Changing Patterns of Security and Stability in Asia*, New York, Praeger, 1980 (63–98), p. 67.

106   S. D. Belenkov and G. S. Ostroumov: *Mirovoi sotsializm i mezhdunarodnye otnosheniya v nachale 80-kh godov*, Moscow, MO, 1982, pp. 3–13.

107   Ch. K. Chase-Dunn: 'The Transition to World Socialism', in *idem* (ed.): *Socialist States in the World-System*, London, Sage, 1982, pp. 271–296.

Chapter 7

1   A.B. Ulam: Expansion and Coexistence. Soviet Foreign Policy 1917–1973. New York, Praeger, [2]1974, p. 123.

2   I. Giritli: Fifty Years of Turkish-Soviet Relations (1920–1970). Annales de la Faculté de Droit d'Istanbul, 1980, No. 43, pp. 429–447.

3   K. K. Orozaliev: Istoricheskii opyt perekhoda Kirgizkogo naroda k sotsializmu minuya kapitalizm. Frunze, Ilim, 1974.

4   V. I. Zuev: Mirovaya sistema sotsializma. Moscow, MO, 1975, p. 151.

5   S. N. Grigoryan and V.G. Georgiev (ed.): *Kritika teoreticheskikh osnov Maoizma*, Moscow, Politizdat, 1973, p. 327.

6   V. E. Chirkin: *Formy sotsialisticheskogo gosudarstva*, Moscow, Jurlit, 1973, p. 219f.

7   H. Piazza: 'Zur Herausbildung der marxistisch-leninistischen Theorie des nichtkapitalistischen Entwicklungsweges' in *Nichtkapitalistischer Entwicklungsweg*, Berlin, Akademie-Verlag, 1973 (61–76), p. 64. The Debates of the Second International in: *Internationaler Sozialistenkongreß zu Stuttgart 18.–24. August 1907*. Berlin, 1907, pp. 22, 32ff.

8   L. Trockij: *Die permanente Revolution*, Frankfurt, Fischer, 1969, p. 116.

9   K. Westen: *Der Staat der nationalen Demokratie. Ein kommunistisches Modell für Entwicklungsländer*, Cologne, Wissenschaft und Politik, 1964, p. 42; R. Biskup: *Sowjetpolitik und Entwicklungsländer*, Freiburg, Rombach, 1970, pp. 167ff.

10 W. Treuheit: *Sozialismus in Entwicklungsländern. Indonesien, Burma, Ägypten, Tansania, Westafrika*, Cologne, Pahl-Rugenstein, 1971, p. 212.

11 H. C. F. Mansilla (ed.): *Probleme des Dritten Weges*, Darmstadt, Luchterhand, 1974, p. 244.

12 R. A. Uljanowski: *Der Sozialismus und die befreiten Länder*, Berlin, Deutscher Verlag der Wissenschaften, 1973, p. 412.

13 D. Ribeiro: *Der zivilisatorische Prozeß*, Frankfurt, Suhrkamp, 1971, p. 259.

14 N. A. Simoniya: 'O kharaktere natsional'no-osvoboditel'nykh revolutsii, *Narody Azii i Afriki*. 1966, No. 6, p. 16; K. N. Bruten *et al.: Sotsialisticheskaya orientatsiya osvobodivshchisya stran.* Moscow, Mysl', 1982, p. 41.

15 M. Schwartz: 'The USSR and Leftist Regimes in Less-Developed Countries', *Soviet Survey*, 1973 (209–244). p. 236.

16 K. Melchers: *Die sowjetische Afrikapolitik von Chruschtschow bis Breschnew*, Berlin, Oberbaum, 1980, p. 207.

17 A. Z. Rubinstein: *Soviet and Chinese Influence in the Third World*, New York, Praeger, 1975, p. 165; On Nicaragua, A. N. Glinkin and A. I. Sizonenko (ed.): *Vneshnyaya politika stran Latinskoi Ameriki*, Moscow, MO, 1982, pp. 180–194.

18 A. V. Kuba: *Strany sotsialisticheskoi orientatsii. Osnovny tendentsii razvitiya*, Moscow, Nauka, 1978, p. 6; V. Chirkin and Yu. Yudin: *A Socialist Oriented State*, Moscow, Progress, 1983, p. 237.

19 N. Ushakova: *Strany SEV i razvivayushchiesya gosudarstva sotsialisticheskói orientatsii*, Moscow, Nauka, 1980, p. 3f.

20 L. V. Goncharev *et al.* (ed.): *Sovremennye problemy i vneshnyaya politika Efiopii*, Moscow, MO, 1982, p. 112.

21 Ushakova, op. cit. (note 19), p. 3.

22 A. V. Kuba: *Nekotorye problemy teorii i praktiki sovremenno sotsialisticheskoi orientatsii*, Moscow, Avtoreferat, 1978, p. 6.

23 op. cit. (note 22), pp. 31, 24.

24 G. F. Kim *et al.* (ed.): *Intelligentsiya i sotsial'nii progress v razvivashiesya stranakh Azii i Afriki*, Moscow, Nauka, 1981, p. 291.

25 *Partiya i gosudarstvo v stranakh sotsialisticheskoi orientatsii*, Moscow, Nauka, 1973, p. 21.

26   V. I. Gubanov: *Politicheskaya organizatsiya obshchestva stran sotsialisticheskoi orientatsii*, Leningrad, Izdatel'stvo Leningradskogo Universiteta, 1981, pp. 56ff; S. P. Nemanov: 'Partii avangardskogo tipa v afrikanskikh stranakh sotsialisticheskoi orientatsii', *Narody Azii i Afriki*, 1979, No. 2, pp. 16–28.

27   G. I. Mirskii: *'Tretii Mir' Obshchestvo, vlast', armiya*, Moscow, Nauka, 1976, pp. 296ff; V. E. Chirkin (ed.) *Vooruzhennye sily v politicheskoi sisteme*, Moscow, Nauka, 1981, p. 10.

28   O. V. Martyshin: *Afrikanskaya revolyutsionnaya demokratiya*, Moscow, Politizdat, 1981, p. 199.

29   cf. W. Spaulding: Checklist of the 'National Liberation Movement', *PoC*, Mar/Apr 1982, 77–82.

30   Kuba, op. cit. (note 78), pp. 34, 37.

31   K. I. Zarodov (ed.): *Natsional'no -osvoboditel'noe dvizhenie na poroge 80kh. S kem ono?* Prague Mir i socializm, 1982, p. 242f. Goncharev *et al*: Sovremennye problemy, op. cit. (note 20), p. 111.

32   V. G. Pavlov (ed.): *Syrevoi krizis sovremennogo kapitalizma. Mirokhozyastvennye aspekty*, Moscow, Mysl', 1980, p. 193f.

33   J. Bielawski: 'The Socialist Countries and the New Economic Order', in R. Jütte and A. Gross-Jütte (eds): *The Future of International Organization*, London, Frances Pinter, 1981, pp. 70–90.

34   N. I. Lebedev (ed.): *Istoriya mezhdunarodnykh otnoshenii i vneshnei politike SSSR 1968–1978*, Moscow, MO, 1979, p. 159.

35   B. S. Gupta: *The USSR in Asia*, New Delhi, Young Asia Publications, 1980, p. 111.

36   B. S. Gupta: *Soviet Asian Relations in the 1970s and Beyond*, New York, Praeger, 1976, p. 87.

37   I. Kovalenko: *Soviet Policy for Asian Peace and Security*, Moscow, Progress, 1979, p. 292.

38   D. Geyer (ed.) *Sowjetunion. Außenpolitik 1955–1973*, Cologne, Böhlau, 1976, p. 614.

39   G. Linde: 'Sowjetische Nahostpolitik nach Camp David', *BioSt*, 1979, No. 23, p. 18.

40   O. M. Gorbatov and L. A Cherkasskii: *Bor'ba SSSR za obespechenie prochnogo i spravedlivogo mira za Blizhnem Vostoke*, Moscow, Nauka, 1980, p. 258.

41   G. Linde: 'Die sowjetisch-syrischen Beziehungen im regionalen Umfeld', *BioSt*, 1982, No. 7, 10.

42   W. Kordt: 'Die Zeit für Beziehungen ist noch nicht gekommen. Das Verhältnis zwischen Riad und Moskau', *FAZ*, 23.12.1982, p. 3.

43   R. H. Donaldson (ed.): *The Soviet Union in the Third World. Successes and Failures*, London, Croom Helm, 1981, p. 185.

44   A. Z. Rubinstein: 'The Soviet Union and Iran under Khomeini', *International Affairs*, 1981, pp. 599–617.

45   Ch. B. McLane: *Soviet Asian Relations*, London, Central Asian Research Centre, 1973, Vol. 2, p. 27.

46   A. S. Kaufman: *Birma: ideologiya i politika*, Moscow, 1973, p. 359.

47   H. A. Kissinger: *Memoiren 1968–1973*, Munich, Bertelsmann, 1979, p. 920.

48   G. Schweigler: *Von Kissinger zu Carter. Entspannung im Widerstreit von Innen- und Außenpolitik 1969–1981*, Munich, Oldenbourg, 1982, p. 93.

49   R. C. Horn: 'The Soviet Union and Asian Security', in S. Chawla and D. R. Sardesai (eds), *Changing Patterns and Stability in Asia*, New York, Praeger, 1980 (63–99), p. 76.

50   R. W. Mansbach: 'The Soviet Union, the United Nations and the Developing Countries', in R. E. Kanet (ed.): *The Soviet Union and the Developing Nations*, Baltimore, Johns Hopkins, 1974 (237–264), p. 258.

51   T. Hovet: *Bloc Politics in the United Nations*, Cambridge/Mass., Harvard UP, 1960, p. 55; Schaefer: *Die Funktionsfähigkeit des Sicherheitsmechanismus der Vereinten Nationen*, Berlin, Springer, 1981, p. 314.

52   G. Baumann: *Die Blockfreien-Bewegung*, Melle, Knoth, 1982, pp. 304ff; M. P. Isaev and Ya. N. Pivovarov: *Vneshnyaya politika sotsialisticheskoi respubliki V'etnam*, Moscow, Nauka, 1983, pp. 160ff.

53   W. M. LeoGrande: 'Evolution of the Non-aligned Movement', *PoC*, Jan/Feb 1980, pp. 35–52.

54   B. Engel: 'Von Belgrad (1961) bis Havanna (1979). Zur Entwicklung der Bewegung blockfreier Staaten', *BioSt*, 1980, No. 45, p. 105.

55   cf. K. von Beyme: *Economics and Politics within Socialist Systems*, New York, Praeger, 1982, pp. 108ff.

56   P. Wiles (ed.): *The New Communist Third World*, London, Croom Helm, 1982, p. 32.

57   A. Ja El'janov: *Razvivayushiesya strany: problemy ekonomicheskogo rosta i rynok*, Moscow, Mysl', 1976, p. 268f.

58   E. E. Obminskii: *Gruppa '77*, Moscow, MO, 1981, p. 242; V. N. Zolobov: *Neokolonializm: finansovyi aspekt*, Moscow, 1982, p. 154.

59   J. D. Beam: *Multiple Exposure: An Amerian Ambassador's Unique Perspective on East–West-Issues*, New York, Norton, 1978, p. 256.

60   J. S. Berliner: *Soviet Economic Aid*, New York, Praeger, 1958.

61   H. Machowski and S. Schulz: *RGW-Staaten und Dritte Welt. Wirtschaftsbeziehungen und Entwicklungshilfe*, Bonn, Europa Union Verlag, 1981, p. 45.

62 'Die Waffen- und Wirtschaftshilfe Moskaus stößt auf ihre Grenzen', *FAZ*, 27.11.1982, p. 3.

63 'Die Entwicklungshilfe der COMECON-Länder im Jahre 1980', *Handbuch für internationale Zusammenarbeit*, *188*, May, 1982 (1–8), p. 2.

64 op. cit. (note 63), p. 5.

65 Die Waffen- und Wirtschaftshilfe, op. cit. 1982, p. 3.

66 R. H. Donaldson (ed.): *The Soviet Union and the Third World. Successes and Failures*, Boulder, Westview/London, Croom Helm, 1981, p. 369.

67 E. Doglopolov: 'Armiya razvivayushchiesya stran i politika', *Kommunist vooruzhennykh sil*, 1976, No. 6, p. 80; W. R. Duncan (ed.): *Soviet Policy in the Third World*, Oxford, Pergamon, 1980, p. 146.

68 R. A. Scalapino and Ch. S. Lee: *Communism in Korea*, Berkeley, University of California Press, 1972, vol. 1, p. 647, vol. 2, p. 944f.

69 SIPRI: *The Arms Trade with the Third World*, Harmondsworth, Penguin, 1975, p. 81.

70 SIPRI: *Rüstungsjahrbuch '81/82*, Reinbek, Rowohlt, 1982, p. 184.

71 A. J. Pierre: *The Global Politics of Arms Sales*, Princeton UP, 1982, p. 78.

72 US Congress, Senate, Committee on Foreign Relations: *Prospects for Multilateral Arms Export Restraint*, Staff Report, 96th Congress, 1st Session, April 1979, p. 11.

73 Pierre, op. cit. (note 71), p. 77.

74 E. Einbeck: 'Moscow's Military Aid to the Third World', *Außenpolitik 1971*, pp. 460–476.

75 Pierre, op. cit. (note 71), pp. 27, 29.

76 SIPRI, op. cit. (note 69), p. 99.

77 A. Grachyov: 'Terrorism as a Method of Imperialist Foreign Policy', *International Affairs* (Moscow), 1982, No. 4, pp. 48–57; V.V. Vituk: 'O ponyatii "mezhdunarodnyi terrorism" *SI*, 1982, No. 2, pp. 59–68.

78 A. S. Grachev: *Tupiki politicheskogo nasiliya. Ekstremizm i terrorizm na sluzhbe mezhdunarodnoi reaktsii*, Moscow, MO, 1982, pp. 177f, 180.

79 op. cit. (note 78), p. 183.

80 M. N. Katz: *The Third World in Soviet Military Thought*, London, Croom Helm, 1982, p. 30f.

81 O. Bykov *et al*: *The Priorities of Soviet Foreign Policy Today*, Moscow, Progress, 1981, p. 93.

82 G. B. Starushenko: *Mirovoi revolyutsionnyi process i sovremennoe mezhdunarodnoe pravo*, Moscow, MO, 1978, pp. 285, 296.

83   O. M. Gorbatov and L. Ja. Cherkasskii: *Bor'ba SSSR za obespechenie prochnogo i spravedlivogo mira na Blizhnem Vostoke*, Moscow, Nauka, 1980, p. 255.

84   A. J. Klinghoffer: *The Soviet Union in International Oil Politics*, New York, Columbia UP, 1977, p. 82.

85   R. O. Freedman: *Soviet Policy Toward the Middle East since 1970*, New York, Praeger, 1978, pp. 334ff; A. Sella: *Soviet Political and Military Conduct in the Middle East*. London, Macmillan, 1981, p. 153.

86   H. Carrère d'Encausse: *La politique soviétique au moyen-orient. 1955–1975*, Paris, PUF, 1975, p. 326.

87   S. S. Kaplan: *Diplomacy of Power, Soviet Armed Forces as a Political Instrument*, Washington, Brookings, 1981, p. 597.

88   Akademiya Nauk SSSR. Institut Afriki: *Sovetsko–afrikanskie otnosheniya*, Moscow, Nauka, 1982, p. 141; Goncharev, op. cit. (note 20), p. 111.

89   W. Kühne: *Die Politik der Sowjetunion in Afrika*, Baden-Baden, Nomos, 1983, p. 246.

90   N. N. Moltsanov: *Zapovedi prochnogo mira*, Moscow, MO, 1979, p. 84.

91   O. T. Darushenko (ed.): *Vneshnyaya politika sotsialisticheskoi Kuby*, Moscow, Progress, 1980, p. 108.

92   N. S. Kolesnikov: *Kuba: Narodnoe obrazovanie i podgatovka natsional'nykh kadrov 1959–1979*, Moscow, Nauka, 1980, pp. 26ff.

93   C. Blasier and C. Mesa-Lago (eds): *Cuba in the World*, Pittsburgh, University of Pittsburgh Press, 1979, p. 55.

94   A. Z. Rubinstein (ed.): *Soviet and Chinese Influence in the Third World*, New York, Praeger, 1975, p. 183.

95   W. M. LeoGrande: *Cuba's Policy in Africa 1959–1980*, Berkeley, University of California, Institute of International Studies, 1980, p. 65

96   op. cit. (note 95), p. 68.

97   Blasier and Mesa-Lago, op. cit., (note 93), p. 73; G. Krabbe: 'Die Kubaner und Namibia', *FAZ*, 13.12.1982, p. 12; For the Soviet point of view: Yu. I. Gorbunov and A. V. Pritvorov: *Namibia, problemy dostizheniya nezavisimosti*, Moscow, Nauka, 1983.

98   A. D. Bekarevich and N. M. Kucharev: *Sovetskii Sojuz i Kuba: Ekonomicheskoe sotrudnichestvo*, Moscow, MO, 1973, p. 232.

99   K. Melchers: *Die sowjetische Afrikapolitik von Chruschtschow bis Breschnew*, Berlin, Oberbaum, 1980, p. 269.

100   D. E. Albright (ed.): *Communism in Africa*, Bloomington, Indiana UP, 1980, pp. 116, 56.

Chapter 8

1   A. A. Gromyko and B. N. Ponomarev (eds): *Soviet Foreign Policy*.

Vol. 2, 1945–1980, Moscow, Progress, 1981; Yu. I. Vorobtsova: *Internat-sional'naya deyatel'nost' KPSS*, Leningrad, Izdatel'stvo Leningradskogo universiteta, 1983, p. 139.

2 *Materialy XXVI s"ezda KPSS*, Moscow, Politizdat, 1982, p. 16.

3 Lenin: 'Poln. Sobr.', *Soch.*, vol. 30, p. 123.

4 H. König: *Der rote Marsch auf Rom. Entstehung und Ausbreitung des Eurokommunismus*, Stuttgart, Seewald, 1978, p. 322.

5 V. V. Zagladin *et al* (ed.): *Dvizhushchie sily mirogo revolutsion-nogo protsessa*, Moscow, Politizdat, 1981, p. 321.

6 H. Weber: *Die Kommunistische internationale. Eine Dokumenta-tion*, Hannover, Dietz, 1966, p. 15.

7 J. Braunthal: *Geschichte der Internationale*, Berlin/Bonn, Dietz, 1978, vol. 1, p. 323ff.

8 S. Serfaty: 'An International Anomaly: The United States and the Communist Parties in France and Italy, 1945–1947', *StiCC*, 1975, No. 1/2, pp. 123–146.

9 Braunthal, op. cit. (note 7), p. 182.

10 V. Dedijer: *Tito speaks*, London, Routledge & Kegan Paul 1953, p. 284f.

11 H. Lademacher (ed.): *Gewerkschaften im Ost–West-Konflikt*, Melsungen, Walter Schwartz, 1982, p. 17ff.

12 Z. K. Brzezinski: *The Soviet Bloc. Unity and Conflict*, New York, Praeger, 1961, p. 61.

13 K. I. Zarodov (ed.): *Kommunisty mira — o svoickh partiyakh*, Prague, Mir i socializm, 1976, p. 5.

14 'Moskau und der Eurokommunismus', translation from *Novoe Vrema*, 1977, No. 26, in *Deutschland-Archiv, 1977* (884–891), p. 886.

15 W. Leonhard: *Eurokommunismus*, Munich, Bertelsmann, 1978, pp. 176ff.

16 W. Leonhard: *Die Dreispaltung des Marxismus*, Düsseldorf, Econ, 1970, p. 354.

17 M. Strübel: *Neue Wege der italienischen Kommunisten. Zur Außen- und Sicherheitspolitik der KPI (1973–1981)*, Baden-Baden, Nomos, 1982, pp. 136ff.

18 W. Markert (ed.): *Jugoslawien. Osteuropa-Handbuch*, Cologne, Böhlau, 1954, p. 165.

19 W. Berner: 'China und die kommunistische Weltbewegung', in *Die Außenpolitik Chinas*, Munich, Oldenbourg, 1975 (335–356), p. 337.

20 B. S. Gupta: 'Communism and India. A New Context', *PoC*, Aug 1981, pp. 33–45.

21 St. Clarkson: *The Soviet Theory of Development. India and the Third World in Marxist-Leninist Scholarship*, Toronto, University of Toronto Press, 1978, p. 259.

22 P. Berton: 'Japan: Euro-Nippo-Communism', in V. V. Aspatur-ian *et al* (eds): *Eurocommunism between East and West*, Bloomington, Indiana UP, 1980, p. 326–362.

23 A. Z. Rubinstein (ed.), *Soviet and Chinese Influence in the Third World*, New York, Praeger, 1975, p. 119; For a chinese description: 'CPC Principles Governing Relations With Other Communist Parties. China and the World, *Beijing Review Foreign Affairs Series*, No. 4, 1983 (113–116), p. 105.

24 R. Tökés (ed.): *Eurocommunism and Détente*, New York UP, 1978, p. 416.

25 T. Draper: *Castroism. Theory and Practice*, New York, Praeger, 1965, p. 148.

26 H. Fabian: *Der kubanische Entwicklungsweg*, Opladen, West-deutscher Verlag, 1981, p. 512.

27 R. E. Kiessler: *Guerilla und Revolution. Externe und interne Faktoren einer lateinamerikanischen Variante des revolutionären Volk-skrieges*, Diss. Tübingen, 1974, pp. 274ff.

28 Quoted in F. R. Allemann: *Macht und Ohnmacht der Guerilla*, Munich, Piper, 1974, p. 411.

29 *Chile 1971: Habla Fidel Castro*, Santiago de Chile, Editorial Universitaria, 1971, p. 268.

30 R. K. Furtak: *Kuba und der Weltkommunismus*, Cologne, Westdeutscher Verlag, 1967.

31 K. von Beyme: *Political Parties in Western Democracies*, Alder-shot, Gower, 1985, pp. 99ff.

32 Strübel, op. cit. (note 17), p. 114.

33 A. Hottinger: 'Arab Communism at Low Ebb', *PoC*, Aug 1981, pp. 17–32.

34 H. Timmermann: 'Methoden und Muster sowjetischer Einflußnahme auf die Westkommunisten', *BioSt*, 1982, No. 27, p. 10.

35 Strübel, op. cit. (note 17), p. 316.

36 op. cit. (note 2), p. 16.

37 Timmermann, op. cit. (note 34), p. 4f.

38 Ju. A. Vasil'chuk and B. I. Koval' (ed.): *Sotsial'no-ekonomicheskie problemy bor'by kommunisticheskikh partii v razvitykh kapitalistiches-kikh stranach*, Moscow, Nauka, 1981, pp. 319ff.

39 Ju. A. Krasin: *Mezhdunarodnoe kommunisticheskoe dvizhenie kak predmet izucheniya*, Moscow, Mysl', 1980, p. 71.

40 N. V. Zagladin: 'Nekotorye aspekty ideologicheskoi strategii imperializma SShA v otnoshenii kommunisticheskogo dvizheniya Zapadno Evropy', in *Mezhdunarodnoe kommunisticheskoe dvizhenie. Pravda protiv vymyslov*, Moscow, Politizdat, 1981 (120–138), p. 129f.

41   Strübel, op. cit. (note 17), p. 108.

42   U. Wagner: *Finnlands Kommunisten. Volksfrontexperiment und Parteispaltung*, Stuttgart, Kohlhammer, 1971, p. 153f.

43   Timmermann, op. cit. (note 34), p. 14.

44   The DKP got about 50 million DM per annum. *Verfassungsschutzbericht 1981*, Bonn, Bundesminister des Inneren, 1982, p. 72.

45   G. Spadolini (ed.): *I partiti e lo stato*, Bologna, Il Mulino, 1962, p. 48; J. Montaldo: *Les finances du P.C.F.*, Paris, A. Michel, 1977, p. 205f.

46   C. M. Hutter: *Eurokommunisten. Lenins treue Jünger*, Krefeld, Sinus, 1978, pp. 15ff; H. Bendikter: *Eurokommunismus. Der große Bluff*, Bolzano, Athesia, 1978, p. 22.

47   *Mondo operaio*, 1981, No. 2, p. 10, quoted in: H. Timmermann: 'Eine widersprüchliche Bilanz für Moskau. Zu den Grußbotschaften ausländischer Delegationen an den XXVI. Parteitag der KPdSU', *BioSt*, 1981, No. 20, p. 38.

48   J. E. Dougherty and D. K. Pfaltzgraff: *Eurocommunism and the Atlantic Alliance*, Cambridge/Mass., Institute for Foreign Policy Analysis, 1977, p. 64f.

49   V. V. Kravchenko: *Obshchestvennye organizatsii SSSR na mezhdunarodnoi arene*, Moscow, MO, 1969, p. 98.

50   I. P. Il'inskii (ed.): *Konstitutionnye osnovy vneshnei politiki sovetskogo gosudarstva*, Moscow, MO, 1978, p. 187.

51   A. Losowski: *Marx und die Gewerkschaften*, Münster, Verlag Kommunistische Texte, 1972, pp. 164ff.

52   Lademacher, op. cit. (note 11), 13–76; H. Lademacher: *et al.: Der Weltgewerkschaftsbund im Spannungsfeld des Ost–West-Konflikts*, Archiv für Sozialgeschichte, 1978; W. Link: *Deutsche und amerikanische Gewerkschaften und Geschäftsleute. 1945–1975*, Düsseldorf, Droste, 1978.

53   U. Scalia: 'Der Weltgewerkschaftsbund und die Beziehungen zur CGIL', in W. Olle (ed.): Einführung in die internationale Gewerkschaftspolitik Berlin, Olle & Wolter, 1978, vol. 1, pp. 170–182; K. von Beyme: *Challenge to Power. Trade Union and Industrial Relations in Capitalist Countries*, London, Sage, 1980, pp. 12ff.

54   G. E. Kanaev and A. S. Protopopov (eds): *Profsoyuzy mira*, Moscow, Profizdat, 1980, pp. 8ff; V. M. Chigaev: *Rabochii klass i profsoyuzy Evropy v bor'be za mir i razoruzhenie*, Moscow, Profizdat, 1982, pp. 30ff.

55   S. A. Ersov and G. A. Cysina: *Profsoyuzy i mezhdunarodnye monopolii*, Moscow, Profizdat, 1980, pp. 203ff; V. Rubtsov: *Sila v edinstve. Mezhdunarodnye monopolii i bor'ba profsoyuzov s nimi*, Moscow, Profizdat, 1974, p. 86.

56   G. D. Georgan: *Profsojuzy SShA i vneshnyaya politika*, Moscow, Profizdat, 1979, pp. 246, 248.

57   W. Galenson: *The International Labor Organization*, Madison, University of Wisconsin Press, 1981, pp. 60, 120f.

58   K. von Beyme: 'Die Entwicklung der sozialistischen Länder und die Ostpolitik der deutschen Gewerkschaften', in *Gewerkschaftspolitik. Reform aus Solidarität*, Cologne Bund Verlag, 1978, pp. 597–613.

Selected Bibliography

Only the most important studies in Western languages are mentioned. Soviet literature and Western studies on detailed problems are included in the notes at the end of each chapter.

General works

H. Adomeit and R. Boardman (eds.): *Foreign Policy Making in Communist Countries*, Westmead, Saxon House, 1979.

C. Bertram *et al.*: *Sowjetmacht der 80er Jahre*, Munich, Bernard & Graefe, 1981.

S. Bialer (ed.): *The Domestic Context of Soviet Foreign Policy*, London, Croom Helm, 1981.

A. Bykov *et al.*: *The Priorities of Soviet Foreign Policy. Today*, Moscow, Progress, 1981.

O. Eran: *Mezhdunarodniki. An Assessment of Professional Expertise in the Making of Foreign Policy*, Tel Aviv, Turtledove Publishing, 1979.

D. Geyer (ed.): *Sowjetunion. Außenpolitik 1917–1955*, Cologne, Böhlau, 1972.

D. Geyer (ed.): *Sowjetunion. Außenpolitik 1955–1973*, Cologne, Böhlau, 1976.

W. E. Griffith: *The Superpowers and Regional Tensions*, Lexington/Mass., Lexington Books, 1981.

A. A. Gromyko and B. N. Ponomarev (eds.): *Soviet Foreign Policy. 1945–1980*, Moscow, Progress, 1981.

P. Hoffmann and F. J. Fleron (eds.): *The Conduct of Soviet Foreign Policy*, New York, Aldine, 1980.

E. P. Hofman: *The Scientific-Technological Revolution and Soviet Foreign Policy*, Oxford, Pergamon, 1982.

E. Jahn (ed.): *Sozioökonomische Bedingungen der sowjetischen Außenpolitik*, Frankfurt, Campus, 1975.

S. S. Kaplan: *Diplomacy of Power. Soviet Armed Forces as a Political Instrument*, Washington, Brookings, 1981.

L. J. Lederer (ed.): *Russian Foreign Policy*, New Haven, Yale UP, 1962.

K. London (ed.): *The Soviet Union in World Politics*, Boulder, Westview, 1980.

B. Meissner and G. Rhode (eds.): *Grundfragen sowjetischer Außenpolitik*, Stuttgart, Kohlhammer, 1970.

R. J. Mitchell: *Ideology of a Superpower. Contemporary Soviet Doctrine on International Relations*, Stanford, Hoover Press, 1982.

J. L. Nogee and R. H. Donaldson: *Soviet Foreign Policy since World War II.*, Oxford, Pergamon Press, 1981.

H. Nolte: *Gruppeninteressen und Außenpolitik*, Göttingen, Musterschmidt, 1979.

R. Rotermundt *et al.*: *Die Sowjetunion und Europa. Gesellschaftsreform und Außenpolitik der UdSSR*, Frankfurt, Campus, 1979.

A. Z. Rubinstein: *The Soviet Union in International Organizations*, Princeton UP, 1964.

A. Z. Rubinstein: *Soviet Foreign Policy Since World War II*, Cambridge/Mass., Winthrop, 1981.

A. P. Schmidt: *Soviet Military Interventions Since 1945*, New Brunswick, Transaction Books, 1985.

M. Schwartz: *The Foreign Policy of the USSR: Domestic Factors*, Encina/Ca., Dickenson, 1975.

T. Schweissfurth: *Sozialistisches Völkerrecht?*, Heidelberg, Springer, 1979.

M. D. Shulman: *Stalin's Foreign Policy Reappraised*, Cambridge/Mass., Harvard UP, 1963.

R. M. Slusser and G. Ginsburgs (eds.): *A Calender of Soviet Treaties 1958–1973*, Leiden, Sijthoff & Norodhoff, 1981.

Soviet Political Sciences Association (eds.): *International Relations. Trends and Prospects*, Moscow, USSR Academy of Sciences, 1982.

W. Taubman: *Stalin's American Policy*, New York, Norton, 1982.

A. A. Ulam: *Expansion and Coexistence. Soviet Foreign Policy 1917–1973*, New York, Praeger, 1974.

W. Zimmerman: *Soviet Perspectives of International Relations. 1956–1967*, Princeton UP, 1969.

Relations to Western countries

G. Adler-Karlsson: *Western Economic Warfare 1917–1967*, Stockholm, Almqvist & Wiksell, 1968.

H. Adomeit: *Die Sowjetmacht in internationalen Krisen und Konflikten*, Baden-Baden, Nomos, 1983.

J. Alford (ed.): *The Impact of New Military Technology*, Aldershot, Gower, 1981.

K. Amundsen: *Norway, Nato and the forgotten Soviet Challenge*, Berkeley, Institute for International Studies, 1981.

A. G. Arbatow: *Der sowjetische Standpunkt. Über die Westpolitik des UdSSR*, Munich, Rogner & Bernhard, 1981.

R. K. Ashley: *The Political Economy of War and Peace*, London, Pinter/New York, Nichols, 1980.

V. Belezki: *Die Politik der Sowjetunion in den deutschen Angelegenheiten in der Nachkriegszeit 1945–1976*, Berlin, Staatsverlag der DDR, 1977.

K. E. Birnbaum: *The Politics of East–West Communication in Europe*, Westmead, Saxon House, 1979.

W. von Bredow: *Vom Antagonismus zur Konvergenz? Studien zum Ost-West-Problem*, Frankfurt, Metzner, 1972.

L. T. Caldwell and W. Diebold: *Soviet-American Relations in the 1980s*, New York, McGraw Hill, 1981.

C. Costoriadis: *Devant la guerre. Les réalités*, Paris, Fayard, 1981.

C. Critchley: *The North Atlantic Alliance and the Soviet Union in the 1980s*, London, Macmillan, 1982.

A. W. DePorte: *Europe Between the Superpowers*, New Haven, Yale UP, 1979.

B. Dismukes and J. M. McConnell (eds.): *Soviet Naval Diplomacy*, Oxford, Pergamon, 1979.

J. D. Douglass and A. M. Hoeber: *Soviet Strategy for Nuclear War*, Stanford, Hoover, 1979.

G. Fahl: *SALT II vor START. Die strategische Grenznachbarschaft von USA und UdSSR*, Berlin, Berlin-Verlag, 1983.

R. Faramazyan: *Disarmament and the Economy*, Moscow, Progress, 1981.

H. Fast Scott and W. F. Scott (eds.): *The Soviet Art of War. Doctrine, Strategy and Tactics*, Epping/Essex, Bowker, 1982.

D. Frei: *Feinbilder und Abrüstung. Die Gegenseitige Einschätzung der Ud SSR und der USA*. Munich, Beck, 1983.

D. Frey and Ch. Catrina: *Risks of Unintentional Nuclear War*, Geneva, UN Institute for Disarmament Research/London, Croom Helm, 1983.

G. Ginsburg and A. Z. Rubinstein (eds.): *Soviet Foreign Policy Towards Western Europe*, New York, Praeger, 1978.

M. Görtemaker: *Die unheilige Allianz. Die Geschichte der Entspannungspolitik 1943–1979*, Munich, Beck, 1979.

D. Halloway: *The Soviet Union and the Arms Race*, New Haven, Yale University Press, 1983.

P. Hanson: *Trade and Technology in Soviet Western Relations*, London, Macmillan, 1981.

A. L. Horelick (ed.): *U.S.-Soviet Relations. The Next Phase*, Ithaca, Cornell U.P., 1986.

A. J. Jefremow: *Die nukleare Rüstung*, Moscow, Progress, 1981.

Ch. Jönsson: Superpower, *Comparing American and Soviet Foreign Policy*, London, Francis Pinter, 1984.

S. Jutila: *Finlandization for Finland and The World*, Bloomington, Europa, 1983.

R. E. Kanet (ed.): *Soviet Foreign Policy and East–West Relations*, Oxford, Pergamon, 1982.

Ch.W. Kegley and P. McGowan (eds.): *Foreign Policy USA–USSR*, London, Sage, 1982.

P. A. Kerber: *Sowjetische Macht und westliche Verhandlungspolitik im Wandel militärischer Kräfteverhältnisse*, Baden-Baden, Nomos, 1983.

H. Kohl (ed.): *Der neue Realismus. Außenpolitik nach Iran und Afghanistan*, Düsseldorf, Erb, 1980.

G. Krell and D. Lutz: *Nuklearrüstung im Ost-West-Konflikt*, Baden-Baden, Nomos, 1980.

R. F. Laird: *The Soviet Union, The West, and the Nuclear Arms Race*, Brighton, Wheatsheaf Books, 1986.

T. B. Larson: *Soviet-American Rivalry*, New York, Norton, 1978.

M. Lavigne: *Les relations économiques est–ouest*, Paris, PUF, 1979.

W. Link: *Der Ost-West-Konflikt*, Stuttgart, Kohlhammer, 1980.

G. Liska: *Russia and the Road to Appeasement. Cycles of East–West Conflict in War*, Baltimore, Johns Hopkins, 1982.

D. S. Lutz: *Die Rüstung der Sowjetunion*, Baden-Baden, Nomos, 1979.

V. Mastny: *Russia's Road to the Cold War. Diplomacy, Warfare and the Politics of Communism 1941–1945*, New York, Columbia UP, 1979.

T. B. Millar: *The East–West Strategic Balance*, London, Allen & Unwin, 1981.

E. Moreton and G. Segal (eds.): *Soviet Strategy Towards Western Europe*, London, Allen & Unwin, 1983.

F. Müller *et al.*: *Wirtschaftssanktionen im Ost–West–Verhältnis*, Baden-Baden, Nomos, 1983.

U. Nerlich (ed.): *Sowjetische Macht und westliche Verhandlungspolitik im*

Wandel militärischer Kräfteverhältnisse, Baden-Baden, Nomos, 1982.

U. Nerlich (ed.): *Die Einhegung sowjetischer Macht, Kontrolliertes militärisches Gleichgewicht als Bedingung europäischer Sicherheit*, Baden-Baden, Nomos, 1982.

G. Niedhart (ed.): *Der Westen und die Sowjetunion seit 1917*, Paderborn, Schöningh, 1983.

J. H. Nun: *The Soviet First Strike Threat*, New York, Praeger, 1982.

R. Pipes: *US–Soviet Relations in the Era of Détente*, Boulder, Westview, 1981.

R. Pipes: *Soviet Strategy in Europe*, New York, Crane, Russak, 1976.

C. Royen: *Die sowjetische Koexistenzpolitik gegenüber Westeuropa*, Baden-Baden, Nomos, 1978.

G. Schiavone (ed.): *East–West Relations. Prospects for the 1980s*, London, Macmillan, 1982.

E. Schulz (ed.): *Die Ostbeziehungen der Europäischen Gemeinschaft*, Munich, Oldenbourg, 1977.

M. Schwartz: *Soviet Perception of the United States*, Berkeley, Univ. of California Press, 1978.

A. Shlaim and G.N. Yannopoulos (eds.): *The EEC and Eastern Europe*, Cambridge University Press, 1979.

G. Simon (ed.): *Weltmacht Sowjetunion*, Cologne, Wissenschaft und Politik, 1987.

U. Stehr: *Wirtschaft und Politik in den sowjetischen Westbeziehungen*, Frankfurt, Campus, 1980.

A. Stent: *From Embargo to Ostpolitik. The Political Economy of West German–Soviet Relations. 1955–1980*, Cambridge/Mass., Harvard UP, 1981.

R. Swearingen: *The Soviet Union and Postwar Japan*, Stanford, Hoover, 1978.

S. Tiedtke: *Rüstungskontrolle aus sowjetischer Sicht*, Frankfurt, Campus, 1980.

G. Wettig: *Die sowjetischen Sicherheitsvorstellungen und die Möglichkeiten eines Ost–West–Einvernehmens*, Baden-Baden, Nomos, 1981.

A. Wildavsky (ed.): *Beyond Containment. Alternative American Policies Toward the Soviet Union*, San Francisco, ICS Press, 1983.

W. Zimmerman and G. Plamer: 'Words and Deeds in Soviet Foreign Policy: The Case of Soviet Military Expenditure', *APSR*, 1983, pp. 358–367.

Relations to socialist countries

T. S. An: *The Sino-Soviet Territorial Dispute*, Philadelphia, Westminster Press, 1973.

K. von Beyme: *Economics and Politics within Socialist Systems*, New York, Praeger, 1982.

O. B. Borissow and B. T. Koloskow: *Sowjetisch-chinesische Beziehungen 1945–1970*, Berlin, Staatsverlag der DDR, 1973.

, London, Allen & Unwin, 1981.

B. Bracewell-Milnes: *Economic Integration in East and West*, London, Croom Helm, 1976.

A. Bromke and D. Novak (eds.): *The Communist States in the Era of Détente 1971–1977*, Oakville/Ontario, Mosaic Press, 1979.

Z. Brzezinski: *The Soviet Bloc. Unity and Conflict*, New York, Praeger, 1961.

H. Carrère d'Encausse: *Le grand frère. L'Union soviétique et l'Europe soviétisée*, Paris, Flammarion, 1983.

Ch. Chase-Dunn (ed.): *Socialist States in the World-System*, London, Sage, 1982.

Ch. O. Chung: *Pyongyang between Peking and Moscow*, University of Alabama Press, 1978.

R. Damus: *RGW. Wirtschaftliche Zusammenarbeit in Osteuropa*, Opladen, Leske, 1979.

K. Dawisha and P. Hanson (eds.): *Soviet–East European Dilemmas*, London, Heinemann, 1981.

R. O. Freedman: *Economic Warfare in the Communist Bloc*, New York, Praeger, 1970.

Ch. Gati (ed.): *The International Politics of Eastern Europe*, New York, Praeger, 1976.

G. Ginsburgs and C. F. Pinkele: *The Sino-Soviet Territorial Dispute 1949–1964*, New York, Praeger, 1978.

J. Glaubitz: *China und die Sowjetunion. Aufbau und Zerfall einer Allianz*, Hannover, Landeszentrale für Politische Bildung, 1973.

J. Hacker: *Der Ostblock. Entstehung, Entwicklung und Struktur 1939–1980*, Baden-Baden, Nomos, 1983.

J. K. Hoensch: *Sozialistische Osteuropa–Politik 1945–1975*, Kronberg, Athenäum/Düsseldorf, Droste, 1977.

G. Ionescu: *The Breakup of the Soviet Empire in Eastern Europe*, Harmondsworth, Penguin, 1965.

J. Kalvoda: *Czechoslovakia's Role in Soviet Strategy*, Washington DC, University Press of America, 1981.

J. Lévesque: *The USSR and the Cuban Revolution*, New York, Praeger, 1978.

P. Lorenz: *Multinationale Unternehmen sozialistischer Länder*, Baden-Baden, Nomos, 1978.

A. D. Low: *The Sino-Soviet Dispute*, Madison, Fairleigh Dickinson UP, 1978.

P. Marer and J. M. Montias (eds.): *East European Integration of East–West Trade*, Bloomington, Indiana UP, 1980.

B. Meissner: *Der Warschauer Pakt. Dokumentensammlung*, Cologne, Wissenschaft und Politik, 1962.

B. Meissner: *Die 'Breschnew-Doktrin'*, Cologne, Wissenschaft und Politik, 1969.

G. Schiavone: *The Institutions of COMECON*, London, Macmillan, 1981.

R. Szawlowski: *The System of International Organizations of the Communist Countries*, Leiden, Sijthoff, 1976.

US Congress, Joint Economic Committee: *Soviet Economy in a Time of Change*, Washington, GPO, 1979, vol. 2.

G. Wettig: *Community and Conflict in the Socialist Camp: The Soviet Union, East Germany and the German Problem 1965–1972*, New York, St. Martins, 1975.

T. Wolfe: *Soviet Power and Europe 1945–1970*, Baltimore, Johns Hopkins, 1970.

D. S. Zagoria: *The Sino-Soviet Conflict*, New York, Praeger, 1962.

G. Zieger: *Der Warschauer Pakt*, Hannover, Niedersächsische Landeszentrale für Politische Bildung, 1974.

Relations to the Third World

D. E. Albright (ed.): *Communism in Africa*, Bloomington, Indiana UP, 1980.

C. Blasier and C. Mesa-Lago (eds.): *Cuba in the World*, Pittsburgh, Pittsburgh UP, 1979.

H. Carrère d'Encausse: *La politique soviétique au moyen-orient 1955–1975*, Paris, PUF, 1975.

S. Chawson and D. R. Sardesai (eds.): *Changing Patterns of Security and Stability in Asia*, New York, Praeger, 1980.

V. Chirkin and Yu. Yudin: *A Socialist Oriented State*, Moscow, Progress, 1983.

S. Clarkson: *The Soviet Theory of Development. India and the Third World in Marxist–Leninist Scholarship*, Toronto UP, 1978.

R. H. Donaldson (ed.): *The Soviet Union in the Third World. Successes and Failures*, London, Croom Helm, 1981.

R. Duncan (ed.): *Soviet Policy in the Third World*, Oxford, Pergamon, 1980.

T. J. Faber: *War Clouds on the Horn of Africa*, Washington, Carnegie Endowment for International Peace, 1979.

E. J. Feuchtwanger and P. Nailor (eds.): *The Soviet Union and the Third World*, New York, St. Martins, 1981.

R. O. Freedman: *Soviet Policy Toward the Middle East since 1970*, New York, Praeger, 1978.

B. S. Gupta: *Soviet Asian Relations in the 1970s and Beyond*, New York, Praeger, 1976.

B. S. Gupta: *The USSR in Asia*, New Dehli, Young Asia Publications, 1980.

W. Joshua and S. P. Gilbert: *Arms for the Third World: Soviet Military Aid Diplomacy*, Baltimore, Johns Hopkins, 1969.

G. Jukes: *The Soviet Union in Asia*, Berkeley, University of California Press, 1973.

R. E. Kanet (ed.): *The Soviet Union and the Developing Nations*, Baltimore, Johns Hopkins, 1974.

S. S. Kaplan: *Diplomacy of Power. Soviet Armed Forces as a Political Instrument*, Washington, Brookings, 1981.

M. N. Katz: *The Third World in Soviet Military Thought*, London, Croom Helm, 1983.

A. J. Klinghoffer: *The Soviet Union in International Oil Politics*, New York, Columbia UP, 1977.

J. Kovalenko: *Soviet Policy for Asian Peace and Security*, Moscow, Progress, 1979.

W. Kühne: *Die Politik der Sowjetunion in Afrika*, Baden-Baden, Nomos, 1983.

B. R. Kuniholm: *The Origins of the Cold War in the Near East: Great Power Conflict and Diplomacy in Iran, Turkey and Greece*, Princeton UP, 1979.

M. Leitenberg and G. Sheffer (eds.): *Great Power Intervention in the Middle East*, Oxford, Pergamon, 1979.

W. M. LeoGrande: *Cuba's Policy in Africa, 1959–1980*, Berkeley, Institute of International Studies, 1980.

R. Loewenthal: *Model or Ally? The Communist Powers and Developing Countries*, Oxford UP, 1977.

H. Machowski and S. Schulz: *RGW-Staaten und Dritte Welt. Wirtschaftsbeziehungen und Entwicklungshilfe*, Bonn, Europa Union Verlag, 1981.

H. Malik (ed.): *Soviet–American Relations with Pakistan, Iran and Afghanistan*, Basingstoke, Macmillan, 1986.

K. Melchers: *Die sowjetische Afrikapolitik von Chruschtschow bis Breschnew*, Berlin, Oberbaum, 1980.

A. J. Pierre: *The Global Politics of Arms Sales*, Princeton UP, 1982.

R. B. Remnek: *Soviet Scholars and Soviet Foreign Policy: A Case Study in Soviet Policy Towards India*, Durham, Academic Press, 1975.

Y. Ro'i (ed.): *The Limits to Power. Soviet Policy in the Middle East*, London, Croom Helm, 1979.

A. Z. Rubinstein: *Soviet and Chinese Influence in the Third World*, New York, Praeger, 1975.

C. R. Saivetz: *The Soviet Union and the Gulf in the 1980s*, Westview, Boulder, 1986.

A. Sella: *Soviet Political and Military Conduct in the Middle East*, London, Macmillan, 1981.

Ch. Stevens: *The Soviet Union and Black Africa*, New York, Holmes & Meier, 1976.

R. A. Uljanowski: *Der Sozialismus und die befreiten Länder*, Berlin, Deutscher Verlag der Wissenschaften, 1973.

J. Van der Kroef: *Communism in South-East Asia*, Berkeley, University of California Press, 1981.

H. Vogel (ed.): *Die sowjetische Intervention in Afghanistan*, Baden-Baden, Nomos, 1980.

W. Weinstein (ed.): *Chinese and Soviet Aid to African Nations*, New York, Praeger, 1980.

K. Westen: *Der Staat der nationalen Demokratie. Ein kommunistisches Modell für Entwicklungsländer*, Cologne, Wissenschaft und Politik, 1964.

P. Wiles (ed.): *The New Communist Third World*, London, Croom Helm, 1982.

D. S. Zagoria (ed.): *Soviet Policy in East Asia*, New Haven, Yale University Press, 1982.

Index

Varga, Eugene 26, 38
Vietnam 9, 65, 73, 89, 99, 110, 112, 131, 144
Vietnam war 90
'Vodka-Cola complex' 92
Voroshilov, Marshall 21

Wallerstein, I. 117
war
  'inevitability' of 94, 113, 114
  nuclear *see* nuclear war
Warsaw Pact 164
  and Soviet hegemony 105, 108–9
  superfluity of 69
weapons, nuclear 52–4, 55, 56, 60, 62–3
  major innovations in 55
  weapon-free zones 67
Western Europe *see* Europe, Western
Wiles, P. 80

'world order', concept of 8
world system perspective 5–6, 7–8

Yakovlev, A. 26
Yemen 112, 113
Yugoslavia 37, 72, 73, 93, 95, 96, 98, 111, 146
  and Comecon 104, 154
  and pressure by Stalin 153
  Communist parties in 152–3
  relations with China 154

Zaire 142
Zamyatin, L. 15
Zaradov, 157
Zarapkin 22
Zhukov, Marshal Y. 31–2
Zinov'yev, G. Ye. 118
Zorin 17